PRAISE FOR

THE MUSIC NEVER STOPS

"An entertaining and often amusing look into the music business."

—*Wall Street Journal*

"The most important concert producer of his day."

—JOEL SELVIN, *San Francisco Chronicle*

"An entertaining insider's tour of the concert business from a likable guide."

—*Kirkus*

"A friendly, enjoyable ramble through live music history as seen from an amiable insider."

—*Booklist*

"Peter thinks like a musician. He understands the spirit of the music I'm trying to make because he wants to create situations for that music that enhance the experience on many levels."

—PHIL LESH, Grateful Dead, author of *Searching for the Sound*

"Peter Shapiro is a unicorn. He has a magical/mythical quality to him. We met back in the days of Wetlands, which you'll read about in this book. You never knew who you were going to see there— some nights it could be Dave Matthews Band, the next night Toots and the Maytals, another night it's Pearl Jam. I don't know any venue that existed that could pull that off. I remember wondering who was behind this, who could make these nights happen—and that was Shapiro."

—JIMMY FALLON, *The Tonight Show*

"Pete is the rarest of personalities in the music industry. He explodes into the room, swinging for the fences, full of unbridled enthusiasm and joy, with huge energy and huge ideas. For Pete, the dream is still alive—the power of live music—and I love him for that."

—TREY ANASTASIO, Phish

"Peter is the reincarnation of the '60's and '70's entrepreneurs. He's as close as we have to Bill Graham."

—STEVIE VAN ZANDT, E Street Band, *Little Steven's Underground Garage*, *The Sopranos*, author of *Unrequited Infatuations*

"I met Pete in the late '90s when he opened his first club. His boundless energy and enthusiasm are infectious. He is so passionate about all that he does and is ready to dive in at the deep end. He has great taste and is a perfect combination of the creative collaborator who has his eye on the business side of things, which is quite a rare quality but so important. One Love."

—CHRIS BLACKWELL, Founder, Island Records

"I've given Peter eleventh-hour surprises, like, 'How about a practice Usher show?' or 'Can we organize a quickie Elvis Costello performance?' Anyone else would have riddled me with bullets for taking such a grand idea and tossing it to him with seconds left to spare. But with him it's always, 'Oh man, I can't wait to get to it.' And it's always magic."

—QUESTLOVE, The Roots, author of *Creative Quest*

"*The Music Never Stops*, like everything Peter Shapiro, inspires and ignites all of our senses—even those we didn't know we had. Peter is a brilliant architect of communities, cultures, and dreams. This book is where you come to grow and for your deal to go down— and if you look at it right—you'll find the next rainbow, at just the right time."

—BILL WALTON, NBA Hall of Famer

"Peter has said, 'I try to think obsessively about the future, and you have to be ready for multiple different paths.' One of those paths has been to make millions of concertgoers more aware of our global environmental movement, while encouraging environmental awareness and commitment by the music industry. He is always collaborative, he dissolves differences, and he makes it happen. He's that kind of guy."

—KATHLEEN ROGERS, President Earth Day Network

"Pete Shapiro has borne witness to the inner workings of the most important cultural events of the last quarter century. Impresario, Innovator, and Beloved Instigator...the stories in his book will blow your mind!"

—DON WAS, President, Blue Note Records

"It's a special person, a magician of the tallest order, who simply figures it out. A person filled with passion for the blessing, the reason we all wake up day after day with a glimmer of optimism and hope: the music. Pete's story is one of dedication, persistence, success, and some failure too. It's an inspiring journey. He always has multiple irons in the fire and dozens of balls in the air. He is an idea person who is on a crusade for the music, with the talent, knowledge, and drive to bring the vision to life. This book could easily be called *Whatever It Takes*."

—BEN JAFFE, Creative Director, Preservation Hall Jazz Band

"I met Pete in 1996. Since then, I've told anyone who will listen that he is the Bill Graham of our generation. He kept my word."

—GREG SCHOLL, Executive Director, Jazz at Lincoln Center

"In an industry filled with hucksters and charlatans, Peter Shapiro is a music promoter with a heart and a soul. He produces music with all the best parts of the good old days and none of the bad. He is a real, live Unicorn."

—ROGER MCNAMEE, Cofounder, Elevation Partners, Moonalice

THE
MUSIC
NEVER
STOPS

THE
MUSIC
NEVER
STOPS

*What Putting on 10,000 Shows
Has Taught Me About Life, Liberty,
and the Pursuit of Magic*

PETER SHAPIRO
WITH DEAN BUDNICK

hachette
BOOKS
New York

Hachette Books
Hachette Book Group
1290 Avenue of the Americas
New York, NY 10104
HachetteBooks.com
Twitter.com/HachetteBooks
Instagram.com/HachetteBooks

First Trade Paperback Edition: November 2023

Published by Hachette Books, an imprint of Hachette Book Group, Inc. The Hachette
Books name and logo is a trademark of the Hachette Book Group.

The Hachette Speakers Bureau provides a wide range of authors for speaking
events. To find out more, go to hachettespeakersbureau.com or email
HachetteSpeakers@hbgusa.com.

The publisher is not responsible for websites (or their content) that are not owned
by the publisher.

Print book interior design by Jeff Williams

Library of Congress Control Number: 2022937303

ISBNs: 9780306845185 (hardcover); 9780306833304 (trade paperback);
9780306845178 (ebook)

Printed in the United States of America

LSC-C

Printing 1, 2023

Thank You . . .

*Andrew & Jon, for accelerating the car for me
at key points along the trip.*

*Mom & Dad, for creating and then feeding the
engine, especially when I was going to places that
were not on the map that you had given me.*

*Rebecca, Roxy & Simon, for being in the car with
me and never asking me to change directions,
wherever we were headed.*

*(and thank you, Larry and Charley, for being
the first to get into the car.)*

*(and Rich Caplan for getting me to
Rosemont Horizon.)*

CONTENTS

THE
MUSIC
NEVER
STOPS

1

RAINBOWS ARE REAL

Fare Thee Well: Celebrating 50 Years of the Grateful Dead
Levi's Stadium, Santa Clara, California
June 27, 2015

While I will never forget the rainbow, the real magic moment might have been the peace sign.

The broken peace sign.

We had hired a skywriter to fly over Levi's Stadium to commemorate the opening of Fare Thee Well.

We hoped to create a spectacle, and that is exactly what happened, although not in the way we'd intended.

But you cannot let yourself get frazzled.

Nothing is ever a straight line.

And even when it is, you still may require course correction.

That is equally true for a bewildered music entrepreneur and an errant airplane pilot who made their way to Santa Clara, California, to celebrate fifty years of the Grateful Dead.

In certain respects, Fare Thee Well began with two shows over one weekend in Santa Clara and ended with three shows the next weekend in Chicago.

In other respects, it began ten years earlier when I unsuccessfully attempted to put together a series of concerts to celebrate the fortieth anniversary of the Grateful Dead. Then again, you could also say it began thirty-two years earlier, when spoken-word artist Ken Nordine freaked me out of a Grateful Dead show and into a snowy Shakedown. But I'll come back to that.

Even though I couldn't get traction in 2005, ten years later, I was able to reunite the Core Four of the Grateful Dead (Bob Weir, Phil Lesh, Mickey Hart, and Bill Kreutzmann), alongside Phish guitarist Trey Anastasio and keyboard players Bruce Hornsby and Jeff Chimenti.

Originally, they were only going to play three shows at Soldier Field in Chicago over Fourth of July weekend. Actually, *originally* originally, the shows were going to be at Madison Square Garden (and somewhere out west), but MSG wasn't available.

Again, nothing is ever a straight line. It is often a long and twisting path (and sometimes a long and *twisted* path). What is key is how you make adjustments on the fly. A lot of times, I will start heading in one direction but things don't quite work out, and that leads to the next thing. You should not let yourself get too high or too low. Stay in the middle.

I repeatedly reminded myself of this during the pandemic, after I suspended operations of my venues and shut down my festival events, leaving no immediate source of income for myself or my team. However, I kept recalibrating and reinventing, pushing in new directions that kept us afloat and added ballast.

Have I acquired a case of PTSD over the past few decades? It's possible. But what I also have is the music. That's the real reward, and it never fails to lift me.

On January 16, 2015, when we initially announced Fare Thee Well, we decided to do three shows in the middle of the country over Fourth of July weekend. We put tickets on sale through traditional Grateful Dead mail order and also via Ticketmaster. However, we were able to fulfill only a fraction of the mail requests, and the online sales nearly overwhelmed the system, setting a new Ticketmaster record for demand.

In response, I scrambled to find another venue so I could add a couple of shows and relieve the pressure. I had initially hoped for Golden Gate Park, but it wasn't available on the dates we had in mind. Thankfully, we found Levi's Stadium in Santa Clara, California, which had a certain symmetry because it was about a dozen miles from what can be thought of as the birthplace of the Grateful Dead: Dana Morgan's Music Store, where Jerry Garcia and Bob Weir first played together (and it was a similar distance from the band's first gig: Magoo's Pizza Parlor). We convinced Ticketmaster to sell all the Santa Clara tickets through an online lottery—the first time they had done anything like that for a stadium show—and in early April, we finally announced the two additional dates.

When people come up to me and talk about Fare Thee Well, the conversation often turns to the rainbow.

What most of them don't remember is that we had attempted to commemorate the opening day with another form of visual spectacle. A skywriter was going to kick things off by creating a peace sign.

Unfortunately, there was a misfire.

It started out just fine. The pilot made the circle, then the line down the middle, and then connected a point on the perimeter with the center line. All he needed to do to complete the design was create one more line from the edge of the circle that intersected with one he had just made.

Except he missed.

Somehow, his bearings were off. So instead of completing the peace sign, he drew a line from the edge of the circle to some other arbitrary point. He flat-out failed to connect.

Whatever he'd created, it certainly wasn't a peace sign.

Part of me wondered if that might be a bad sign.

I was standing next to my copromoters, Mike Luba and Don Sullivan, as this all went down. I remember collapsing into collective, convulsive laughter that blended nervous energy with a tinge of horror.

Thankfully, all of that has been forgotten. Looking back, it seems like our luck turned in that moment.

These days, people don't talk about the mangled peace sign; they ask about the rainbow.

It happened during the last song of the first set. I can remember looking up at the sky moments earlier, and although it wasn't raining, orange clouds had started to roll in, making me feel slightly uneasy. Weather is the major unknown at an event like this, and my track record hadn't been perfect. Just a few years earlier, I'd been forced to cancel the Earth Day celebration I was producing on the National Mall midway through the event, due to thunderstorms.

Shortly after spying those vivid, tangerine clouds in Santa Clara, I heard a low rumble in the crowd. I've learned to stop and pay attention whenever I hear that sort of clamor from an audience. It means that something's happening and things are about go one of two ways.

I could see that people were starting to crane their necks upward, transfixed by something above them.

That's when I first caught sight of the rainbow.

I felt a wave of positive energy flow over me.

It seemed like all seventy-five thousand of us were sharing a moment of wonder and jubilation that amplified the energy coming from the stage.

As Shirley Halperin wrote in her *Billboard* review, which posted shortly after the show, "The set ended with a 17-minute 'Viola Lee Blues' that segued into a deep jam accentuated by a glorious rainbow encircling the venue in the sky. Said one longtime Head: 'This is the band that jams with God.'"

But then she added, "Whether it was Mother Nature stepping in became an instant debate, intensified by *Billboard*'s own report citing an insider who claims the production sprang for the effect, at a cost of $50,000."

Unfortunately, that insider was me.

I've known Shirley since the mid-1990s, when I became owner of the New York nightclub Wetlands Preserve. Our musical tastes are typically in alignment. On this day, though, our senses of reality were out of sync.

While the rainbow was still in full effect and people were freaking out, Shirley texted me and asked, "How'd you do that?"

"What do you mean?" I responded.

"The rainbow!" she answered me.

I sent her back a text informing her that it wasn't possible to make a rainbow, but she countered, "Come on . . ."

We went back and forth a bit more until I finally gave in and quipped, "Okay, I paid fifty grand for it."

That ended the text thread along with any further discussion of the topic.

Or so I'd thought.

Until I saw her story later that night while we were in the van heading back to our hotel after the show.

By the time I woke up the next morning, the *Billboard* report was everywhere.

I felt obliged to call Shirley, who, to her credit, revised her account: "This article has been updated to include the continuing debate over the appearance of the rainbow, which upon further investigation appears to have been real. Turns out this band really does jam with God."

Later that afternoon, I received an email from Mickey Hart in which he joked, "How did you do that rainbow trick? I won't reveal your power. Not even Bill Graham could do that."

Mickey kept it going the following day, poking fun with another email asking the same question that I couldn't seem to avoid:

> Just tell me the truth . . . How did you pull it off?
> I will never reveal your very clever illusion . . .
> P.S. how much did it cost?
> Your friends at the NSA

Over five years later, the story of the rainbow still finds its way onto lists of the world's craziest music conspiracy theories.

These days, I have a different response when someone asks me whether the rainbow was man-made.

My answer is yes . . . and the man who made it was Jerry Garcia.

2

AND MILES TO GO

Grateful Dead
Rosemont Horizon, Rosemont, Illinois
March 11, 1993

I can point to a specific moment when music changed the trajectory of my life. It was March 11, 1993, at the Rosemont Horizon arena in Chicago.

If I don't see the Grateful Dead that night, then I don't go to the library the next morning, and I don't make *And Miles to Go*, my film about touring Deadheads. This means I don't meet Larry Bloch and I don't take over Wetlands—I hadn't even been to Wetlands at that point. It also means no *All Access* or Jammy Awards or *U2 3D* or Brooklyn Bowl or LOCKN' or Jazz & Colors or Rock and Roll Playhouse. I certainly don't take over the Capitol Theatre or *Relix*. I'm not even sure I meet my wife, Rebecca, which certainly complicates matters for our two amazing kids, Roxy and Simon. One thing leads to another . . .

On March 11, 1993, I was a sophomore at Northwestern University in Chicago, the same city where I would return to produce Fare Thee Well. I was a double major in radio/television/film (RTVF) and political science. A lot of what I was studying was on the business side of media. I remember reading quite a bit by Ken Auletta, as well as books about Roone Arledge, Howard Cosell, and Peter Jennings on the rise of ABC News and Sports divisions.

I had started exploring my interest in television a few years before I arrived at Northwestern. I did some play-by-play for my high school basketball team, although whenever I think back on this, my mind turns to a moment at a road game when the kids from the other school saw us in front of the video camera and started chanting, "Ne-rds! Ne-rds!" while we were standing there like piñatas (I suppose this prepared me for some occasional piñata moments to follow). I also hosted a weekly high school sports wrap-up show that aired on New York City public access. I even attended Bill Raftery broadcasting camp.

My first internship was with the *National*, the all-sports daily paper. I would go into bodegas and try to convince them to carry the *National*. I thought this was the coolest job in the world. In retrospect, it's not so different from joining a street team to spread the word about your favorite band or a venue. It's also similar to working the *Relix* table at an event.

During the summer of 1990, I was an intern at WNYC-TV, our public television station. This provided me with an opportunity to work on a number of programs, including *Video Music Box*, the first show of its kind built around hip-hop. Ralph McDaniels had created it in 1983, five years prior to *Yo! MTV Raps*.

I went on a few memorable shoots for *Video Music Box*, including an interview with Bootsy Collins at the Gramercy Park Hotel. Bootsy opened the door to his room with those glasses on, making me appreciate that some artists are in full-on star mode 24-7, but you can't be rattled; you need to engage them on their terms.

Ralph McDaniels is still at it today, and I was able to reintroduce myself and share some appreciation when he came to Brooklyn Bowl a couple of years ago.

The first concert I attended was Madonna with the Beastie Boys at Madison Square Garden in 1985. I was twelve years old, and my brother Andrew brought me (I'm the youngest in my family, Andrew is four and a half years older than I am, and our brother, Jon, is three years older than he is). I had been to plenty of sports events at the Garden, but this was a different type of energy. The experience of being in the moment and connecting directly with the artist was very different from watching my favorite hockey team vanquish an opponent (even if I still get a dopamine hit from the "Let's Go, Rangers!" chant). I also remember all the moms dressed up in black lace just like their daughters, which in its own way said something about the power of live music.

While I was growing up in NYC, my friends and I were really into Jane's Addiction and My Bloody Valentine. When I saw MBV at the Ritz, staffers handed out earplugs at the door, and at the end of the set, more than half the room fled during the fifteen minutes of white noise that accompanied "You Made Me Realise."

In 1992, I attended a formative Lollapalooza show in Scranton, Pennsylvania, with Red Hot Chili Peppers, Pearl Jam, Soundgarden, Ice Cube, the Jesus and Mary Chain, Cypress Hill, and Porno for Pyros. It was an incredible day that nearly ended on a sour note when we got lost and I drove the wrong way down a road, but I course-corrected just in time.

Twelve years later, I hooked up Lolla cofounder Perry Farrell with the String Cheese Incident at The Jammys. I've gone on to do a number of shows with him, including a 2015 Jane's Addiction gig at Brooklyn Bowl when they performed *Nothing's Shocking*, their 1988 album I had heard so many times in high school.

During my first two years at Northwestern, my musical tastes started to shift. While I saw Charlatans UK and Inspiral Carpets at Chicago's Metro, I also began checking out bands like Col. Bruce Hampton and the Aquarium Rescue Unit, Leftover Salmon, Rusted Root, and God Street Wine at smaller clubs, like Biddy Mulligans and Otis's.

I was also starting to get into the Grateful Dead. The music took hold of me in a way that seems equally accidental and inevitable, as my friends dropped live tapes into boom boxes while we were throwing Frisbees or hanging out. I also was in the audience when Mickey Hart gave a talk about the power of percussion to unite people across cultures (these days, I'll still hear him give that talk, it's just that sometimes I'll be an audience of one—ha!).

When I was a freshman, the Dead didn't make it to Chicago during the school year. They played two nights at Soldier Field in the summer, but by that time, I was back in New York. However, I was able to go to my first show, at Giants Stadium, with my friend

Alex Cornfeld, who, like myself, had grown up in the city and was attending Northwestern.

While that Giants Stadium show didn't completely knock me on my ass, it still set me reeling. That's where I experienced the glory of seventy thousand people singing, "You know our love will not fade away," while the band harmonized in response. That was the energy I later hoped to revisit at Fare Thee Well, and I had chills when "Not Fade" closed out set two on the final night.

My second Dead experience was the one that forever scrambled my DNA. The evening started out with that special Grateful Dead kismet I've since experienced so many times over the years. By the spring of 1993, I had started hanging out at a local head shop called the Parking Lot, a reference to the vending village (a.k.a. Shakedown Street) outside Grateful Dead shows. The store's slogan was "Where the '60s Meet the '90s," and it was owned by a married couple named Bill and Coertje. They were the only people I knew at that time, other than my Northwestern crew, who would possibly have been at a Grateful Dead show in Rosemont, Illinois. So, of course, when we got to our seats, I turned around to see that Bill and Coertje were right behind us.

I was much more familiar with the music than I had been at Giants, so I figured I was primed and ready. I may have gotten a little too primed before the show because I was not ready for what went down.

The first set started out with "Help on the Way" > "Slipknot" > "Franklin's Tower," the classic GD trifecta that blends a snaky intro with an intricate instrumental section and builds toward an iconic sing-along chorus. It was Jerry at his most appealing. So, too, was the wistful "So Many Roads," which popped up a bit later (he would perform the poignant final version of this song at Soldier Field in 1995 during the band's last show).

The second set opened with a spirited "Aiko Aiko" that had the entire venue moving in unison. However, it was the jam during "Space" that set me in motion. Literally. The poet Ken Nordine took the stage with the band for some of his "word jazz," using the deep, resonant baritone that had made him a successful voice-over actor for commercials and movie trailers. It was during "Flibberty

Jib" that I began to feel claustrophobic. The walls were starting to constrict, and I needed to take a breather from the intensity of it all. So I left my seat, then my section, then the arena.

I stepped into the parking lot, where it had started to snow. I immediately ran into some Deadhead kids who put me at ease. They were about my age, but it soon became clear they weren't going back to school the next day. They were living the life of the road, savoring the adventure, and sharing a sense of community that often seemed absent from daily life. I hung out with them for a while in a drum circle in the snow.

I never gave much thought to the fact that I was separated from my friends, who had driven me to the show, but shortly after I came to this realization, I ran into them. Again, that's the sort of serendipity that I've come to expect from the good ol' Grateful Dead.

Eventually, we made it back to Northwestern.

However, I never made it to bed that night.

In the concert industry, we talk about being there at doors, which means being outside a venue waiting to be admitted as soon as it opens. Well, the next morning, I was at doors when the college library opened, for the first and only time in my life.

I needed to learn more about what I had just experienced.

Nothing would be the same for me.

3

COLD-CALLING KESEY

Grateful Dead
The Palace, Auburn Hills, Michigan
June 8, 1993

The adventure began in Auburn Hills.

I had convinced my friend Philip Bruell to join me traveling from show to show on the Grateful Dead's summer tour recording footage and interviewing Deadheads in the lot for a documentary. He was a fellow RTVF student who had a Hi8 video camera and an editing system in his dorm room. He had never seen the Dead and didn't know what to expect. We ended up spending four weeks on tour together and then heading west to land some additional interviews.

The idea for the film had come to me following my all-nighter three months earlier. As soon as the Northwestern library opened, I walked in and started researching Deadhead culture. Back then, I wasn't googling it; I was using the card catalog and microfiche. I discovered that Rebecca Adams, a sociology professor in North Carolina, had been writing about Deadheads, but there wasn't a major examination of the early '90s scene. It was larger than prior decades, filled with twentysomethings hitting the road with the band.

When I first stepped into the library, I didn't realize I was doing film research. I just wanted to learn more, maybe for a research paper. I had never previously contemplated making an hour-long documentary. However, after poking around for a while, I convinced myself that this would be a worthy project for a film.

Then I convinced Phil as well.

We were going to make a documentary for school credit. That was as far as we thought it would go.

So we hunkered down in Evanston after the spring semester and prepared to join the circus when it arrived in Auburn Hills, Michigan, on the third date of Dead's '93 summer tour.

We plotted out our travel plans, readied our gear, and rented a van.

Then, on the afternoon of June 8, we drove into a parking lot outside the venue, amped up and ready to go.

There was only one problem. We had rented an all-white van with no windows. As soon as we pulled into the lot, I could hear the cries of "DEA! DEA!"

The obvious is obvious until you miss it.

When Phil and I had picked up the van, we failed to recognize that Deadheads would view us as Drug Enforcement agents.

"Pull out! Let's get out of here!" I yelled at Phil, who was behind the wheel.

We made a quick U-turn and drove up the road to find a less conspicuous spot. Then we grabbed our recording gear and walked back to the lot to begin shooting the film that eventually would be called *And Miles to Go Before I Sleep: On Tour with the Grateful Dead Summer 1993.*

We were figuring it all out on the fly, which continues to be my MO. It's important to do as much preparation as possible, but then there comes a moment when you have to take a deep breath, let it all go, and prepare to react. As the scale of the event increases, so does the intensity, but there's stress at any level, particularly when something leaves your hands and you pivot to pure response mode.

We relied on the kindness of others. I asked my friends for whatever help they could offer, and it turned out one of them was the nephew of Louisville's mayor, which is how we were able to ride with undercover police officers in the lot. However, it was just as important to meet Sunshine Bear out there in Shakedown, who shared his story and made introductions for us.

You can't see it if you're not there. It's important to show up.

We were committed to being out there in the lots shooting every day, no matter how easy it might be to get distracted (and for a college kid on a Dead tour, it was plenty easy—perhaps easier for me than for Phil). However, we stuck to it, which is how we captured a riot in Buffalo.

We were at Rich Stadium around 1:00 p.m. when this one guy stood outside the fence and told the security guards, "I'm going, I'm going . . ." The guards didn't think much of it, and they told him, "Yeah, right." We kept coming back to shoot additional footage of him because he never left. Then around 7:30, just after dusk, a bunch of people crashed through the gate from that very spot, and the original guy was the one who started it.

This was one of the few times we witnessed friction or hostility. Despite the initial "DEA!" chants and the Buffalo gate-crashing incident, most people were open-minded and welcoming, even if the wind did blow strange.

We were never able to get any band members to participate, but twenty-two years later, I experienced another moment of Grateful Dead serendipity via Justin Kreutzmann. Justin is a filmmaker who also happens to be the son of Grateful Dead drummer Bill Kreutzmann. We were discussing the videos that he was going to create for us to screen during the set breaks at Fare Thee Well. That's when he told me that he had been on the summer '93 tour shooting behind the scenes.

I would have loved to have shared his vantage point, but as I told him, "I was out there in the lot. I couldn't get in."

Justin responded, "Well, I was backstage with Jerry, so I didn't go out."

We realized that we had filmed the same shows, which allowed Justin to intercut some of our footage for Fare Thee Well, moving back and forth from his backstage perspective to my viewpoint from the lots.

Two months after the summer tour, Phil and I again took to the road, traveling west in search of interviews with cultural figures who could lend context to the story. Our first stop was the Universal Amphitheatre in Los Angeles on September 2 for the MTV Video Music Awards. We didn't have credentials because we were two college kids making a student film, but we were able to sneak into the backstage artist compound. We lugged in the gear, avoided eye contact, and made it appear like we belonged. Our variation on the Jedi mind trick. I later pulled the same move to get into the men's soccer final at the 1996 Olympics and the 2001 Super Bowl. These days with barcodes and scanners, it's almost impossible to make it work. Almost.

After we made it into the compound, we soon scored an interview with Chris Barron. This was when the Spin Doctors were at their commercial peak and they performed "Two Princes" on the show. Chris was supercool after we explained we were renegade students on a stealth mission. We've become friends, and in the final days of Wetlands, I pushed the Spin Doctors guys to get past some personal differences and reunite for one of the club's last shows.

Something else happened en route to the VMAs. We went to a video store to pick up some tape, and while we were standing in line talking about the project, a random guy heard us and asked, "You're working on a Dead thing? You want to interview Timothy Leary?" I told him we'd been trying to get to Leary, and he said, "I'm having a party tonight after the VMAs, and he's going to be there."

He wasn't.

However, his girlfriend *was*, and she invited us to drop by his house the next day at 5:00 p.m.

That's how we were able to film this crazy conversation with Timothy Leary and his twenty-six-year-old girlfriend.

Our biggest interview happened a few days later in Eugene on my twenty-first birthday. Ken Kesey's number was listed in the phone book, so I had called him after we'd come home from tour, asking for an interview. His wife, Faye, answered the phone and gave me a polite pass.

I waited until August and tried again. But this time, I said, "I'm going to be in Oregon in early September, and I was wondering if I could stop by, since I'll be there anyways."

She responded, "Well, if you're gonna be in the neighborhood, then give us a call when you're nearby."

I wasn't going to be in Oregon in September . . . until I made that phone call. I have used that move once or twice since then— "Hey, I'm going to be in the neighborhood" can be very effective. If the person you want to meet understands that you're already going to be there, it is a lot easier for them to say, "Okay, come on by." It's a good one to keep in your quiver.

So we went up to Eugene on September 7, 1993, my twenty-first birthday. When we got to the house, Kesey said, "I will talk a bit about your project, but I don't want to do an interview." I told him this was fine.

Something I took away from my time with Kesey was not to be overeager and to try and follow his lead. That is important when interacting with legends who do not suffer fools gladly. Hanging with Kesey helped me learn to hang.

We were sitting on his porch around 6:00 p.m. having a smoke when he suddenly told me, "Okay, go get your camera. I'll talk a bit, but I don't want to talk about the old days. I want to talk about the kids today; I think it's important."

And it was.

We jumped from topic to topic, but here's something that's always stuck with me. After demonstrating a magic trick with a coin, he explained, "There's a moment when you see something like that [where] there's a crack in your mind and you know it's a trick, but you can't figure it out. And that crack lets in all the light. It opens up all the possibilities. When that little split-second thing happens when the Dead are playing and everybody in the audience goes, 'Wow! Did you see that?' that's the moment. And the kids will watch five hours of mediocre music to have that one click happen because that puts them in touch with the invisible."

Kesey's words ring as true to me today as they did back then.

Phil Bruell and I returned to school and began editing the film. Phil's roommate Dave Gioiella pitched in as well because they had their own equipment. This was linear editing where you had to find the proper spot on the videotape to make an edit. You couldn't just zoom around from place to place like you can today, assembling and disassembling a potential edit with the click of a mouse. If you look at the final film, there are a few spots that look slightly blown out because of the wear and tear.

The process of editing *And Miles to Go* lasted well over a year because we were juggling other things. However, I can never stand idle, so we kept adding interviews with folks like Al Franken.

In the midst of all of this, I received a phone call that guided me to the next step on a path that eventually led to Wetlands.

4

AMERICAN ROAD

Phish
The Vic Theatre, Chicago, Illinois
December 5, 1992

I saw my first Phish show in December of my sophomore year at Northwestern.

The connection was immediate, and I ended up traveling to Boston later that month for their New Year's Eve gig at Matthews Arena.

I am still drawn to the music, and I'll take it whenever and wherever I can. In February 2020, I called an audible and hopped on a plane to Mexico at the last minute on a Thursday afternoon to check out the first night of their festival and was back in the office the next day for three nights of Joe Russo's Almost Dead at the Capitol. A few years earlier, I wrapped up a family vacation in Rome with a visit to the Sistine Chapel and then made it to Denver in time for a Phish gig at Dick's (before continuing to Vegas in the morning).

There's something about seeing live music in general and Phish in particular that seems to enhance my mental capacity. Watching them perform is candy for my brain waves. It adds additional effectiveness to my ability to figure things out—whether that's a problem I'm already turning over in my mind or something that all the additional effectiveness helped me realize I needed to figure out (ha!).

Over the years, I've been at Phish shows where the ideas have started flowing, but because of the way my brain works, when the music stopped, all those thoughts disappeared. There were a few occasions in the '90s when I'd assembled a complex plan of action with interlocked pieces like a LEGO skyscraper, only to have it all collapse in an instant after the lights came on.

Nowadays, it's easy to put things down in the notes section of my phone, which I'll do throughout the set as a precautionary measure. However, during the pre-iPhone era, there were instances when I'd walk over to the concession stand and buy a pretzel just for the napkin. Then I'd borrow a pen to jot down what I was thinking before it dissipated. There may even have been some nights when I was so deep in it that I handed over my wallet and said, "Take what's needed," while balancing a tower of thoughts. That may have happened.

In the spring of 1995, a Phish-related idea occurred to me outside of a Phish show that would have reverberations for years to come. I was at a party shortly after reading *On the Road* when I heard "You Enjoy Myself" blasting out of a deck tape. In that single moment, a film concept came to me—I envisioned a travelogue, presenting images of the country set to the beginning of that song. While many of my ideas develop through a series of iterations, this was a rare one that arrived fully formed and would become the short film *American Road*.

I suppose I had film on my mind because I had recently been to Sundance with a Grateful Dead documentary—not *And Miles to Go* but *Tie-Died*, a project I had become involved with because of *And Miles to Go*.

In the spring of 1994, I was contacted by some film producers in Los Angeles who were preparing to shoot a documentary about touring Deadheads. At this point, we were still editing *And Miles to Go*. No one outside our circle had seen it. But someone—I still don't know who it was—identified me as someone who could navigate the lots to land interviews.

So the filmmakers offered me the title of associate producer and a small salary to join them on tour that summer. As it turned out, the associate producer title required me to do little more than approach Deadheads and see if they'd speak on camera. That's also pretty much all the associate producer title *allowed* me to do. Still, it was a fun summer job.

After tour ended, the filmmakers returned to LA to begin editing what was originally called *Dead Heads*. The documentary was accepted into the 1995 Sundance Film Festival, but after a screening for the Grateful Dead staff, the group's management informed the producers that they would need to remove all intellectual property, including the title, along with the five Dead songs that had appeared in the rough cut.

I heard about this well after the fact, but it slightly curtailed my enjoyment of the renamed *Tie-Died* when it premiered at Sundance on January 21, 1995. I don't have too many memories of the experience, although looking back, I can now appreciate that I was an associate producer of an official Sundance selection while still a college student.

I returned to Northwestern for my last semester, during which we finally completed *And Miles to Go*. I briefly explored making a companion film that would delve into the Lollapalooza scene but eventually decided to let it go.

If you're interested in the arts, then actively pursue this while you're still in college. Don't wait until after you graduate, and certainly don't drop out to launch your own company, because the additional economic pressure could prompt some bad decision-making. If you want to be a music promoter, then find a way to put on a show while you're still an undergrad, ideally as part of a concert committee, so that your own money isn't on the line. The checklists that you'll have to walk through are the same ones that we have at the Bowl, the Capitol, Radio City, or even MSG; it's just the scale is different.

If you're putting on a show in a fifty-cap room, you are making many of the same decisions that somebody is making at a fifty-thousand-capacity festival. You still have to engage with the talent and make an agreement with their representative. You need to promote and execute the onsale and continue to sell tickets—this may involve creating ads or some other form of marketing, as well as the potential pursuit of press coverage. On the night of the show, you have to load in the band, open doors, provide security, take tickets, allow for sound check. There are also backline requirements and production specs. You need a head of sound, a lighting person, a stage manager, production people, box office staff. The fundamentals are the same no matter the scale of the event.

Similarly, if you're a college student with an interest in music and film like I was, then find an academic adviser who will sign off on an independent study allowing you to make a documentary. In my case, that was Professor Richard Maxwell, who remained patient and supportive throughout the process. Thank you, Rick.

While we were completing *And Miles to Go*, I received a call from someone on the *Tie-Died* team who explained that our film represented a problem for them. They'd hired two guys who had successfully repped *Hoop Dreams*, the breakout film from the previous Sundance, to find them a distributor. However, when *Tie-Died* didn't generate the same level of interest, the film reps decided to raise money and release it themselves. They viewed *And Miles to Go* as potential competition, although I certainly didn't see it that way.

Still, we negotiated a deal, in which I agreed not to pursue a distribution deal for *And Miles to Go*. In exchange, my interview with Ken Kesey would appear as a short film prior to *Tie-Died* and would be acknowledged on the official concert poster ("Bonus Attraction: *A Conversation with Ken Kesey: A Short Film by Peter Shapiro*"). I also received $20,000, which I immediately rolled into *American Road*.

My initial Phish show at the Vic in December 1992 was unlike anything I'd ever seen before. The band's energy was incredible, and the crowd responded in kind. I had heard a few Phish originals, which connected with me, but I wasn't prepared for the full-on animated intensity of the live show. Plus trampolines!

I've always enjoyed seeing shows at the Vic. Unlike the Cap, which has a great raked floor, the Vic has multiple flat levels, which I also appreciate as a concertgoer. I was in the center, first level up with a fine angle on the action.

By the spring of '95, I had seen Phish many times over, and I was altogether familiar with their music. But it wasn't until that one moment when I heard "You Enjoy Myself" at a party that I had the epiphany about how I would build a film around it.

So I wrote a letter to Dionysian Productions, the band's management. Remembering what had happened with the Dead's music in *Tie-Died*, I wanted to clear this in advance. Plus, there was no second choice for me. My vision for the film was intertwined with "YEM."

John Paluska, who was the manager at the time, handed it off to Jason Colton, who remains part of the Phish team (and manages many other bands I work with regularly). Jason contacted me, and I explained that I wanted to drive across the forty-eight states in the continental United States and then set that imagery to the first seven minutes of "You Enjoy Myself." They gave me permission, and that's the film I made.

My running buddy for this one was Alex Cornfeld, my fellow Northwestern student with whom I'd attended my very first Dead show in June 1992. I had enjoyed working with Phil Bruell, but by this point, he had relocated to Manhattan and launched Northern Lights Post, an editing house, with his roommate Dave Gioiella. Northern Lights became an immediate success, although Phil took ill and died from kidney disease in 2002.

Phil and I had shot *And Miles to Go* on video using the camera that he already owned. For *American Road*, I wanted to use film, so we rented a Super 16 millimeter camera with my proceeds from *Tie-Died*. Beyond that, we kept our budget tight. No special lighting. It was just Alex, me, the camera, and film. We spent some nights in cheap motels and others in the white van that we rented (which thankfully inspired no "DEA!" reprise).

In June '95, we set out from Nectar's in Burlington, Vermont (a nod to Phish), then traveled through New England and New York, down into the Southeast and the Deep South. From there, we headed through Oklahoma, Texas, and the Southwest, then up the West Coast through Seattle and back east, touching every state we'd missed. We figured out a lot of our stops on the fly, with a Rand McNally in front of us.

The van was crucial. We rented it for one month through a deal that offered unlimited mileage. When we returned it thirty days later, it had 13,254 additional miles on it. The guy behind the counter freaked out a bit when he saw what we had done, but we were just playing by the rules. Plus, if there's one thing

I've come to appreciate after years of experiencing the profound heights of improvisational music, it's that unlimited really means *unlimited*.

Alex and I returned to New York to begin the arduous process of assembling the film. Although *American Road* would only be seven minutes long, there was an abundance of raw footage, which Dave Gioiella edited between gigs at Northern Lights. Meanwhile, I started an internship at New Line Cinema, thinking that I might pursue a career in the movie business.

We had a rough cut ready by the summer of '96. *American Road* tracks our linear trip across the country, and when I hear "You Enjoy Myself" today, it takes me back to that time. The images flash past in a few beats, but over seven minutes and ten seconds, you'll see the Ben and Jerry's factory, Buddy Cianci hawking marinara sauce, Harry Caray outside Wrigley Field, the Lincoln Memorial, Little Rock Central High, the Corn Palace, the Vegas Strip, the Badlands, 710 Ashbury Street, Pike Place Fish Market, President Clinton, the license plate on Kesey's *Furthur* bus, Wall Drug, Nectar Rorris, and plenty more. We submitted it to Sundance, and shortly before Thanksgiving, we learned that we'd been accepted.

I showed up in Park City in January 1997 for the five screenings of *American Road*. I was honored to be there, but my mind was somewhere else as well because the countdown was well underway for April 1, 1997, the day when I would become the new owner of the legendary rock club Wetlands Preserve.

5

WETLANDS PRESERVED

After Dark
Roanoke College, Salem, Virginia
February 8, 1996

While growing up, I never had dreams of becoming a concert promoter.

The idea didn't enter my head.

I didn't really understand what a concert promoter did until I *became* a concert promoter (and I'm still trying to figure some of it out).

However, when it happened, I didn't just dip my toe in the water; I became the owner of the largest Manhattan music venue open for business seven days a week.

When I hear the stories of other people's career paths, their journeys can feel inevitable. Listening to Trey Anastasio, Derek Trucks, Questlove, or Jimmy Fallon, it's clear how they ended up where they are today.

The same cannot be said of me.

But for a particular quirk of history, a fortuitous moment in time, things would have been dramatically different.

Come to think of it, there have been a few of those moments, going back to my decision to flee Rosemont Horizon mid-show, after Ken Nordine got inside my head.

The next pivotal event—literally an event that prompted a full-on career pivot—was my conversation with the fill-in bass player for a Grateful Dead cover band.

On Thursday, February 8, 1996, I traveled to Roanoke College in Salem, Virginia, for a presentation on the Grateful Dead, following Jerry Garcia's passing the prior summer.

Jerry died of a heart attack on August 9, 1995, at age fifty-three. I was twenty-two at the time, and fifty-three had felt ancient to me, although less so these days. Over a quarter century has passed since then, during which Phil, Bobby, Mickey, and Billy have all remained active and vital. Jerry was in rehab when he died. If he could have made it through, imagine all the new songs that would fill the air. That's a given, since his genius songwriting partner Robert Hunter lived until September 2019.

Jerry's death led the *Tie-Died* team to push out the film with additional fanfare, including a full-page ad on the back page of *Entertainment Weekly*. *Tie-Died* opened on September 22 in nearly one hundred theaters, which was impressive for a documentary released by an independent distributor.

The reviews were moderately positive, although no one said much about my film. One memorable exception was the Friday morning I opened the *New York Times* to discover that Janet Maslin had described *A Conversation with Ken Kesey* as "poignant."

By February 1996, *Tie-Died* had long since concluded its theatrical run, and the team was hoping to build momentum toward a VHS release. As a result, I was permitted to tour colleges and screen *And Miles to Go*, along with portions of *Tie-Died*.

I created an event called The Music Never Stops (!).

We pitched it to college student activities committees as a multimedia experience reflecting on the legacy of Jerry and the Dead. In addition to the documentaries, I delivered a brief presentation and facilitated a discussion. This was followed by a performance from After Dark, a leading Grateful Dead cover band.

After Dark's bass player was unavailable to perform at Roanoke or Bloomsburg University in Bloomsburg, Pennsylvania. So they had asked Marty Bostoff—who normally played in his own Dead tribute act, Tiberius—to fill in.

I didn't know Marty, but he approached me with a bold suggestion: "Dude, you should take over Wetlands."

"What do you mean?" I responded.

I had no idea at the time that Wetlands founder Larry Bloch was thinking about shutting down the club. He had opened Wetlands with his wife, Laura, in February 1989, as a nightclub with a social mission. To quote Larry: "Wetlands was a new frontier. It was setting aside from eighty to one hundred thousand dollars a year as an overhead expense to fund a full-time environmental and social justice organization, originally called the eco-saloon and eventually renamed the Activism Center at Wetlands. The idea was that the monetary cost of running an effective activism center wouldn't be impaired or tied into the profitability of the nightclub. It would be a necessary expense. Just like if we didn't pay the rent, we would be shut down. If we didn't fund the social and environmental activism center, we wouldn't be Wetlands."

With these principles and a passion for the Grateful Dead, Larry and Laura built the club from scratch in a former warehouse at 161 Hudson Street in a section of Lower Manhattan. The area would soon become the trendy neighborhood known as Tribeca (Triangle Below Canal Street) thanks to Robert De Niro and a few other folks.

Wetlands gained notoriety for the converted 1966 VW bus located inside the club that served as a merch booth, as well as its role in nurturing a new generation of improv-based bands (starting with groups like Phish, Blues Traveler, Widespread Panic, the Spin Doctors, Col. Bruce Hampton and the Aquarium Rescue Unit, and later, moe., Gov't Mule, Dave Matthews Band, God Street Wine, and many others).

I had only set foot in Wetlands once. I grew up on the Upper East Side of Manhattan but never much went below Fourteenth Street. I attended sporting events but didn't step up my live concert game until I arrived at Northwestern.

Finally, in September 1995, I attended a performance by Merl Saunders and the Rainforest Band (Marty Bostoff's group, Tiberius, opened that show, but we didn't meet).

At first, I brushed off Marty's suggestion. I appreciated he thought I could run Wetlands, but it seemed implausible.

What did I know about being a club owner? The closest I had come was producing the Hamlin Street Block Party in Evanston when I was a senior at Northwestern. I had secured the permits and organized this outdoor gathering, but there was no headline music.

Plus, how could I even afford it? The only resources I had available to me were some shares of IBM that my grandfather had given to me for my bar mitzvah. I didn't have the kind of money required to purchase and operate a nightclub.

Still, after Marty put the idea in my head, I kept coming back to it.

I believed that following Jerry Garcia's death, people needed to be lifted. I also understood that those who loved the spirit and improvisational vibe of the Grateful Dead would be seeking out new bands and experiences. All of this was true of me as well.

So I decided to learn more about the situation at Wetlands.

I discovered that Larry was going to shut down the club unless he identified a successor who could meet his exacting standards. He was burnt out and relocating to Vermont, following a divorce, to live closer to his son.

As Larry later recalled, "It was a process I didn't think would happen necessarily. It wasn't clear someone would shoulder the responsibility to contractually bind him- or herself to a licensing agreement that would bind them to fund the Activism Center and carry on the independent no-selling-out policy, which was what Wetlands was all about."

My first point of contact was Otis Read. He had been general manager of the club for about four years, and he was now the incoming point of reception for all purchase inquiries. I laid it all out for him, acknowledging my enthusiasm and ignorance.

Apparently, I passed muster because I was allowed to meet Larry, who was living in his father's apartment in Murray Hill. Larry was going through quite a bit at that time and seemed slightly distracted as I made my pitch: "I know nothing about the club business; I don't know much about the music business. I'm twenty-three; I just graduated college. I believe in the culture because I went on the road with the Grateful Dead, and I want to see if I can be involved and maybe part of the team to keep Wetlands going."

Thankfully, he'd seen *And Miles to Go*, and he believed that I could successfully maintain the musical mission of the club. That was the easy part.

For Larry, it was far more important that the new owner support the social and environmental activism center. Even though I had no background in any of that, I think *And Miles to Go* helped convince him that I respected the ethos.

There was, however, one complication that made my advisers nervous: Larry wouldn't let me see the books.

My advisers were my parents, Ellen and Daniel Shapiro. They were somewhat mystified because I had graduated from Northwestern as a TV and film student. I was interning at New Line, preparing to submit *American Road* to Sundance, and now I wanted to run a nightclub?

My parents had plenty of questions for me, and I fielded those questions most every night because I was still living at home. The decision to return home after college had enabled me to avoid paying living expenses and keep my options open.

I encourage interns to do the same, whenever possible. I also tell them that they don't need to pick their careers until they've been out of college for a number of years. People don't retire at sixty-two or sixty-five anymore. They don't get married at twenty-four. Everything's been pushed back. You want flexibility to try things, and if that means living at home for a little while, you should give it a go.

In my case, as I considered taking over Wetlands, my parents offered both support and skepticism. In addition, my father was a leading tax attorney and the founding partner of Schulte Roth & Zabel, a firm with over one hundred lawyers. He would provide me with much-needed legal advice and enlist a few of his colleagues to do the same.

I first brought my parents to Wetlands on a Tuesday night. It was in between sets, and they didn't know what to make of the fact that the audience members in this rock club were sitting cross-legged in front of the stage, waiting for the next band.

While Larry permitted Otis to show me the monthly expenses, he wouldn't allow me to see the tax returns or anything that identified whether he was turning a profit. Still, I did have a real sense of what it cost to operate Wetlands: the rent, the staffing, the garbage, the water, the unemployment insurance, and the like.

Otis also helped me understand how the club generated income. He explained that most of the revenue came from the bar, along with a split of the door proceeds, with 70 percent typically going to the band and the remainder to the club, although certain headliners would receive a higher percentage (that 70 percent has drifted higher over the intervening years).

By forbidding anyone to see the numbers, Larry sought to eliminate candidates who viewed Wetlands solely as a business proposition. I was not one of those individuals, so I remained undeterred. I am not sure if I would proceed the same way today (buying the business without numbers is pretty cray), but I believed in Wetlands.

It took a little while for Larry to believe in me. Even after I demonstrated my willingness to move forward with limited financials, our conversations didn't advance to the subject of my transition. I would also experience this later with Marvin Ravikoff at the Capitol Theatre. Before Marvin or Larry would expend any energy on deal points, I needed to earn their trust. I sensed that if I rushed it, I'd blow it.

It often felt like Larry was administering a series of tests. He'd ask me for my thoughts on a variety of subjects, from the practical considerations of running a nightclub to environmental concerns to house music. (A quintessential Larry story is that he was out of town one Saturday night and then called to check in. While most club owners would immediately ask about the bar proceeds or the paid attendance, Larry wanted to know what was the first song that the DJ played immediately after the headlining band had completed its opening set.) As you can imagine, I was nervous about saying the wrong thing. Larry was an idiosyncratic guy, and I suspected that if I screwed up, he'd say, "The kid's out."

We got to the point where he informed me that I could have a small ownership stake in Wetlands. I wouldn't be the principal owner, but I could join the team. This made perfect sense to me, particularly since I had no experience and limited capital.

The individual Larry had selected as the majority partner was older and could contribute far more resources. The financial component was important to Larry because he was particularly concerned that there would be enough money to fund the Activism Center.

The owner-in-waiting was a professional bridge player, a vocation in alignment with some of Larry's recreational habits. (Larry enjoyed betting on horse racing, in particular, and in 2005, he hit on a superfecta at the Kentucky Derby, picking the top four horses in order of finish and winning a cool $864,253, which he then donated to multiple causes, keeping all of this quiet until he allowed his ex-wife, Laura, to report on it for *HorsePlayer Magazine.*)

I was introduced to my new partner, although it felt like he was keeping me at arm's length. I assumed this was because he was the lead investor and I would only have a limited role.

But then in the early fall of '96, Larry called me with an update.

To gain favor with the people running the Wetlands environmental center, the prospective owner had hired one of the organization's volunteers to clean his apartment. In the process of doing this, the volunteer found a letter that the card player had written to his girlfriend, who was living in Europe at the time. This letter explained that he was going to purchase a New York nightclub at an amazing price because he had promised to fund its in-house activism center. However, he revealed that after he closed the deal, he was going to shut it down.

The Wetlands volunteer ran out and made a photocopy of the letter at a nearby print shop (espionage required a bit more hoofing in the pre-smartphone days). Then he returned to the apartment, replaced the original, and brought the copy to Wetlands.

When Larry saw the letter, he immediately shuffled the deck.

The ongoing series of fortuitous events continued.

Larry called to let me know that the bridge player was out and he was bumping up my role.

I had recently turned twenty-four years old, and I was about to take over Wetlands.

6

TEN THOUSAND SHOWS

Marty Balin
Wetlands Preserve, New York, New York
April 16, 1997

W hat's that phrase?
It's all fun and games until someone loses five grand at the door?

It's all fun and games until someone loses 10 percent of their bank account on a Wednesday night?

It's all fun and games until your big gig tanks?

Here's what I do know: Just over two weeks after becoming full-time owner of Wetlands, we put on our first high-ticket show (it cost a whopping twelve dollars). The date was April 16, 1997, and the performer was Marty Balin.

I was so excited to have a founding member of Jefferson Airplane in my club that it never occurred to me that not everyone else in the tristate area would share my enthusiasm.

That was the moment when I first appreciated the uneven risk exposure in the concert industry. The promoter pays a guarantee to an established headliner, and the artist is permitted to keep the money no matter how many people attend.

So if only a handful of folks make their way to Wetlands to see Marty Balin on a Wednesday night (not so hypothetically, alas), then the promoter is out the full sum of money. There's no form of remediation.

Beyond the artist's guarantee, there are costs associated with opening the doors, such as utilities and staffing. If there is low turnout (again, not hypothetically), it's unlikely that proceeds from the bar will offset these expenses.

Which is how I lost 10 percent of my bank account when Marty Balin played Wetlands, two weeks after I took over.

I enjoyed meeting him, though, and it *was* a good show.

It was also less stressful than the phone call I had received from a reporter at the *New York Post* on the morning of April 1—my first official day as owner—inquiring about a shooting incident at the club.

Although I officially took over on April 1, I had been a steady presence in the venue for a few months. After Larry decided not to sell to the bridge player, he recommended that I come in as part of a three-headed leadership team along with Chris Zahn, who had been booking the club for a few years, and James Hansen, who ran the environmental and social justice center. We began meeting during the fall of 1996 to chart a collective course, but we were all so strong-willed that Larry realized it wouldn't work.

That's when he structured a deal in which I would be the sole owner. To take things easy on me, he agreed to accept $75,000 per year for four years, which I paid in monthly installments after my initial deposit. That deposit represented most of the bar mitzvah money, with a little extra in the bank for operating expenses (which would become a little less extra following the Marty Balin show).

Larry went out of his way to make things work for me. As long as Wetlands was successful, there was a good chance that I would be able to pull the additional payments out of the club's profits when I paid him each month.

He also decided to enter into a handshake agreement and then postpone the formal changeover by six months, allowing for a gradual transition. Meanwhile, he moved up to Brattleboro, Vermont, where he opened Save the Corporations from Themselves, which sold environmentally sustainable clothing and fair-trade goods and became a hub for people who embraced an eco-friendly lifestyle.

When it came to Wetlands, though, he was fried. As I've come to learn, it's tough to do a venue every night of the week. It's even tougher when you're the little guy in a competitive market like New York. Plus, on top of the challenges associated with running a music venue, Wetlands also featured an in-house activism center that utilized an aggressive, direct-action-oriented approach.

So with Larry up in Brattleboro, I moved forward with a slow roll. Since I had no background in the concert business, it was helpful to spend time at Wetlands before I was responsible for what happened at the club.

I am a believer in the ten thousand hours thing. You need to put in the time. In *Outliers*, Malcolm Gladwell identifies plenty of people, from the Beatles to Bill Gates, who thrived after devoting ten thousand hours to their pursuits. There's nothing more important than rolling up your sleeves and getting into it. To succeed, you need to fail.

In my case, after all the years at Wetlands and then the Brooklyn Bowls, which are seven days a week, as well as the Cap and Garcia's, I haven't just logged ten thousand hours, I've put on ten thousand shows.

It all began when I was the owner-in-waiting at Wetlands.

During this period, I familiarized myself with the day-to-day operations. There were about fifty people working at Wetlands, and I was younger than all of them. The advice some folks had given me was that when you take over an existing business, you're supposed to fire everyone, reinterview them, and then rehire the ones who seem worthy. That just wasn't going to be the move for twenty-four-year-old Pete Shapiro when he became the new owner. So I made an effort to spend time with everyone and understand the nature of their jobs.

Based on their initial reactions, I also went out and bought business cards. I thought it might be useful to have these on hand when people doubted that I owned the place.

In general, I think I handled myself pretty well, aside from the time I nearly killed Wavy Gravy. He had come to the club for an afternoon sound check, then he wanted to go to a magic shop to buy an invisible dog leash. So we hopped in a cab to Abracadabra, where he purchased a few items, then walked into a nearby Papaya King for a hot dog. By this point, it was raining and turning dark. There were no taxis available, but I noticed one on a cross street.

So I said to him, "You stay here, and I'll run over, get the taxi, and bring it to you."

With traffic stopped due to a red light, I ran over to the cab. As I opened the door and turned back to Wavy, I realized that he'd been slowly following me, holding his hot dog and his bags.

Then the light turned green, and suddenly, he was stranded in the middle of the street. I could see the confusion on his face as he realized that three lanes of cars were flying at him on the slippery pavement. He began spinning around to avoid them. His bags went flying, and he dropped the hot dog. Somehow, he avoided getting hit, though, which is part of that Wavy Gravy magic. If he had gone down on my watch, it would not have been cool.

Another memory of that era is that we didn't have voice mail in the club; we had physical in-boxes. If you missed a call, someone would jot down the message and place it in your box. I remember the thrill I experienced on my first official day as owner when the box that previously held Larry's messages now held mine.

That was later in the day, though.

Before I made it to that point, I was woken up by a call from the *New York Post* (I'm still not sure how they got my number). The reporter wanted to know if I had any comment on the shooting that had taken place the prior evening at Wetlands. I had little to say because I was still trying to wrap my head around the potential repercussions.

I wasn't at the club on Monday night, March 31. Instead, I was at my new apartment, anticipating Tuesday's ownership transition. I remember sitting in the living room, which doubled as my bedroom, when the phone rang. It was the transitional GM Larry had brought in to bridge the gap from Otis Read to my eventual GM, Charley Ryan (with whom I would later cofound Brooklyn Bowl).

The transitional GM explained there had been a shooting, but everything was fine and that I should remain where I was. I agreed to do so, in part because I was paralyzed by dread. As I've said, I believe that I suffer from a mild case of PTSD, and it may very well have started in this moment.

What I learned the next day was that someone had been kicked out of Wetlands and, in a fit of rage, drove past the club and fired a few shots into it. The front doors were open, and the bullets entered the vestibule, but thankfully, no one was hurt.

We did the right thing and contacted the police, which is presumably how the reporter at the *Post* discovered it. That kind of incident results in a violation of the ABC (Alcoholic Beverage Control) law known as "disorderly premises." I held my breath waiting for the article to appear in the paper, but it never did. I suppose that's because without an injury, there was no real story.

I also was worried about potential impact on the liquor license transfer, but nothing happened. I now assume that when the "disorderly premises" was logged and processed, it appeared on Larry's license, which, as of April 1, was no longer the active one for the club. If it had gone on my record, there would have been repercussions.

One of my initial goals as Wetlands's new owner was to improve our relationship with the local community. When Larry left, he was not on the greatest terms with the neighbors. His contention was he had opened the club in a section of Manhattan classified as an M-1 manufacturing zone—a mixed-use space, where nightclubs were permissible. Larry was particularly contentious when it came to issues of gentrification. For him, any debate about the neighborhood impact of running a music venue in an area where warehouses were being converted into lofts began and ended with the official zoning designation.

As I would be reminded fifteen years later when I attempted to build a kid-friendly music venue in Gowanus, Brooklyn, the reality of the situation can be more complicated. While I eventually won over my local critics at Wetlands, they were initially skeptical that a twenty-four-year-old neophyte would do anything to remedy their concerns about noise and litter. So although the club was properly zoned to operate at 161 Hudson Street, they had pursued every available legal recourse to shut it down.

Thankfully, the incident on March 31 basically disappeared, since it occurred on the final day of Larry's liquor license, which he forfeited the next day when mine took effect. It was never used against us. Sometimes you've just got to hold your breath . . . and hope you get lucky.

The transfer went through the next day, and I celebrated by getting the drunkest I've ever been in my life, with Jake Szufnarowski, the longtime Wetlands staffer who remains a friend and occasional creative partner to this day.

As it turned out, an extended legal battle with the New York State Liquor Authority still loomed, but I was blissfully unaware of that at the time.

Larry had long established Tuesdays at Wetlands as Dead Center, presenting Grateful Dead cover bands for free. He paired this with the Eco Saloon, an informational meeting and planning session led by the Wetlands activist team, which opened the night. This way, he was able to build awareness for the club's various working groups prior to shows that drew hundreds of Deadheads.

The thing about Wetlands is that it was a living, breathing social network. It drew together people eager to learn more about the latest musical happenings, as well as the current social and political developments.

Wetlands was a pre-internet place. You came to the meetings to get the latest information about what Rainforest Action Network was doing. There was no Meetup and no way to sign a petition on your phone. You'd go to Wetlands, pick up the petition, fill it out, and mail it in.

So before the music kicked off on Tuesdays, the Activism Center hosted meetings and presentations from the Student Environmental Action Coalition, the Federal Land Action Group, the Animal Rights Action Team, and many others.

All of this continued under my watch. It could be nerve-racking because they approached their objectives with a single-mindedness and intensity. They were always telling me that our phones were tapped by the FBI because big companies didn't like the optics of kids leading boycotts outside their businesses or chaining themselves to the doors. I didn't interject my own political views or offer counsel on their techniques, because I viewed my role as that of a caretaker.

I did, however, feel comfortable interceding when it came to the musical programming, and my confidence grew over time. I was inspired by my experiences at those early Grateful Dead shows, and my goal was to take that magic in the air and bring it to a new setting.

I have also always made a point to return a favor and pay things forward. This is why on my very first evening of Wetlands ownership—Tuesday, April 1, 1997—we all got down to the sweet sounds of Marty Bostoff and his band, Tiberius.

With the previous night behind me and my new liquor license in hand, I was feeling no pain.

This sentiment would linger for about two weeks until another Marty B. took the stage.

That is when I began to appreciate that I had no business owning a nightclub with fifty employees, given my lack of financial wherewithal.

Even though I had been in the on-deck circle for nearly six months, there's no substitute for learning on the job.

Thankfully, I had 9,984 shows ahead of me.

7

A GUEST AT MY OWN PARTY

Strangefolk
Wetlands Preserve, New York, New York
July 26, 1997

In March of 2012, I was on a family vacation in Southern California. After spending the day at Disneyland, my six-year-old daughter, Roxy, asked, "Can we go back tomorrow?"

I told her, "There's good news and bad news. We can go back, but not tomorrow. We'll go the day after tomorrow because Daddy has to fly home to New York to visit some old friends."

Those old friends were Strangefolk: Reid Genauer, Jon Trafton, Erik Glockler, and Luke Smith. They were going to open their reunion tour at Brooklyn Bowl. The last time I had seen the four of them perform a show together was at their Eden Festival over Labor Day weekend 2000.

I couldn't miss the Brooklyn Bowl date. Not only had I set their reunion in motion a couple of months earlier, but Strangefolk was the first band I ever booked at Wetlands. Some of my closest friendships I can credit to Strangefolk.

I was at Deadhead Heaven over Memorial Day weekend 1996 when I initially encountered the Folk. By that point, although I was talking with Larry about taking over Wetlands, I was still interning at New Line and continuing to screen *And Miles to Go*, which was what I was doing at Deadhead Heaven.

Ken Hays, the longtime owner of Terrapin Tapes, had launched the fest, which was subtitled A Gathering of the Tribe, to bring

Heads together nine months after the passing of Jerry Garcia. Over seven thousand people made their way to SUNY Purchase for the event that Ken would move to Croton Point Park the next year under a new name: Gathering of the Vibes. One of my earliest efforts at marketing Wetlands on a grander scale would later be sponsoring a stage at the Vibes (I would also do this at the Berkshire Mountain Music Festival, which helped extend our reach beyond Lower Manhattan).

In 1996, though, I was just there to show my film and take in some music. I enjoyed Strangefolk's rootsy, melodic, Dead-infused sound, although I didn't interact with them that day.

It was a little over a year later on Saturday, July 26, 1997, when I sat down for dinner with Strangefolk manager Brett Fairbrother to finalize details of their New Year's run. Brett and I had first met in January at a Strangefolk gig while I was working toward the transition that would follow on April 1. Now I was fully in charge and fired up to confirm plans for a signature year-end celebration at the club. So Brett and I had a meeting at the Thai House, located on the block between Wetlands and the North River Bar, three places where I'd already become a steady presence.

Brett and I were simpatico and soon found ourselves crossing the country to see live music together, particularly Phish and the latest projects from the Grateful Dead guys. These worlds entwined at San Francisco's Warfield Theatre in April 1999, when we traveled west for the Phil Lesh & Friends run where Phil was joined by Trey Anastasio and Page McConnell. Brett would later work with me at the Capitol and is probably best known these days as DJ JerrBrother, who spins at the Jerry Dance Parties, including some immersive late-night audiovisual experiences we've hosted in Garcia's Forest at LOCKN' and online at FANS.

I also started hanging with John Moore, who was working for Mammoth Records. The label had relocated from North Carolina to Tribeca in 1996, and we began crossing paths. Like myself, Jomo was a Strangefolk enthusiast, although his tastes also ran from the Dead and Phish to the indie rock world. I had started thinking about launching a Wetlands record label with Strangefolk as my flagship act (which, in retrospect, probably would have been an overreach), but I was happy to cut bait after Jomo signed Strangefolk in 1998.

I still wanted to help out, though, and I thought Nile Rodgers would be a great fit to produce the album. I had recently met him, so I invited him to see one of their shows (and, for the record, it wasn't even a Wetlands show). Nile liked what he heard and agreed to work with them.

Then things became complicated. First, Disney purchased Mammoth and began purging the artist roster, including Strange-folk. Then, Reid decided to leave the group and enroll in business school at Cornell. The band eventually self-released the aptly titled *A Great Long While* in September 2000.

Meanwhile, Jomo changed course as well, moving over to the venue side in 1999, booking shows at the Mercury Lounge and then the Bowery Ballroom. The Bowery became the trendy, go-to venue within the industry, and I used to joke with him how easy he had it. While I needed to chase shows, all he had to do was pick up the phone and take holds.

The Bowery, which opened in 1998, was designed as a showcase venue. It had perfect sight lines, along with a balcony that could be shut off to the general public and limited to VIPs, which held great appeal to record labels. At Wetlands, we struggled at times to land certain gigs because we didn't have a VIP area (the best we could do for actual VIPs was the DJ booth). Plus, the entire capacity of the club couldn't simultaneously watch the band, because the stage was low to the ground and didn't face out into the club—it was tucked into the far corner.

Here's what Larry had to say about that: "The stage was first of all always envisioned to be a low stage, to create intimacy, even though I understood that most stages were higher than our stage, and higher meant you could see the band better. I regarded that as less important than the intimacy of band and audience. As well as everything else was supposed to be less ego-oriented, and when a band is onstage, it's more like band worship. I wanted it more like people playing cool music for their friends."

Although I did contemplate moving the stage, I ultimately yielded to Larry's vision.

We did part company on the air-conditioning, though. The system he had originally installed was inadequate for the room. The club would get so humid on certain nights that John Popper dubbed the place Sweatglands. I think Larry was honored that Popper came up with the nickname because Blues Traveler was so essential in establishing the club's reputation. However, it would have been okay by me if the air-conditioning had worked and Popper busted chops about something else.

There's no question that we were the struggling little guy, and while it was a challenge to compete, we were scrappy, creative, and usually pulled it off.

Although I was initially a bit defensive about our perceived limitations, I've come to appreciate Larry's foresight. He hadn't designed Wetlands as a perfect music venue. Instead, he'd created a village, with many different spaces where people could congregate. Even though it was only 7,500 square feet spread out over two floors, there were a lot of different gathering points. Larry had even designated a section of the basement as a chill zone known as the Inner Sanctum, with plush sofas and throw pillows, where the live music would be piped in from upstairs but the volume wasn't overbearing, to facilitate conversations.

This is why you'd meet your future spouse at Wetlands, but you never would at Bowery, because you wouldn't have a chance to speak while you were standing in front of the stage, craning your neck to stare at the band. It's also why Wetlands had a vibe and an energy that existed independently of the musical performances. So while it wasn't necessarily the best place to see a show, it was the best place to experience a show. I kept this in mind years later when developing Brooklyn Bowl.

In 2004, Jomo cofounded Bowery Presents, which eventually became part of AEG. Bowery helped me book Brooklyn Bowl early on, and we'll occasionally do some copromotes, such as Vulfpeck at Madison Square Garden.

Jomo and I remain avid live music fans. When we're standing side by side at Phish or Guster or My Morning Jacket, there are probably no two friends in the venue who collectively have seen more shows (unless Concert Joe is in the house with Everynight Charley or TicketStub Stu—respekt).

As for the Strangefolk dates that Brett and I confirmed at the Thai House, they represented the first time since I had taken over Wetlands that I made the deal myself. By that point, I had developed a feel for how the business worked. Not only that but I believed the moment had arrived for me to be more active in defining the creative mission of the club. When December 30 and 31 finally arrived, it was almost like opening night for me all over again.

A writer who followed me around during a Trey Anastasio show at the Capitol Theatre described me as "a guest at his own party." I guess the point is that I was out there in the audience enjoying the music as much as anyone else. I do that most every night at my venues because I still love the shows.

However, even though I'm out there as a fan for a portion of the evening, there are a few occasions when I've cut loose for an extended period of time. One of those was Strangefolk at Wetlands on December 31, 1997 (and the evidence is available on YouTube via a Burly Bear Network report on the night—enjoy!).

As I've said, I was a Strangefolk true believer. I traveled out west in February 1998 to see them in Santa Cruz and at the Great American Music Hall. Later that year, I caught them at the Capitol Theatre, my lone show at the venue before I closed the deal to take it over in late 2011.

When I began thinking about who would open the Cap, Strangefolk came to mind. So we set up a phone call. I made my pitch and convinced them to let bygones be bygones.

However, while everyone was game, it turned out that the Capitol Theatre was not.

As Strangefolk finalized plans for their March 2012 reunion shows, I eventually realized that our construction would not be complete by then.

Sometimes you can do it right but not right away.

Once the band heard about the delay, they offered to open their tour at Brooklyn Bowl.

And that is why I left my family for the day and flew across the country for one more chance to be a guest at my own party.

8

BECCA & COMPANY

Michael Ray & the Cosmic Krewe and Moon Boot Lover
Wetlands Preserve, New York, New York
December 29, 1997

I believe part of the reason Larry Bloch sold me Wetlands at a reduced rate is because I was twenty-three years old and I didn't have a wife or children. This meant that I didn't feel the financial pressure that comes with raising kids in New York City. I wouldn't need to run Wetlands in a way that would require me to pull money out to pay for private school tuitions.

Still, Wetlands did play a significant role in my future domestic life. I brought Rebecca, my future wife, to the club on our very first date. I met her at a party, then reached out and invited her to Phish, who were opening a three-night MSG run on December 29, 1997. Rebecca is a music publicist, who at the time worked for Fran Curtis at Rogers & Cowan. She said that she'd get back to me, but she didn't, so I followed up and said, "Hey, do you want to come to this Phish show? It's a pretty good ticket." She finally relented.

Rebecca is not much of a Phish person. Her taste runs more to Brit-pop and New Wave. She probably would not have hesitated if it had been an invitation to see New Order, the Jesus and Mary Chain, or the Stone Roses. I later found out that she asked her sister, who *is* a hippie, what to wear on a Phish first date.

We went to the first two-thirds of the Phish show, and then I brought her back to my club. I suppose that's not something everyone can do. We were standing in the DJ booth during Moon Boot Lover when I held her hand for the first time.

I met Rebecca during a moment when I felt that I was coming into my own as a club owner. Beyond the day-to-day particulars inside the walls of the venue, I had been working to shore up Wetlands's relationship with the local community.

As I've mentioned, Larry had not been sympathetic to the noise or crowd grievances of area residents because the location was zoned as a mixed-use neighborhood. He believed that the neighbors didn't have the right to complain about Wetlands because they were on notice when they moved in.

This nearly had a devastating effect on my ownership. The people who lived close to the club were politically savvy, and they approached the head of the city council with a barrage of complaints, attempting to shut us down. I was operating under a temporary liquor license, and this politician contacted the New York State Liquor Authority to see if there might be a way to deny me a permanent license. On August 8, 1997, the SLA did just that, rejecting my application because we did not serve food. This was a technicality on the books that had not been enforced for years.

The explanation for their ruling hinted at some of the neighbors' complaints: "It has been the Authority's experience that premises such as these which have the capacity to accommodate this number of patrons (in excess of 300), which do not serve food and which offer alcoholic beverages to the patrons, have a propensity for quickly going out of control and, if not properly supervised, they become the scene of disorders, escalating violence and even loss of life."

Thankfully, as I've mentioned, my father was an attorney. If he hadn't helped us or if we hadn't known to ask for legal assistance, we would have been out of business. We successfully filed for a temporary restraining order against the SLA, preventing it from closing the club. Then, we began offering some menu items: veggie burritos and chili (which we microwaved), salad, trail mix, organic fruit, and Ben & Jerry's. It wasn't Blue Ribbon (and I wouldn't recommend the chili), but it satisfied the minimum legal requirement. By early fall, we'd won our license.

I didn't take a victory lap. Instead, I walked the neighborhood reaching out to any disgruntled residents. It didn't make sense to protect the rain forest and yet pollute our local environment. So we discouraged our patrons from milling around outside the club and mitigated the noise. I attended community board meetings where I gave everyone my number and told them to call me if there was ever a problem, which they did, pressing me to respond.

About a year after I bought the club, the *Tribeca Trib* ran an article that opened, "When Peter Shapiro took over Wetlands last year, he made it his business to win over the club's worst enemies. Now even arch foe Carol DeSaram counts Shapiro as a friend and calls him a 'good boy.'" *Good boy* was in really large print, making those two words pop. I felt like a beagle.

Thankfully, Rebecca had grown up with a mutt ("Duke!"), so she decided I'd be an acceptable companion. We began dating and got married in 2002.

Our relationship helped set the tone for me during the Wetlands years. I was the owner of a club that continued to gain heat during my tenure, but I didn't use that position to look for women. For those of us in jamband land, it wasn't about the party, it was about the music. Okay, maybe it was about the party, but the *music* was the party.

I never saw coke at Wetlands, even though I assume it was probably there somewhere. I did drink a lot of beer, though. And some tequila . . .

While Rebecca and I both worked in the music industry, we occupied different worlds (although they have converged a bit over time). She has represented some great artists that I enjoyed getting to know, like Zac Brown, Kesha, and Bonnie Raitt (I soon discovered that Bonnie's manager, Kathy Kane, had started her career at Wetlands, focusing on environmental activism). I first met Elvis Costello over twenty years ago through Rebecca. He's gone on to play my clubs quite a few times, and we even hosted a birthday party for his kids at the Bowl.

The fact that Rebecca didn't care about jambands was helpful to my career and probably my sanity. I hang out with enough people in the scene—I don't need to be married to someone in the middle of it. Becca didn't want to go to the Gathering of the Vibes, so it was easier for me to geek out with the music, then talk to agents and managers without worrying if she was doing okay.

But since Rebecca's a great publicist and knows a ton of people, I would be insane not to enlist her on occasion. She's now the senior VP at Shore Fire Media, where she's helped represent my venues. I've worked with other publicists like Ken Weinstein, but Shore Fire does the venues, which is a good way to balance things. It would be an error to overlook her expertise, but it's important to maintain some separation.

Getting married helped me to toe the line, and what *really* helped was being a parent. My kids, Roxy and Simon, have kept me honest because they don't get too caught up in what I do. In 2019, I dropped Simon off at Keewaydin, the same summer camp in Vermont that I had once attended. A counselor there who was from Chicago and had attended Fare Thee Well approached us and said, "Thank you for everything you do," but Simon was like, "Come on, let's go."

That's fine by me.

A couple of years earlier, he brought a picture from Fare Thee Well into class for a presentation on his parents' jobs. He told everyone, "This is something my dad does. It's called Grateful Dead."

What also helps keep me grounded is taking my kids to school. If I weren't married with kids, I'm not sure where I'd be today because of all the hedonism that comes with late nights. But when you have that responsibility in the morning, there's a strong incentive to go home (relatively) early. So that's what I do, typically by 1:30 a.m. I don't stay out till 4:00. And honestly, anything that goes on after 1:30 is probably not something that's going to help the cause.

When I'm on the West Coast, this also applies, as I'll be on a plane by midnight so that I'm back in time for 7:00 a.m. soccer.

Fun is fun, but too much fun is still too much.

As I get older, it becomes more of an issue. I can't quite bounce back the way I did twenty years ago. Some mornings, I wake up with what Jimmy Fallon describes as the afterglow of fun. But when you play varsity ball, that's part of the game.

Rebecca and I have been together awhile, and our family stability has kept me heading down the highway, without taking many wrong turns.

I appreciate that Rebecca's been so supportive over the years, even if she might have wondered what she was getting herself into back in 1997 when Michael Ray & the Cosmic Krewe hit the stage. After the Phish show let out, the circus traveled to 161 Hudson. That's when the room started to vibrate, transforming the Wetlands environment. This atmospheric shift led to Becca's first Wookie sighting, with plenty more to follow.

9

SEVENTY-TWO HOURS

High Plains Drifter
Wetlands Preserve, New York, New York
January 27, 1998

"**Y**o, new guy!" Blues Traveler bassist Bobby Sheehan called out to me.

High Plains Drifter had just completed the first of their two sets at Wetlands, and as they walked to the band room, he indicated that I should join them.

So I followed Bobby and his fellow musicians into the small space adjoining the stage that had originally served as the Wetlands kitchen before Larry eliminated food service early in the club's first year.

"Everybody else out!" came Bobby's gruff follow-up, dispersing anyone who wasn't a member of High Plains Drifter or self-identified as Peter Shapiro.

I wasn't quite sure what was to follow, but I could tell that Bobby had something urgent on his mind.

Now that I was ten months into the job at Wetlands, I thought I was hitting my stride.

It's not that I didn't have setbacks now and then, losing shows to other venues or having some nights when the turnout was soft. Nonetheless, I felt that when it came to my role as club owner, I had finally come to understand and embrace the job description.

However, as I looked at the grim faces that now surrounded me in the band room, I could only reach one conclusion: Blues Traveler wasn't entirely in agreement.

A few weeks earlier, on relatively short notice, we had booked High Plains Drifter, the project that featured Jono Manson of Joey Miserable and the Worms, who had been a godfather to Blues Traveler and the Spin Doctors when they were just starting out in the late '80s. Both Traveler and the Spin Docs were entwined with the Wetlands DNA, performing numerous memorable shows during the club's first few years, including some evenings that went to dawn, when Larry closed the bar and pulled down the roll gates while the band continued to play (if you were in, you were in).

The High Plains Drifter lineup included Blues Traveler's John Popper and Bobby Sheehan along with Eric Schenkman of the Spin Doctors. I had no idea who else would be in the group, but just having these guys was a gratifying nod to the early days of the club.

It had been a scramble to announce the band members in our *Village Voice* ad. The show had a fifteen-dollar ticket price, which was at the high end of what we were charging in those days. Coupled with the fact that it was on a Tuesday night, I thought we'd have trouble if we were only able to identify the group as High Plains Drifter without identifying any of the musicians.

That was a different world when it came to promoting a show. These days, if we have a huge last-minute underplay or a pop-up, we can press a button and notify potential audience members via email or socials. Back then, you had to get your ad in the *Voice* by 5:00 p.m. on Thursday for the issue that would appear the following Thursday. We'd also send out a street team to hand out flyers and cards, but so much turned on the *Voice* strip ad.

While it's easier to hit fans directly nowadays, I find that it's harder to know what else is going on in New York without the *Village Voice* (1955–2017, RIP). It used to be one-stop shopping. I would seek it out each Thursday and immediately turn to the ads for a comprehensive look at the shows taking place that week. I think that's missing in this current digital environment. Ironically, it was easier to remain on top of concert listings in the pre-digital age.

As for ticket prices, before I began at Wetlands, I had no idea how they were formulated. I probably assumed that the concert venue set the amount and the artist had no awareness or input. That's not quite how it plays out. While musicians may be unaware of the figure (although over the past few years, they've become increasingly tuned in), their team is fully cognizant. The ticket price is a direct product of the amount a promoter pays an artist and is stipulated by a contract. It can be a point of negotiation with the artist's agent because more expensive tickets generate higher proceeds, which trigger potential bonuses.

Here's a real-world example from an epic Flaming Lips show that took place at Wetlands on September 27, 1998. It was one of the Lips' "Boombox Experiments," in which the group distributed baggies full of cassettes and portable tape players to fifty people, who followed the band's instructions, transforming those fifty folks into both instruments and performers. Our initial offer to the band's booking agent (sent via fax—old-school!) indicated that the ticket price would be $12, and we offered a guarantee of $3,000. However, when that was rejected, we revised our offer, with a new ticket price of $15 and a guarantee of $5,000 (when making these calculations, we set the room capacity at six hundred patrons, so the additional $3 per ticket would theoretically generate $1,800, then we rounded up to $2,000, which is how we moved from $3,000 to $5,000). The agent accepted our offer, which also included a bonus clause, by which the band would receive 80 percent of any door receipts over $7,000.

This is how national headliner deals often worked at Wetlands. On other occasions, to entice an artist who otherwise wouldn't play the club, we'd go with a straight "versus deal." For instance, in July 2000, we offered the Dickey Betts Band $10,000 versus 90 percent of the gross door receipts. Dickey and his group would receive $10,000 with the potential to earn more (this limited our opportunity for profit—unless the bar crushed, which we thought it would). We were aggressive with this one because Dickey had never played Wetlands. In fact, he was already booked the previous night at B. B. King's in Times Square, so we even promised to advertise that gig in our own ads. That's something you don't normally see, but we wanted the show.

With local headliners or artists who had a less established track record in the market, there often would be no guarantee, and we would split the gross box office on a percentage basis, typically around 70 percent to the band, 30 percent to the venue (which was riskier for the musician, although it enabled a higher upside). Support acts received a flat-rate deal.

These days, there are a few additional variants on these models, many of which factor in net proceeds rather than gross funds, but the fundamentals are the same.

I learned the finer points of all of this during my early days at Wetlands. As a result, I can now do most promoter math in my head. My multiplication skills are top-notch, which allowed me to impress my kids . . . until they reached fifth grade.

While I'm on the topic of economics, throughout my run at Wetlands, I was always on the financial edge. One trick I learned is that if you charge something on a credit card, the money hits the vendor's account pretty much immediately. However, as the cardholder, you don't have to pay the bill for at least thirty days. If you need some quick money, charging $10,000 at your own bar is a handy method of short-term financing. (You gotta do what you gotta do.)

Eventually, I realized that additional operating capital would help cushion me against unexpected cash outlays. So I met Joel Bluestein, who owned Dreamland Recording Studios in Woodstock (he still does), and I sold him 10 percent of the club for a hundred grand. I think owning a small piece of Wetlands made sense for Joel, as it was a nice thing to tell potential studio clients. The relationship was mutually beneficial, and things were only less than ideal when Joel's friends would come to the club and announce, "We know the owner!" and expect free drinks. It was never Joel, he was always cool, but it's always best to have a pre-existing relationship with partners.

I had come to terms with something else as well. I was beginning to contemplate additional projects outside the club, and I realized that I needed to conserve my energy.

I was taking the subway back and forth from my apartment, and by the end of the day, I would be exhausted. There were a number of times I would get on the subway at the end of the night intending to get off at Seventy-Seventh and Lex, but I'd fall asleep and miss my stop. I'd end up at 160th Street, and then I'd need to go back downtown to make it home.

So I finally decided to make a short-term financial trade-off with some larger goals in mind. When I first took over Wetlands, I'd often stay until 3:00 a.m. But eventually, I picked some nights to leave a couple of hours earlier. I understood that my presence was probably helpful to minimize breakage, but if I lost 4 percent by going home early, it allowed me to make more than that amount by waking up early in the morning feeling refreshed to work on new projects.

Things are different now. It was a bigger cash business back then. There's less slippage these days with credit cards and POS machines. Plus, at Wetlands, we had a bare-bones crew. I have a more robust staffing structure these days, but I still believe in the basic principle—I'm willing to give up 4 percent to get 20 percent. I think that's a successful trade-off, and at Wetlands, this just meant going home a few hours earlier during select shows. That said, High Plains Drifter wouldn't be one of them.

Since I have been talking about numbers, here's another one that is important to me: seventy-two. The magic that I experience during an inspiring night of music lasts for seventy-two hours. It stays with me forever, but I can feel it directly for about three days. Then I'm chasing it again. Thankfully, owning Wetlands, Brooklyn Bowl, and the Capitol has made it pretty easy for me to maintain that infusion of energy by having another show to attend the next day (and sometimes even the same night).

Our High Plains Drifter show supplied plenty of that fuel. When we had booked them, I was aware that Jono Manson would be joined by John Popper, Bobby Sheehan, and Eric Schenkman. Given their musicianship, as well as their Wetlands lineage, that was more than enough for me.

But during set break, I discovered an additional old-school surprise. While half of Blues Traveler had taken the stage during the first set, the two other members of the group were in the house as well.

When Bobby Sheehan ushered me into the band room, we were joined by Chan Kinchla and Brendan Hill. I sat there with the four of them for an awkward moment while Bobby made some pretty intense eye contact, until he moved over and put his arm around me. I felt a surge of relief, because with this simple gesture, Bobby was saying, "You're one of us now. You're part of it. Congrats." He didn't grill me with questions, because he knew I was the guy that Larry had picked, but he did offer a brief lecture about the legacy of the club I had come to own. He detailed the importance of Wetlands to his group, to other groups, and to the wider community.

When Bobby called me in, I thought he was going to take me to task for something I had done wrong. Instead, he offered encouragement for what I should continue to do right. He was a football coach at halftime. I've given versions of that speech in the years to follow. They've come from my own perspective, but the message has been the same: welcome to the family.

Bobby Sheehan passed away in August 1999, and while Popper has always been Blues Traveler's front man, I think Bobby was the leader who continued to propel them forward. I would love to be doing shows with him today. Thankfully, I have continued to do shows with the other guys, both individually and as a group, whenever I can.

Popper never fails to get me riled up in the best way possible. I think my relationship with him is best summed up by a note I found in my office at *Relix* a couple of years ago after he had stopped by while I was out of town. It read something like "Dear Pete, I left a knife in your desk. Cops are asking questions, so I needed to get rid of it." Plus, he once compared me to Batman in *Wired*, so there's that, too.

We all emerged from the band room forty-five minutes later for the start of the second set. Three songs into it, Chan and Brendan joined High Plains Drifter for "Carolina Blues." Then there was a mass exodus from the stage, leaving only the members of Blues Traveler, who made their triumphant return to Wetlands as a quartet for the first time in five and a half years to play "As We Wonder," "Sweet Talking Hippie," and "The Devil Went Down to Georgia."

I had won their blessing.

Larry Bloch created a place unlike any other, but it was Blues Traveler who put it on the map.

And now they were confirming that it was still a worthy destination.

I was feeling good.

I might have gotten eighty-two hours out of that one.

10

YOU CAN'T SEE IT
IF YOU'RE NOT THERE

The Disco Biscuits
Wetlands Preserve, New York, New York
February 19, 1998

A few weeks after my glimpse at Wetlands's storied past, I was invited to check out its promising future.

We were hosting a twenty-fifth anniversary concert for *Relix* magazine (eleven years before I would become publisher). The bill featured the South Catherine Street Jug Band, Jiggle the Handle, and, finally, the Disco Biscuits. It was a Thursday during an era in which I was easing up on my late nights at the club because I was spending my days trying to move forward with new projects.

I had been there for a while that night when Biscuits bass player Marc Brownstein approached me (six years before he would launch HeadCount with Andy Bernstein and I would become a founding board member). I was on friendly terms with Brownie, as the Biscuits had already played the club five times during my tenure.

"You've got to stay," he said. "We've got a new sound, and we really want you to see it." This would keep me far later than I had originally intended, but I promised that I would.

He, in turn, fulfilled *his* promise.

It *was* a new sound.

What they did that night was nothing I had seen before, adding techno to their Zappa-infused improvisational blues rock.

The music was intense and unexpected. It felt like the future.

That evening, they played most of their forthcoming *Unciv-ilized Area* album, which would be released three months later. They also closed out their first set with the debut of "Mindless Dribble," a song written after the *Uncivilized Area* material that would quickly become a signature tune and an archetype of a new style called jam-tronica. Their sound finally evoked the name *Disco Biscuits*, although, like many others, I would come to refer to both the style and the group as *Bisco*.

Marc and I still talk about that night.

It solidified our connection and embodied something that I believe in quite strongly, which is that you can't see it if you're not there.

If you work in the concert industry, you need to see shows—not only for the exhilarating moments that can inspire you but for the professional connections that can yield additional opportunities.

No one's necessarily taking attendance, and folks will under-stand if you're absent, but bands, managers, and agents do notice if you're there.

Plus, when it's your venue, you can make adjustments and enhance the experience for everyone. I was at Brooklyn Bowl during an event for Kamala Harris, tweaking the lights and sound to best suit the room. I can also recall a late-night Lettuce set at LOCKN', where a bright security light was flooding a portion of the audience. I was standing in the crowd and knew that turning it off would create a better environment for the fans, so I sent a quick text and took care of it.

These days, if a band is going to play multiple nights at one of my venues and I need to be out of town, I try to make travel plans that will allow me to attend either the first or last night (otherwise, I watch the stream).

If it turns out that I can't see the show (and there is no sub-stitute for seeing the show), I've worked out a way that I can still touch base, particularly if it is a big night for the group. When I'm there, I like to toast the band by throwing down tequila shots. When I'm not there, I enlist technological assistance to do the same.

I have found that as long as I have phone service or Wi-Fi, I can FaceTime in while holding a shot to make a toast. I can be almost anywhere, as long as it's relatively quiet. Although the truth is that when I'm FaceTiming into a room with multiple people, no one can really hear each other anyhow. So as long as they can see me making the toast, that works.

I typically do this at the Cap, where the production manager will bring a tray of shots to the band in the green room or side-stage. Then I will call in via my cell for the remote toast. Not only do the musicians appreciate it, but when I'm somewhere else in the world, I enjoy a home visit as well. I can remember toasting Chris Robinson when I was in Laurel Canyon and he was at the Capitol Theatre, so things were kind of reversed.

Something else we do at the Capitol is we have a welcome book that we ask artists to sign. We've been doing that since day one. The room's history seemed to call for it. We want everyone to feel like it's a warm environment—like a hotel or inn—where they're connected not only to us but to everyone else who has already stopped by. We've had multiple books, and I think Brian Wilson's signature was the smallest while Bob Dylan's was the largest—make of that whatever you will.

Back to the Biscuits (with whom I've certainly shared plenty of toasts, both in person and remotely). After they changed their sound, they became a signature band at Wetlands. All told, they performed twenty-one shows with me at the club. They were there in April 1997 during my first month and in September 2001 during my last month.

The room was electric whenever they'd take the stage.

When I speak with people who were at Wetlands shows throughout its run from 1989 to 2001 and ask them to name the bands where the magic ran the deepest, two of the names I hear most often are Blues Traveler and the Disco Biscuits.

We blended those worlds at the 2001 Jammys, when John Popper sat in with the Biscuits for a version of Jane's Addiction's "Three Days." It was a satisfying moment even if they did turn their backs on me when I attempted to inform them that we were up against curfew (I'll come back to that).

Another thing the Disco Biscuits and Blues Traveler had in common was that the music would go late. On Bisco nights, forget about counting the money at 4:30 a.m. They were often still in the middle of their second set at 4:30.

As Biscuits' guitarist Jon "the Barber" Gutwillig recalled in an interview for the 2008 documentary, *Wetlands Preserved: The Story of an Activist Rock Club*: "I don't think anybody ever played later than the Disco Biscuits at the Wetlands. I think we broke the record. And the nice thing about Wetlands was the staff, the security, the bartenders, they were part of the family. They wanted you to play all night just like the fans wanted you to play all night. They wanted you to do your thing as long as you wanted to do it. Whereas in other clubs, you'd be on this production schedule and have to stop. Wetlands was like, 'You're in our house, and we don't ever want you to stop. Eventually you're going to pass out, and that's when we want you to stop.' That was the rule there. I remember being thrown onstage at Wetlands, but I don't remember being thrown offstage at Wetlands, and we pushed it as much as we could."

All of that is true from my perspective, although I can recall a single awkward moment to the contrary. At one Biscuits show, there was a manager who had been there since 3:00 p.m. who started to lose it around 6:00 a.m. and wanted to pull the plug. I had to physically block him from the stage. He was prepared to tackle the band, and I stood in his way, so he quit right then and there.

The fact that this was a one-off incident says something about what the Biscuits were able to do in that room.

If the Biscuits were the signature act during my era, then my signature contribution was opening up the Wetlands lounge as a music space. Larry didn't believe in bands downstairs; for him, it was a relaxation chamber. However, by the time I took over, the Inner Sanctum was slightly beat-up and ready for reinvention. So I decided to add a dimension by bringing in live acts.

This added to the village. The vibe in that lounge with one hundred people, a low ceiling, and dim lighting was like an Amsterdam coffee shop. It was unique to New York. There were other rooms of that size in the city, but it was another world down there.

It was also a great place for new groups to develop without any pressure. They didn't need to demonstrate that they were able to draw upstairs. Sometimes they'd be given the choice of playing a single opening set upstairs or else multiple sets downstairs. If I were a band looking to build a fan base and I had the material, then the lounge would be the way I'd go.

As a music fan, I appreciated having that second musical option. If you wanted a break from what was happening upstairs, you could head to the lounge and experience something totally different yet complementary. On a few rare occasions like the 1999 Jambands.com tour, rather than one band in the lounge, we had three, along with four more acts upstairs, creating our own festival atmosphere.

During my time at the club, there were plenty of memorable lounge shows. That's where I first saw many of the groups that I continue to work with today. On any random night, you could experience Soulive, Umphrey's McGee, STS9, Lettuce, the Slip, the New Deal, Fat Mama, RANA, and many more.

For some of our regulars, the lounge was their primary destination. It became its own scene.

As Derek Trucks once pointed out, "It always happened downstairs. You'd see some acid jazz trio, making music you didn't know was going on in the world."

You can't see it if you're not there.

11

MMMBOB!

Bob Weir, Rob Wasserman, and Jay Lane
Wetlands Preserve, New York, New York
February 13, 1999

he tenth anniversary of Wetlands was approaching in February
of 1999, and I wanted to do something special.

Larry always believed that the Grateful Dead should have
played at 161 Hudson. There's a moment in the Wetlands documentary when he addresses this very topic: "A band that we
thought we should be able to book that never played the club.
Hmmm . . . you mean aside from the Grateful Dead?" Then he
laughs, but you can tell he's altogether serious. While some might
say this was a reach, he thought it made perfect sense; the Grateful
Dead helped birth the club in the same way that the club helped
birth the jamband scene.

I was determined to have Bob Weir perform at Wetlands for
the tenth anniversary. It was a multiyear mission. I repeatedly
approached Cameron Sears, Bob's manager, and I also went
through John Scher, the Dead's longtime tour coordinator and
New York promoter who continued to work with the band members after Jerry's passing.

I would get a no, and then I would get another no.

That was fine. I was never discouraged.

Nos lead to yeses. You often can't get to a yes until you've had
a few nos. There are a lot of reasons for that. Sometimes it's about
building awareness for what you're doing. Artists want to feel

comfortable with the situation on every level, from the technical elements to the promotional aspects to the crew interactions. Agents and managers recognize that they're on the line when they recommend a new venue or promoter. So in many cases, you need to run that gauntlet before a musician learns about your proposal. Then, even after you win the team's support, the timing can be off or the tour routing changes. You should never take it personally when you get a no, particularly if you've made a strong pitch.

Here's a more recent example of how a no led to a yes. When we were working on our initial schedule for the Capitol Theatre, we asked Bob Dylan to play our first New Year's. Bob's agent said he couldn't do it but came back a couple of days later and said, "Sorry it didn't work out, but what about if Bob opened the venue?" That wouldn't have happened without our New Year's offer.

Sometimes it all comes together at the right moment, which is what happened in February 1999 when we celebrated the tenth anniversary of Wetlands with Bob Weir, Rob Wasserman, and Jay Lane.

Three-night runs were rare at Wetlands because once you had an artist who could blow out three nights, there was an impulse for that performer to "graduate" to a larger venue where there could be higher revenue opportunities for one night. Of course, when someone like Bob played three nights at Wetlands, this was an underplay envisioned by the performer as something special for the fans and, in this case, the club then as well.

I picked up Bob at the airport in a limousine with a joint in my pocket. Five years later, when Bill Kreutzmann flew in to cohost The Jammys with Mickey Hart, he had had a long, frustrating flight, and we delivered calming medicine as well.

From the airport, I brought Bob to the Waldorf Astoria. I had convinced the guy in charge of corporate groups that I'd be a big client in the future, so he gave me a crazy-low rate for the Presidential Suite—like $400 or $500 for what was normally $10,000–$12,000 a night. The room was nuts, more like a three-thousand-square-foot apartment than a hotel suite. I'll bet Bobby vaguely remembers it. Presidential suites are definitely a good way to begin a twenty-plus-year relationship.

When Bob arrived at Wetlands on the afternoon of the first day, he showed up in a taxi with his guitar in the trunk. As he approached the club, a guy was waiting for him outside who kept saying, "Bob, you're God! Bob, you're Jesus!" I remember thinking how difficult it must be to deal with such extreme adulation. I've seen Bob in action for over two decades now, and he's always calm and collected in that type of situation, with a hint of his wry, prankster humor.

On occasion, people have said some really nice things to me, particularly after Fare Thee Well. It hits you for a minute and it does feel good, but it also fades away pretty quickly. I don't allow myself to dwell on it because it will become a distraction.

For me, the creative process is iterative and ongoing. So once I confirmed Bob, Rob, and Jay, I began thinking about who else I could toss into the mix to ramp things up even further.

I understand that some venue owners stop thinking about things like this once a show sells out, but I can't help myself. I'm always wondering what a fan would want to see, which is pretty easy to imagine because I am that fan, and the energy of trying to make something happen still fuels me to this day.

So I put pressure on myself to try to pull off something that is unexpected, since Wetlands had facilitated all these spontaneous, unanticipated moments over the previous ten years. I thought about it 24-7, not just during the day, but while lying in bed at night staring at the ceiling.

Then I woke up one morning and said, "It's Hanson."

Since the three Hanson brothers played instruments and wrote their own songs, I thought it would work. I didn't delude myself into thinking that Bob would be singing high harmonies on "MMMBop," but I figured they could hang with him.

The way I was able to get to them was the same way you get to anyone in the music business—relationships. I had a connection through my friend, photographer Taylor Crothers, who had shot Hanson a number of times and put me in touch with their managers, one of whom was a Deadhead, which always helps the cause. So they were in, and Bob signed off as well.

Hanson appeared on the final night, but the two preceding shows also included appearances by a more intuitive guest: Warren

Haynes. He would later tour with Bob Weir as a member of The Dead, including an appearance at President Obama's Mid-Atlantic Inaugural Ball. However, Warren had performed with Bob for the first time less than five months earlier as part of a Robert Johnson tribute put on by the Rock & Roll Hall of Fame. Warren was also a Wetlands regular who spanned the run of the club from Larry's ownership to mine, so it was fitting to see him onstage with Bob.

Speaking of Larry, on the very first night of the run, I invited him to introduce Bob and the band. None of us would have been there but for Larry's efforts. To this day, I remain grateful that Larry believed in me.

The final night of the run offered more than the climactic Hanson collaboration. It also featured a performance by the Tuvan throat singers Huun Huur Tu. When asked about this aspect of the night, Bob later recalled, "Somebody came to our management and said they were going to be in town and would we be amenable to their opening up. I said, 'Sure, that would be plenty weird enough for me.'"

As for his overall experience at Wetlands, he added, "I'd been hearing about it for years, but I never did manage to get down there until I went down there to play. I remember a place that had a lot of different spaces, a lot of different rooms, and stuff like that—unusual for a concert facility, but from every little nook, you could still see the stage somehow, which was kind of cool." I think he was generous in his assessment of the sight lines, but I'll take it.

As for Hanson, toward the end of the second set when Bob began the intro to "Wang Dang Doodle," he played it pretty close to vest, stating, "We've got some friends coming up." As Isaac, Taylor, and Zac walked out, there was a range of responses. Most people had no idea who these kids were. A few others chuckled, and I imagine some folks shook their heads. It was no joke, though, they could hang, which they did throughout the remainder of the set ("All Along the Watchtower," "Goin' Down the Road Feeling Bad," and "Gloria"), and then they returned for the "One More Saturday Night" encore.

As Taylor later recalled, "You always want to dispel people's ideas of who they think you are, and for the people who don't even know who you are, that's a great way to start their idea of Hanson."

It was a rare night at Wetlands where the mainstream media noticed us as well. Serena Altschul reported on the sit-in for MTV News: "No, bewildered Grateful Dead fans, those were not blond dancing bears backing Bob Weir onstage at New York's downtown club the Wetlands the other night. It was Hanson." The *New York Times* headline was "Teen-Age Idols Come Alive at a Temple for Deadheads." Yahoo! Music led with "Isn't It Weir? Hanson Jams with Dead Guitarist." Still, the MTV website won the day with "MMMBob!"

Looking back, I defer to Taylor, who reflected, "In the end, it just comes down to musicians playing with each other. I think Wetlands has a great history of letting that happen, and a lot of the music that comes through there fosters that. It's been great that we've been able to play a part of that history in some way."

Respekt.

12

BLACK LILY

The Roots and Friends
Wetlands Preserve, New York, New York
June 6, 1999

Wetlands is best known for its role supporting a few gen-
erations of the jam scene, from Blues Traveler to the Biscuits.
The venue offered welcome terrain in the most important media
market, which helped these acts gain visibility and build fan bases.
From the beginning, Larry Bloch required headliners to perform
two sets, which helped push these musicians to new creative
heights.

However, Wetlands also was a home to other music scenes that
often found it challenging to plant their flag in Manhattan. A good
example of this occurred during the first weekend of June 1999.
On Friday and Saturday, we hosted two nights of my coauthor's
Jambands.com tour. For those shows, we utilized all 7,500 square
feet of the club—I still can't believe it wasn't bigger than that—
with five bands upstairs each night (including Percy Hill with special guests Butch Trucks and Oteil Burbridge, as well as Ominous
Seapods and the Biscuits) and three in the lounge (STS9, Lake
Trout, and ulu were among these acts). Then on Sunday, we had
two separate shows. At 4:00 p.m., we hosted ska heroes the Toasters as part of a June residency in which they would appear for
three out of the four weeks. We followed this at 9:00 p.m. with
the Sunday debut of Black Lily, which became a Wetlands staple
until the club closed.

Black Lily was an open-ended jam session, so in certain respects, it was similar to the jam sessions that took place over the course of Wetlands's history. However, there were a few things that were special about it. First off, it was the creative brainchild of The Roots, and they would drive up from Philadelphia on Sunday afternoons to serve as house band. It was also ahead of its time because it was designed as a showcase for women, striving to break down some of the artificial barriers in hip-hop and music in general. The core participants included Jazzyfatnastees (who helped set it all in motion with The Roots crew), Jill Scott, Jaguar Wright, 3 7000 9 and Kindred the Family Soul, with Erykah Badu, India.Arie, and Macy Gray also among the alumni. A few males were allowed to take the stage on rare occasion, such as Bilal and Musiq Soulchild. The priority was always female artists, though, and as Questlove recalls, "John Legend used to come and try to get on and get fleeced."

Black Lily originated at Questlove's house in Philadelphia. However, it soon outgrew this space, which is when Richard Nichols, The Roots' manager, contacted us about the possibility of hosting a residency. The band had already played at Wetlands a few times and felt comfortable with what we could offer.

After some Monday test runs, Black Lily finally claimed the Sunday slot on June 6.

Here's Questlove's recollection of the events: "In late 1998, we were fortunate enough that the Wetlands let us host what would become our weekly Sunday-night jam session. By that time, our so-called movement was coming together. That's when all of us would pile sixteen, seventeen, eighteen deep into a van—we would rent three vans—and you would have a young unknown, a Jill Scott come up from Philly to test out new material or an upstart named India.Arie. So many people would come and get on the stage and rock with us, but back then, that was their woodshed.

"There were a lot of legendary moments in the career of The Roots at that particular venue. The stage was very small, and sometimes the units would be as big as Earth, Wind & Fire, but as long as you can get in where you fit in, that's all that mattered. I like the idea of cramming a million people onstage to work out songs. A lot of the material that ended up on our fourth album was developed onstage at Wetlands.

"I think the thing that won us over to Wetlands is it had a kick-ass sound system. Hip-hop is a bass-heavy music, and you have to treat it sonically like dub-style reggae—you need a lot of wooden cabinets. We went from 10:00 to 5:00 every Sunday, and the only reason we stopped was Wetlands closed."

I wasn't creatively involved in Black Lily, but I did help make it happen. I worked with Richard Nichols, who managed The Roots from the beginning of their career until he passed away from leukemia in 2014. He pitched the idea, and I said, "Let's do it." That's the best part of my gig. I get to help make things happen.

Richard was a very bright guy, and we had a good relationship. He commanded respect, and it felt good to have *his* respect. I remember his phone number and I can still hear his low baritone voice calling out, "Yo, Petey!"

Rich would often run the soundboard at these shows, and at times, the levels would be quite high, causing some people to complain. I trusted him, so we just let it go. Sometimes there's a push and pull, so even if the volume was ebbing into the uncomfortable zone, it's important to have a sense of when to let it go.

Questlove has acknowledged, "We were banned at a lot of clubs because The Roots are the guinea pigs for testing the sonic limits. The law typically limits the decibel level to 118, and you get complaints at 122, but the average Roots show was 138. What I've learned over the years is that people respond to noise. Plus, once they fill in a space, they serve as human Styrofoam and absorb it. We trained a lot of sound guys on the Wetlands sound system."

The Black Lily residency led to a long relationship with The Roots. If you treat people right, then time begets respect. You have to earn it, but then it's there for you. Beyond Wetlands, we continued to work together, starting with my IMAX film *All Access*, when I paired them with B. B. King and Trey Anastasio. We've done so many things together over the years—Earth Day 40, Brooklyn Bowl, opening night at Bowl Vegas—and all of that came out of our relationship at Wetlands.

Black Lily was free the first year. Eventually, we began charging five dollars so we could kick a little extra compensation to the staff and crew who helped pull this off. Plus, another thing that I learned at Wetlands is that sometimes you'll have much better energy in the room if you sell five-dollar tickets. With a free show, there's no commitment to attend, so people might not show up if it rains or a friend calls with a dinner invitation—it's easy to bail without losing anything. There's no downside. Even that five-dollar ticket price has an impact.

Plus, there's a psychological aspect. When you buy a ticket, you're making a commitment. You're putting it on your calendar and planning out your pregame. This leads to an energized audience who will show up earlier in the evening rather than waiting it out to make a last-minute call. When people actively want to be there, you can feel the difference in the room. So a five-dollar ticket (in 1999; I aim for fifteen or twenty dollars these days) can have a significant impact on the overall vibe.

I wasn't at every Black Lily. Sometimes I'd use that Sunday night to refresh and recharge for the week, which could be challenging at Wetlands given the intensity of what was taking place. However, every time I went, I would always come away impressed with what was happening onstage and the scene that was coming together offstage—plus the two could be entwined since you'd have members of the audience performing and performers becoming members of the audience. If you're interested in looking back on that scene, you can check out Episode 2 of *Roots TV* from Okayplayer Films.

Looking back to June 6, 1999, I'm still amazed that we were able to clear the room between the Toasters and Black Lily. We didn't skimp on the ska that day either, as we also had two other bands on the bill.

That early show was all ages, a longtime Sunday tradition at Wetlands. We often alternated between ska and hardcore from week to week. The hardcore shows were probably the only ones at the club that made me feel squeamish. I'd be standing by the bar watching the mosh pit, and I'd see people come out covered in blood. Those matinees could be tough on the staff, with all the flailing limbs and hardly any tips for the bartenders because most of the people in the club were underage. However, we continued to do those shows because that's what Wetlands was about—providing an environment for music lovers who were otherwise disaffected and disenfranchised by the established venues that didn't see the money in these "fringe" scenes.

Wetlands was occasionally mocked because it had such a hippie spirit, but it was that same hippie spirit that made us open to everything. Wetlands was for hip-hop heads and punk heads and ska heads and Deadheads.

Wetlands was for Heads.

13

SOLDIER FIELD: PART 1

Dave Matthews Band with Al Green
Soldier Field Chicago, Illinois
June 30, 2000

On July 3, 2015, Fare Thee Well kicked off the first of three nights at Soldier Field in Chicago.

While the scale of that event was unlike anything I had previously attempted, it was not my first production inside the massive venue.

Fifteen years earlier nearly to the day, I was on-site with a collection of oversize cameras to shoot Dave Matthews Band perform a song with Al Green. And when that went off the rails, I put my body on the line, refusing to allow Al Green's limo to flee the premises until he did it all again before a slightly befuddled audience of sixty thousand.

The performance would appear in our IMAX film *All Access*, and the path to that moment quite literally crisscrossed the country.

It all began with *American Road*.

I attended Sundance in January 1997 with Alex Cornfeld, and we hustled around Park City trying to drum up interest. Not all that much came out of it, though, as most everyone's attention was reserved for the feature-length films (and there were far fewer Phish fans than if it screened today). *American Road* did eventually air on MSNBC, though, and when it happened, I was able to experience the simulcast on a massive screen in Times Square.

After I returned home from Sundance, I began the work of prepping for the Wetlands handoff. Still, in the back of my mind, I thought there might be something else that I could do with *American Road*. (And that's still true twenty-five years later—ha!)

Wetlands was an all-consuming endeavor. But by late 1997, I began carving out some time to think about additional projects. This was the point when I had started leaving the venue a couple of hours before close so that I could be up the next morning pacing around my bedroom / living room rolling calls. That's pretty much how I continue to do things, even though the locations have changed. I am still walking, and I am still making my own calls—I have no assistant getting people on the line and saying, "Hold, please, for Peter Shapiro," the way they do in Hollywood. If you ever get that call from me, please hang up.

In late '97 and early '98, I began thinking seriously about remaking *American Road* in the IMAX format. This was at a time when IMAX films offering visual tours of the Grand Canyon and Niagara Falls had been successful. I hoped to capture the imagery of America set to a score that reflected the music of each area (with Phish certainly representing Vermont).

I had previously met the head of IMAX, so I contacted him about the idea. He invited me to a meeting where he was so enthusiastic that he gave me a distribution deal on the spot. He even offered an advance of a few hundred grand. I was going to make an epic IMAX version of *American Road*.

Or so I thought.

It turned out that IMAX's offer was contingent on my securing the remaining financing from other sources. I had a really cool promise but little else.

I quickly came to understand that the film would cost several million dollars. The technology was expensive, and IMAX cameras could only shoot for three minutes at a time, which added to the complexity and the budget.

Alex and I eventually decided to raise a quarter million for a test shoot in New England during the fall of 1998. Then, once we had proof of concept, we figured we'd be able to finance the rest.

We received our initial seed money from Alex's father, Arthur, the founder of a real estate management firm, as well as an entrepreneur who had promoted concerts at the outset of his career.

Most of the remaining funds came from Chris Blackwell, the founder of Island Records and early champion of Bob Marley, Steve Winwood, U2, Toots and the Maytals, Burning Spear, and many, many others. He was inducted into the Rock & Roll Hall of Fame in 2001 by Bono.

I met Chris through the Disco Biscuits.

Technically, that's accurate, although I really met Chris through the Disco Biscuits' manager, Jonny Zazula. Jonny Z had founded Megaforce Records in the early '80s and managed Metallica, Anthrax, Ministry, and a number of other bands but was trying to get into the jam world, so he asked if I wanted to meet Chris.

Chris came to Wetlands, and we hit it off. He's a hip, thoughtful guy who carries himself with grace. I think he's the coolest guy on the planet and remains a role model to this day. I've been lucky enough to spend a few nights at GoldenEye, his spectacular home and resort in Jamaica, which previously belonged to Ian Fleming, who wrote all his James Bond books there.

I brought Chris to see *Everest* at the IMAX theater on Sixty-Eighth and Broadway. He had a longtime interest in film, having helped finance *Stop Making Sense*, *Koyaanisqatsi*, and *Kiss of the Spider Woman* via Island before founding Palm Pictures in 1998. He's also remained a lifelong music fan, so he loaned us $250,000, which would be enough to finance our initial shoot and allow us to make a trailer.

We ended up with great fall foliage visuals, but we couldn't quite land enough additional funding. After scrambling for a few months, just when we were starting to despair, we learned that Certs, the breath mint company, was interested in becoming the title sponsor. However, while they would work with us, they were focused on the music side and wanted to lose the imagery-of-America element.

While this would lead to a different film from what we had envisioned, the idea of a live concert film shot in IMAX was exciting to me, so we decided to move forward. Certs contributed $4 million, and we found someone to help us gap the other $2 million required to produce the IMAX film that eventually would be called *All Access: Front Row. Backstage. Live!* (yes, that's quite a title, with plenty of punctuation).

My partner on this project was my oldest brother, Jon. He's another Northwestern alum, who as an undergrad had cofounded the Niteskool Project, a student-run music video production house that is still in existence. We have complementary skill sets. Jon spearheaded the financial and organizational aspects of *All Access*, and I did my vibe thing.

I enjoyed working with Jon because we already knew each other, so there would not be any unpleasant surprises or distractions. That is one of the reasons I like to collaborate with friends and family members.

I spent a lot of time sleeping at Jon's house in California—another good reason to work with him, particularly at that stage of my career—and I certainly couldn't have done it on my own.

We were both fans of the IMAX format, but we also thought existing films were not fully utilizing the sound system, which blew away anything else out there at the time. We thought we could showcase this capability and complement it with larger-than-life visuals from some larger-than-life performers.

I became the music director. I didn't have the credentials of a Don Was or a Steve Jordan, but the film's producers decided to take a chance on me (ha!). I selected myself for the role . . . well, because I could. I was twenty-six years old, and no one else would have given me the job. There's only a small community of music directors out there—people like Don, Steve, Greg Phillinganes, T Bone Burnett, and Paul Shaffer. I decided to add my name to the list.

This is where owning Wetlands helped. The club had real credibility, and after nearly two years on the job, I had a fair number of contacts. The fact that I was the owner also enabled managers to understand that I wasn't a random film producer who would take the musicians for granted or put them in awkward situations. This was important, as it protected everyone's interests.

Carlos Santana was the first one to commit. He was crucial to assembling the roster of performers because you can't get a second without a first. Yes, that is obvious, but it's no less true. The first get is always the hardest, and the next hardest is the second, and then they roll down a little from there.

Over the years, I have also found it's often easier to get legends on board rather than younger buzz acts. I think that is because the legends appreciate how hard this business is and that it can be fleeting.

Carlos was also in promo mode around the release of *Supernatural* when I began speaking with him during the summer of 1999. If you're looking to land someone for a project, keep that in mind as well. You can get that person during the promo cycle even if your project won't hit for a while.

I later found out that owning Wetlands, with its mission of supporting social causes, mattered to Carlos. This was after the Bob Weir tenth-anniversary shows, which also bumped up our profile.

Following Carlos's commitment, we confirmed B. B. King and George Clinton in relatively short order.

I paired B. B. with The Roots and Trey Anastasio, and we filmed them at the Grand Olympic Auditorium on the day after the Grammys. This was the first time I met Trey. Although it was nearly two months after Phish's seven-hour New Year's Eve set at the Big Cypress Reservation in Florida, he still looked back on it with a real sense of awe.

We brought in an audience for this performance. There was no private sound check or rehearsal; the musicians just walked out and began finding their way into "Rock Me Baby," which had been B. B.'s first top 40 pop single back in 1964. We started rolling while they were still figuring it all out, and that's the version we used in the final film. I remember a couple of people weren't entirely sure if we'd gotten it, but I had faith. I've found that magic is often strongest when the music is not rehearsed.

We scheduled other shoots with artists who were in town for the Grammys, including Mary J. Blige with George Clinton & Parliament Funkadelic, Santana with Rob Thomas, Kid Rock, Moby, and Macy Gray. We were trying to be efficient, particularly since the cameras were so unwieldy and expensive to set up.

By the summer of 2000, we had most of *All Access* in the can. We shot Sting with Cheb Mami at the PNC Bank Arts Center in Holmdel, New Jersey. Then it was on to Soldier Field for Dave Matthews Band and Al Green. I had not only selected the artists for this one but I had also picked the song, Al's "Take Me to the River." So I was psyched when they crushed it during rehearsal.

The problem was that in the heat of the moment during the actual show, in front of a packed Soldier Field, Al Green ratcheted up the intensity. This was appreciated by everyone in the stadium, except for those of us recording him for an IMAX film because he blew out the microphones, which had been set based on how he sang at rehearsal.

It was certainly a high-energy performance, and when Al walked offstage, he figured he had given it all he had.

While that might be true, he hadn't given us all we needed.

So in my role as music director, I pleaded with him and explained that we needed to do it one more time.

When I first met Al Green, he was the nicest guy in the world, but he had come offstage hot, and now he was bothered.

I tried to explain the problem, but he was unresponsive to my increasingly urgent pleas.

Then he stepped into his limo and prepared to leave.

I couldn't let that happen.

So I ran in front of the vehicle and stood there.

I wouldn't budge.

I couldn't see his reaction behind the tinted windows of the limo, but I am sure he could sense my desperation.

We were at a stalemate for a few minutes until he finally got out, slammed the door, and walked back toward the stage.

Moments later, he reappeared with DMB for a true encore performance of "Take Me to the River."

When *All Access* finally was released in the spring of 2001, Al Green with DMB was one of the standout moments in a film laden with standout moments.

All Access received plenty of positive press, but it didn't receive much positive box office. It grossed $70,000 on opening weekend in the US and never quite reached $1 million in global receipts.

There were a few reasons for this.

One major problem was the name.

Officially, the title was *All Access: Front Row. Backstage. Live!*, but when it appeared in film listings, this was often truncated to

All Access. Everything else was cut off, meaning that no one saw the tagline. Unfortunately, *All Access* was rather generic and didn't convey much about the film.

That is a lesson I took with me moving forward: Say what it is. I try to apply that to everything I do. It is also why the next film that Jon and I worked on together would be called *U2 3D*.

A second issue was the business of IMAX. When IMAX released *All Access*, the company had high hopes. It had recently built some new theaters in larger entertainment complexes, and after concentrating on nature films, IMAX was looking to expand its reach.

However, *All Access* would become the last film of its kind. What IMAX realized was that while their $2 million marketing budget was a significant outlay for them, it was a far cry from the $50 million that the major studios spent to promote *Batman*, *Spider-Man*, and other tentpole movies. So IMAX decided to stop competing with these films. Rather than releasing their own movies, they began piggybacking on the $50 million marketing spends through a process called DMR (digital media remastering) that allowed them to convert these blockbusters to the IMAX format.

All of which is wonderful for IMAX but didn't do much for us and, more importantly, for our investors. This became a major source of anxiety because I owed quite a bit of money with no immediate means to repay it.

But then, just when things were looking dire, our imperfect movie title became the perfect movie title.

This transformation occurred when Verizon decided to launch a new phone plan called All Access.

Verizon swept in and offered an exclusive *All Access* movie soundtrack to everybody who signed up.

This was at a moment when the end of Wetlands was looming. My parents were starting to pressure me about what I would do next. I also wanted to propose to Rebecca but couldn't afford an engagement ring.

Thanks to Verizon's new All Access phone plan, we were able to sell a million CDs at full wholesale. Everyone walked away with smiles on their faces, including the artists.

Not only was I able to buy the ring, but I was able to buy some time. In the end, I made enough to keep going for a few years post-Wetlands while working from home and setting some other plans in motion.

The Verizon deal also allowed me to pay off my debts.

It had been two years since Chris Blackwell loaned me the money for the *American Road* trailer, and I paid him back with a smile on my face. I owed him quite a bit of interest, which he waived, explaining that most people didn't pay him back the principal. He still mentions this to me.

I also delivered a check to Arthur Cornfeld, who was facing a total on his investment but now made a profit. He was appreciative and as a result proved willing to take another chance with me a few years later when I presented an investment opportunity for a new project called Brooklyn Bowl.

14

WHERE GETTING INTO A JAM IS A GOOD THING

The Jammy Awards
Roseland Ballroom, New York, New York
June 28, 2001

I was pacing around my apartment on Twelfth Street when the phone rang.

"Peter, this is Bruce Hampton. I need some help."

I could empathize with him. We were a few hours away from our second-annual Jammys, and help was in short order.

"I'm lost," the deep, husky voice continued.

That made two of us.

We had sold out the 3,200-capacity Roseland Ballroom, our guest list was MIA, and our load-in was behind schedule. Or so I had been told; I hadn't made it over to the venue yet.

"Peter, who's picking me up?" my caller continued.

In that moment, everything clicked, and I realized that Col. Bruce Hampton had been abandoned at the airport. Well, not quite abandoned, because that would have implied that we had made plans to pick him up, which we most certainly had not.

Like Bruce, I was in need of help, and unfortunately for both of us, none was immediately forthcoming.

I could feel a ball of anxiety throbbing in the pit of my stomach.

We had not assigned anyone to pick up Colonel Bruce.

How many other artists would be stranded at LaGuardia? Would all of them have my phone number?

And where was that guest list, anyhow?

All in all, there were seven installments of The Jammys. We debuted at Irving Plaza in 2000. We eventually moved to the Theater at Madison Square Garden for four shows between 2004 and 2008. However, the two most challenging Jammys, by far, were the two at the Roseland Ballroom in 2001 and 2002. Thankfully, the music more than made up for all the stress (although at times it was close).

The Jammys originated with a pitch from my coauthor, Dr. Dean Budnick. We had been discussing the mainstream music media's minimal interest in the bands thriving at Wetlands that he was covering at Jambands.com. So we teamed up on the Jammy Awards, which launched with the tagline "A Celebration of the Scene." We would give out trophies and showcase the improvisational heights attained by these acts through live performance sequences.

To emphasize the community aspect, we allowed fans to choose the winners via an online vote (from the six to eight final nominees selected by a committee comprised of journalists and a few other people with their fingers on the Jam pulse). At the time, there were no other comparable events doing anything really like this.

Otherwise, The Jammys riffed on a traditional awards show. We had a host, prepped and accompanied by Dean, who rented a tux and functioned as our emcee. He'd fill in gaps whenever our host participated in the musical segments interspersed throughout the night.

Each award category was preceded by a roll-in video that introduced the nominees. Jonathan Healey, who created these, later served as cinematographer/editor of the Wetlands documentary and still works with me today, overseeing our livestreams at the Capitol Theatre, FANS.live, and the Relix Channel on Twitch/YouTube. This points to something that might be helpful to people who are aspiring to work in the concert business: Treat any task that's presented to you as a career opportunity, no matter how minor it may seem. If you do the job right and people enjoyed working with you, it increases the odds that you'll get another chance. I've seen too many interns or entry-level hires make it clear that certain chores are beneath them or half-ass their way through them to get to the fun stuff. That's not the right answer.

All the little details are important. I try to keep in mind that everything is everything.

Or to put it another way, as Irving Azoff once said to me before his client Don Henley played the Capitol: "Don't fuck up the salmon."

When we have an opening, we will often turn to people who have earned our trust. We keep track of this throughout my company Dayglo, developing from within as it is something I believe in. Because it works.

After the roll-in videos, a guest presenter then stepped onstage, holding a CD jewel case that was our version of the awards envelope. This person then opened the case, announced the winner's name that had been written on the CD, and gave out the Jammy.

The award itself varied over the course of our run. Initially, we handed out bowls—engraved trophy bowls of the sort designed by Paul Revere, but yes, the pun was intentional. From there, we went with custom metal sculptures in the form of a *J* that incorporated a Fender guitar neck. We later moved to Jammys fashioned from a classic Gibson headstock.

Even though there were some playful elements in all of this, we were quite serious with our intent. I think the musicians responded to that, which is why they performed solely for travel expenses, and the winners made an effort to accept the awards in person. Voting closed a day before the show, and if it looked like a member of a winning band wouldn't otherwise be on hand, we would inform them of the results so that they could send us an acceptance speech if no one could be there.

In 2000, Phish was in Tennessee on the night they won the Jammy for Best Live Set (December 31, 1999, Set II—over seven hours of glory, I mean, come on!). But Mike Gordon sent a message on the group's behalf to Irving Plaza with a couple of hours to spare. His remarks were similar to what Trey had described to me at the *All Access* shoot. Mike wrote: "Being able to play all night was something we've always wanted to try. For us, the idea of going out there for seven hours without any sort of plan whatsoever seemed to encapsulate the essence of improvisation. The location was beautiful and the jamming was relaxed. And, from my perspective, watching the sun come up over Page's piano was sublime."

That same year, the members of the Grateful Dead were scattered to the winds, but when their *So Many Roads* box set received Release of the Year, they hand-delivered an acceptance on official band letterhead via publicist Dennis McNally.

The first Jammys at Irving Plaza offered plenty of memorable musical pairings. The Disco Biscuits and Les Claypool met for the first time during sound check a couple of hours before their collaborative appearance. Soulive performed with John Scofield, anticipating many Bowlives to follow. Strangefolk interpreted the Grateful Dead, alongside Merl Saunders, connecting my Wetlands experiences. Butch Trucks commandeered a tour bus on his day off from the Allman Brothers Band tour for a performance by Frogwings with special guest Susan Tedeschi.

I had first met Butch Trucks when he brought Frogwings to Wetlands in December 1997. This project demonstrated his creative vision, as a couple of years before Derek Trucks joined the ABB, Uncle Butch teamed him with Jimmy Herring, Marc Quiñones, Oteil Burbridge, and Kofi Burbridge (who later joined Derek's band and also left us too soon). Edwin McCain was on vocals in 1997, but when I had them return for three shows during the club's tenth anniversary in 1999, John Popper was the singer (Frogwings' improvised ode to the club, recorded live onstage during that run, appears as the theme song to the Wetlands documentary).

Butch lived life large and was entertaining company. He was a true force both as an entrepreneur and a drummer. He founded Moogis, a streaming service that was about fifteen years ahead of its time. About a month before he passed away, he reached out to me about producing a potential Allmans 50 event. He intended to celebrate the band's golden anniversary in a manner akin to Fare Thee Well, and he wanted me to be part of it, which was an honor I wish I could have experienced.

As for The Jammys, tickets to the first year sold out a couple of hours before doors, and the show even generated some national press, via MTV news online. The *Village Voice* also took notice with a story titled "Prizewinning Jams," which observed, "Irving Plaza mimicked the Dorothy Chandler Pavilion last Thursday for the First Annual Jammys Awards, what with separate queues for revelers, press, and jam-scene potentates. Wetlands owner Peter Shapiro even offered the Lifetime Achievement Award to B.B. King 'via satellite.' Jambands.com honcho Dean Budnick wore Converse sneakers with his penguin suit."

Satellite meant a handheld video camera. I recorded B.B. earlier that afternoon when he was in town for the opening of the B. B. King Blues Club & Grill in Times Square. I presented him with his award and some commemorative Jammys jammies before hustling over to Irving Plaza. I didn't even have time to preview the footage—I just handed the tape over to the person running video—but it turned out just fine.

We were quite happy with year one and decided to step it up in 2001. The biggest change in philosophy and execution was the range of artists that we added to the bill. The first year delivered on our initial vision, but we had worked with most of the performers in the past. The goal for year two (and for every Jammys thereafter) was taking bands from within our scene and pairing them with notable players from the wider music community with whom they had never previously performed.

Working on the 2001 lineup helped to build my growing confidence to where I could raise my hand and say, "How about this?" When I think back to this era, I picture myself pacing around the apartment, chucking spaghetti at the fridge. To be clear, that's a metaphor (the chucking, not the pacing).

Dean and I would toss ideas back and forth, make phone calls, and fax letters to management. Since we were not paying the artists, I generally bypassed the agents. However, when I had an existing relationship, I might go that route, particularly if we could tack on a paying gig like the official Jammys aftershow, which could be a nice financial addition and was a great way to blow off steam following the big show.

Our 2001 roster of performers set the tone for what would follow. It included Paul Shaffer and Junior Brown with Les Claypool's Fearless Flying Frog Brigade, Michael Franti with Tom Tom Club, Marky Ramone and Jerry Only with Lake Trout, Robert Randolph and DJ Logic (Jason Kibler) with the Del McCoury Band, New

York Yankees center fielder Bernie Williams with the Jazz Mandolin Project, and John Popper, Stanley Jordan, and DJ Logic with the Disco Biscuits.

In certain respects, though, all that work was the easy part.

The problem was that we were understaffed and overwhelmed, which is why we hadn't assigned anyone to pick up Col. Bruce Hampton. Eventually, I gave him directions to the cab stand at LaGuardia and informed him that we would pick up his tab when he arrived.

As for the missing guest list, it was riding shotgun on the seat next to Dean as he drove into the city from Rhode Island on the afternoon of the show. People would call him en route with additional names to add and he'd pull over the car to scrawl them down. This was the final year that he handled this aspect of the show, because by the time he arrived at Roseland, all the names still needed to be entered manually into the system. We had such an extensive guest list (this was something we could offer the performers in lieu of payment) that this took far longer than expected. A technical hiccup on-site compounded the problem, which meant that by the time I arrived at Roseland, there was a line around the block.

While I am better at regulating my stress these days (a bit!), I still get nervous before the big shows. I can feel it in my gut when I'm headed over to the venue. However, once I am inside, it usually goes away and I feel at home and relaxed.

I don't love to hang around on-site too long before it's go time. Speaking of arrivals, I have some vague recollection of a Disco Biscuits show at Wetlands when I showed up following some other event in the city. As my taxi was pulling up, I could see flashing white strobe lights, and the street was filled with people. I knew that someone had set off the smoke alarm, but since I didn't see any flames coming off the walls of 161 Hudson, I could tell that the situation was under control, so I ducked down and told the driver to keep going. I'd be back.

During the preshow countdown, I like to be alone in my cockpit, which is pretty much anywhere quiet that I can be on my own, free to pace around while on my phone. When it came to The Jammys, I held off coming to the venue until the last possible minute.

So when I rolled up to Roseland and saw everyone standing outside, my physical discomfort went up a level. I already had that uneasy feeling in my stomach from the Col. Bruce phone call a few hours earlier.

It was time to switch into show mode. I found a few Wetlands staffers and people who worked at *Relix* and told them to pick their friends out of line and walk them to the check-in table so that we could expedite the entry process. There are a few tricks you can do if the line is really long, particularly at a GA venue. You can initiate a procedure where you just look down at the list and then let the people in without taking the time to actually find their names. Just look down and let them pass. This is not something that I recommend, and there are certainly situations where it can get you in trouble. However, when the line's around the corner, then sometimes you have to do what you have to do.

As a venue owner, though, I do appreciate that not all delays are created equal. The bar will be the busiest right before show-time. So your production manager may want to hold the lights a few minutes to give everyone a chance to wait in line for their drinks and then make their way to their seats or their spots on the floor. You can't let that go on for too long, though. Ten or fifteen minutes is about right. I call that a Respectful Delay.

With our problem at the Roseland doors sorted (or at least in the process of being sorted), I walked into the venue, where I soon experienced that moment when the train leaves the station. That's what it feels like when something you've been working on for months suddenly takes off on its own momentum. It can be jarring, and sometimes your heart seemingly stops for a moment (come to think of it, this repetitive stress may have contributed to the need for emergency stent surgery twenty years later).

There's also a moment of release when you realize that things are beyond your immediate control. You need to trust in everything you've done to set this in motion and ready yourself to respond on the fly. You should be prepared to handle the known unknowns.

In 2001, when the train left the station, it was pure "Joyful Noise," courtesy of the Derek Trucks Band. The DTB served as our house band in year two. Roseland had been renovated in the early '90s, creating a larger stage to allow for bigger bookings; however, the original stage remained intact, at a forty-five-degree angle from the new one (the old stage typically was closed off by a curtain or converted into a VIP seating area). We used this second stage to hand out awards, and it's also where we placed the house band.

Derek Trucks was a presence at the first four Jammys, but in 2001, he was a true gamer. Jim Breuer was our host and a perfectly fine guy who immersed himself in the show, from making ample use of the Randy's rolling papers provided by one of our sponsors to enlisting the DTB as his backing band on a few musical bits later in the night. At some point between "Goat Jam" and "Party in Your Stomach," I'm pretty sure I saw Derek grimace, which is rare for such a stoic performer (although, for the record, his guitar speaks with eloquence and passion, and Derek's got a great sense of humor).

The first performance from the main stage that night affirmed we were on the right track. The Del McCoury Band, who had yet to make inroads with our scene, appeared with Robert Randolph & the Family Band and DJ Logic. In this case, due to scheduling issues—Del had another gig that night—he had not even sound checked with his new collaborators. So when they broke into "Swing Low, Sweet Chariot" and Logic began scratching a version of the song they were then performing, Del did a triple take.

Someone else who really opened my eyes (and ears) that night was Bernie Williams, who joined us during an off day between games on a Yankees homestand. His guitar work alongside Jazz Mandolin Project on a version of Ornette Coleman's "Ramblin'" was spot-on. He was also a humble presence backstage, signing autographs for musicians and deftly relocating whenever someone pulled out those ubiquitous Randy's rolling papers. In retrospect, I wonder what Jim Breuer, a lifelong Mets fan, thought of this (when Red Sox fan Jeff Waful appeared on the awards stage, he name-checked the Sawx and was greeted by boos). Thanks to Bernie, some Jammys footage even made it into the JumboTron at Yankee Stadium the next day—where, it's important to note, he went three for three in a Yankees victory.

This was also the year that I walked onstage in the middle of a jam and tried to cut things short (the first of two times I would attempt this move—not a fun job, but someone's got to do it). As a result of the delay getting people into Roseland, we started about fifteen minutes late, which initially threw off our schedule. While we had built in some cushion, I began to get anxious toward the end of the show. If we missed our curfew, we were required to buy an entire hour of overtime, which was quite expensive.

Heading into the Disco Biscuits performance with John Popper, Stanley Jordan, and DJ Logic, we were up against it. They were second to last before our Meters lifetime achievement speech by George Porter Jr. and then his climactic closing set. I didn't want to short-shrift George, one of the all-time greats on every level.

The Biscuits and guests opened with a version of Jane's Addiction's "Three Days," which was awesome and connected with my own musical journey. However, it was nearly twenty minutes long, and their entire set was slated for twenty minutes. So maybe ten minutes into their subsequent cover of Led Zeppelin's "Bring It on Home," I couldn't control myself. I walked onto the corner of the stage and swirled my finger, indicating that they should wrap things up. John Popper and Biscuits guitarist Jon Gutwillig repeated this gesture at me and shrugged as if they were unfamiliar with this signal. Then when I stepped farther out onstage and repeated myself, they turned their backs on me. In the end, things were a bit rushed, but we did finish on time, and they definitely enjoyed watching me grimace.

In 2004, I tried the same thing at the Theater at MSG. It was the close of the night, and our lifetime achievement award winner, Steve Winwood, was onstage for the "Gimme Some Lovin'" finale with Warren Haynes, Michael Kang, Robert Randolph, and James Carter. It looked like they were going to continue past curfew, so again I walked onstage, and this time, I gestured to Warren. He didn't turn his back on me; he just squinched up his face as if to say, "What do you mean?" I stepped closer and repeated the gesture, which elicited a Cheshire cat grin from Warren, so I was still anxious. But of course, they were pros, who could see the digital clock on the side of the stage without any prompting from me, and hit that final climactic note precisely at 1:00 a.m.

The 2001 Jammys also achieved our objective of raising awareness for musicians who deserved the attention. Jon Pareles wrote a review for the *New York Times*, which itself was a victory. I am always psyched when a top writer or photographer attends one of my shows. Danny Clinch has been showing up for over two decades now (including the Roseland Jammys), and his presence never fails to excite me because I know the event is being captured forever in proper form.

Pareles's piece ran with the headline "Where Getting into a Jam Is Considered a Good Thing." When I saw that, I knew we'd delivered. Here is his final paragraph, which really captured our intent in creating the show: "The best jams assume that the musicians have a shared musical heritage. At the Jammy Awards, that heritage spanned Ornette Coleman and King Crimson, James Brown and the Carter Family, the Beatles and Jane's Addiction. At a time when most rockers are belligerently defending tiny niches, jambands promise to keep a broad musical spectrum sound within earshot."

We also received an *Entertainment Weekly* review that concluded, "Memo to cable execs: Let's see the third Jammys on TV!"

Now we had a new goal for 2002 . . .

15

THE NIGHT BEFORE

Project Logic Power Jam
Wetlands Preserve, New York, New York
September 10, 2001

I had a sense from the start that my time at Wetlands would be relatively short-lived. This had nothing to do with my own interests or desires but rather my reading of the tea leaves. Or perhaps an examination of the lease.

It became clear to me early on that I would likely have a limited window as the owner, because in a couple of years, the lease would lapse, and the person who owned the building would raise the rent so high that the club would be forced to close. Tribeca was in the middle of a transformation.

Larry had selected 161 Hudson Street as the ideal home for Wetlands, thinking that he had picked a spot in Manhattan where no one would want to live, ensuring that Wetlands could live forever. It was located within a sector of working warehouses, which meant clatter and truck traffic. The Holland Tunnel exited across the street, which compounded the noise issues (while making it convenient for patrons to pop in from the New Jersey suburbs—at times, they had it easier than I did when I was traveling to the club from my apartment).

However, around the time I took over Wetlands, Tribeca was becoming a trendy residential neighborhood. Many of the warehouses were being converted into condos with the latest in modern amenities, including state-of-the-art soundproofing.

So I suspected my run would be finite, even though I didn't let this get the best of me.

If I were presented with a similar opportunity today, I am not sure that I would do the deal. However, when I was twenty-three, it represented a great opportunity.

I never got too upset about my limited run at Wetlands because if there had been a really long lease, I don't think I would have become the owner. The business would have been worth so much money that someone else would have swept in to make Larry an offer he couldn't refuse.

In mid-2001, the landlord informed me that the end was near. He was in the process of converting the building into multimillion-dollar lofts that one day would be sold to Jon Stewart and Mike Piazza. I kept pushing for additional time until I could push no further. Finally, it became clear that our last night of music would be September 15, 2001.

We went to work trying to put together a lineup for the home-stretch that reflected the full sweep of Wetlands history. It soon became a challenge because so many artists contacted us about participating (a turn of events from my early days at the venue).

Ultimately, we booked a mix of classic Wetlands performers. The Spin Doctors, who represented the club's first era, reunited with guitarist Eric Schenkman after seven years apart, and they've been at it ever since. A number of other groups also came back together during the final weeks, including God Street Wine, Ominous Seapods, Screamin' Cheetah Wheelies, and Fat Mama (the jazz-fusion group that originally brought Joe Russo, Erik Deutsch, and Kevin Kendrick to the Wetlands stage). Other returning regulars during the final few weeks included the Disco Biscuits, Black Lily (with Toshi Reagon, Jaguar Wright, and Jazzyfatnastees), Fishbone, the Toasters, and the Zen Tricksters with Merl Saunders. We captured the present-day Wetlands vibe with the groups who had performed our recent New Year's Eve gigs: Strangefolk, Deep Banana Blackout, and the New Deal.

I made a couple of memorable stage introductions during this final stretch. We booked a showcase with Maroon 5, who were playing their first New York gig after changing their name from Kara's Flowers. The manager knew that Pearl Jam and Oasis had performed their initial NYC dates at the club and wanted to set a similar tone.

On August 23, Robert Randolph & the Family Band recorded their dynamic debut album *Live at the Wetlands*, which opens with my onstage introduction.

Wetlands helped me become comfortable speaking onstage. I learned to talk extemporaneously based on preparation. I would often jot down a couple of notes on a napkin (these days, it's the notes section of my phone), and then I would walk out, grip it, and rip it.

The idea is to think a lot but not to think too much.

This is something I apply to many different contexts. I have heard Trey Anastasio describe how he prepares for improvisation, and what I do is similar in a way. It is important to put in the work that will enable you to be on your toes to anticipate and respond. However, there also comes a point when you have to let it all go and have faith that what you've done has made you ready for the moment. That's how I run my business, coming up with ideas and then executing them like a jam.

The last act we confirmed would allow us to go out in style. After quite a bit of hustling, we landed Bob Weir's RatDog for the final two shows on Friday, September 14, and Saturday, September 15. We announced them on Monday, September 10, and put tickets on sale that day. Our *Voice* ad trumpeted, "One more Friday night!" and "One last Saturday night!"

For the evening of September 10, we booked Project Logic, the band led by turntablist DJ Logic, someone else who has remained a steady presence at my shows over the years to follow. Since we were now in the homestretch, I decided to add another element to this one, and I invited a series of guests to join the band as a nod to the classic Wetlands Power Jams over the years.

Putting together those Power Jam rosters was like assembling all-star teams. One of my favorites took place around our tenth anniversary and included Warren Haynes, Rob Wasserman, Col. Bruce Hampton, Vernon Reid, Melvin Sparks, Bernie Worrell, Robert Bradley, and Buddy Cage. Another memorable Power Jam occurred two years later and drew together members of moe., the

Disco Biscuits, Lettuce, Guster, Deep Banana Blackout, and Brothers Past (our longtime staffer the late, great Rodney Speed sat in as well, which made for a particularly special night).

The Wetlands layout facilitated Power Jams because the back door on Laight Street opened directly into the backstage area. So an artist could show up on Laight, knock on the door, and roll right in. That aspect kept things loose and easy. Musicians would arrive over the course of the night and pop into the band room or watch from the back hallway. It became a fun hang.

On September 10, the evening peaked with an extended, open-ended improvisational jam featuring DJ Logic, Mike Gordon, Warren Haynes, and Stanley Jordan. They shared a vivid musical conversation that electrified everyone in the room. It was an instant classic. No one wanted it to stop, including the musicians, so they kept going well past midnight.

I was there for the entire show and made it home around 6:00 a.m. I crashed for a few hours, and then on the morning of 9/11, the phone started ringing. By this point, I was living with Becca on Mulberry and Houston, and her father called to ask if we were watching TV. This was before the second plane hit the tower. I saw that happen in real time, and it was devastating. I stepped out for a walk shortly afterward, and I felt the ground rumble beneath me when both towers collapsed.

That morning impacted all of us in profound ways. I was mostly speechless as I watched the events unfold on TV.

My thoughts didn't turn to Wetlands right away. My head didn't go there given the scope of tragedy and loss that we were all experiencing in real time.

I kept fielding calls from people checking in on me, and I made a few of my own to friends who could have been down there that morning. Thankfully, all of them had been spared.

In the days to follow, I received two letters from people who had worked in the World Trade Center but had attended the Project Logic show on September 10. Since the evening had gone so long, both of them had called in late the next morning. As a result, they'd been at home rather than at the office when the planes hit. They both credit Wetlands with altering the course of their lives.

It's hard to know what to say in response to that, but I like to think the energy in the room had manifested some positive impact on the world within the larger darkness.

Wetlands was located in Lower Manhattan, less than a mile from the World Trade Center, but 161 Hudson Street was far enough away from the towers that the building experienced no physical damage from the attacks. However, the entire club was covered in ash, which was a sobering sight.

Eventually, we had to accept the obvious: there would be no more shows that week. It wasn't even possible to access that section of Manhattan unless one lived there or was serving as a relief worker.

As the days carried on, I held out hope that we could open for one final night, to have some measure of closure. Live music offers salvation—that is one of its finest qualities.

With some respectful persistence on my part, we were eventually permitted to have one more Saturday night: September 29, 2001. Bob Weir was unavailable, so I decided we'd go out in classic Wetlands style with a final jam session.

Then, at the very last minute, there was a slight change of plans, so we'd go out in another classic Wetlands style with a special surprise guest. Someone had told me that Jerry Garcia's longtime writing partner Robert Hunter was in the city because his daughter's boyfriend had died in the towers. The club had been built on the spirit of the songs he had written, and I realized that he might be the single most appropriate person to perform on the closing night.

I can't quite remember how I ended up with his email address—that period is a daze to me—but I sent him a heartfelt message about how he would be the perfect individual to supply our coda. And even though at that point in his career he had retired from live performances, he agreed to do so.

As he said at the time, "I'm very thankful that Pete asked me to play because it's a way to express some kind of oneness with the city and what went down. It's a focus, and I can use a focus right now. So I decided to be unretired for the evening."

Hunter opened with "Box of Rain," and his final benediction came a few songs later with "Ripple." He gave way to a night of upbeat grooves that featured some of the musicians who have continued on this journey with me: Eric Krasno, Neal Evans, Joe Russo, Scott Metzger, Jeff Mattson, Jen Durkin, Fuzz, and many others.

As dawn approached, I had become physically and mentally exhausted, so I turned things over to Larry. He offered a final few words, then stepped into his longtime home away from home, the DJ booth, to spin sweet songs and rock everyone's soul until 8:15 a.m.

There was a beauty and symmetry to all of this because he opened the club, I took it over, then he closed it out.

One decision that I lingered over during Wetlands's final weeks was what to do with the VW bus. Some people suggested that I sell it on eBay, but that wasn't the Wetlands way. Eventually, I contacted Terry Stewart, the president of the Rock & Roll Hall of Fame, to see if they might want it, and thankfully, they did.

So a day after the final Wetlands show, we busted through the wall with a sledgehammer to get the bus out so we could send it to Cleveland on an eighteen-wheeler. After it arrived, they didn't dump it in storage; they put it on display in the atrium next to Janis Joplin's psychedelic Porsche.

As for Larry, we remained in touch. I will never forget that he was first one who believed I could do this.

I used him as a sounding board for my various ideas and initiatives, including Brooklyn Bowl, which took inspiration from Wetlands in many respects. I would solicit his opinion and he'd tell me, "That's cool!" or explain why it wasn't.

Larry found happiness in his own intense, driven way, running Save the Corporations from Themselves and contributing to Brattleboro Community Radio as a board member and on-air host.

Unfortunately, in 2012, he was diagnosed with pancreatic cancer. Even as he experienced the ill effects of the disease during those final months, he continued to pursue his passions with vigor.

We stayed in touch until the end. I had invited him to come to the Capitol Theatre to DJ the Blues Traveler / Spin Doctors show on October 13, but he wasn't quite feeling up to it.

He passed away on November 4, 2012, at age fifty-nine.

Of Wetlands's closure and legacy, he said, "I don't view it as a loss. I think people shouldn't focus on the absence but rather on the fullness of twelve and a half years of Wetlands. That fullness is sprinkled in consciousness all around the world. That's how I view the world now, as a better place as a result of Wetlands. I put my attention on how it has fueled me for the work I'm doing now. And I hope the same transfer of energy can occur for people who were touched by Wetlands instead of focusing their energy on the absence of Wetlands."

To this day, in certain situations, I'll still ask myself, "What would Larry think?"

16

OPERATION KINKO'S

The Jammy Awards
Roseland Ballroom, New York, New York
October 2, 2002

The decision to move The Jammys to Roseland Ballroom had some implications for me.

After many years of experience as an independent promoter, I realized that there were certain occasions when I could benefit from help.

We had big plans for Roseland. We intended to fill two stages with musicians and maintain a steady flow of changeovers and guest players. We also hoped to conclude the evening with a massive jam in which the artists would interact from across the room, which meant we needed to ensure that they could hear each other and that the audience could hear everyone. No one had previously used the venue this way, which made it both daunting and potentially gratifying.

To pull all of this off, we established a partnership with SFX (the future Live Nation). This was my first time working with them, and they were actually pretty good to us.

The Jammys were expensive. We didn't pay for any of the artists to perform, but we also didn't want any of them to dip into their pockets to participate. So we took care of all their travel and hotel accommodations, along with whatever backline equipment they needed (and there were a lot of artists, which meant a lot of backline). Keep this in mind if you're ever doing an event in which the musicians are donating their time: free is not cheap.

By the time we moved to the Theater at MSG in 2004, the costs were north of $500,000. With ticket sales and some sponsorships, we turned a small profit once or twice, but most years, we were a little short. I can recall a couple of times when we still owed something to SFX / Live Nation eight months after the event. I'd get a call, but they never came at me too hard. By then, we'd be close to putting tickets on sale for the next one, so $100,000 would come in to pay the $62,000 we owed them for the previous year, and now we had a $38,000 credit for this year.

None of this was part of our official deal. No one at SFX formally agreed that they were going to be a source of financing, but they were willing to let it float. Now to be clear, you can't get away with something like that unless you eventually make good on what you owe. It also helped that they had real respect for what we were doing. We were putting on an awards show featuring top-name touring acts with minimal personnel—a comparable event typically had over one hundred people working on it.

The Jammys started with Dean and me. By year two, though, his website Jambands.com had been acquired by *Relix*. That is when *Relix* publisher Steve Bernstein became a partner in the show. However, at that point, Steve was working a full-time job on Wall Street, so *Relix* was a bit of a side hustle, so we did not have much of a Jammys team.

I can remember a meeting that took place at the Madison Square Garden offices in 2004. We were preparing to move The Jammys from Roseland to the Theater at MSG, so we sat down to discuss budget and logistics. We were in a giant conference room, and there were at least two dozen people on their side and only three on ours (KindBud, *Relix* head of marketing Jonathan Schwartz—who is now the General of Jam on SiriusXM—and me). They had more interns in the room than we had us.

One of the benefits that came with stepping up into this prestigious new venue (with a capacity of 5,600) was working with the legend, Dan Parise. He served as line producer for our four Jammys at MSG and he was a pro's pro (Danny passed away following a heart attack in August 2020—I took it pretty hard, and it was a major loss to live music). He embraced the challenge of running a seamless production, and I never saw him sweat. I just pulled out one of his old color-coded Jammys show rundowns, and it's a thing of beauty, with artist performances in blue, onstage announcements in yellow, offstage announcements in green, video roll cues in pink, audio cues in purple, and stage moves in orange. Like I said, Dan was a pro's pro (and a budding artist—that thing is eye candy).

By 2002, we were starting to get some real forceful pitches from managers on behalf of their acts, so the impulse to add yet another high-caliber segment was overwhelming.

Here's a fun fact about The Jammys: John Popper is our longest-serving host. No, he only did it once, just like everyone else, but he's our longest-serving host because in 2002, when he was on the job, the night lasted for seven hours. As a bonus, he agreed to do it in pajamas (this was an idea that he came up with while we were riffing backstage before the show, and we sent out a runner to find some jammies for him).

Our main stage lineup for the 2002 Jammys looked like this:

1. Rob Wasserman and DJ Logic
2. Rusted Root with DJ Logic and Melvin Sparks
3. John Scofield, Stanton Moore, Skerik, and Andy Hess
4. Blind Boys of Alabama with Robert Randolph & the Family Band, Derek Trucks, and John Mayer
5. Particle with Fred Schneider and Kate Pierson of the B-52's
6. moe. with Eric Bloom, Buck Dharma, and Allen Lanier of Blue Öyster Cult
7. Mike Gordon and Leo Kottke
8. Gov't Mule with Oteil Burbridge, Stefan Lessard, John Scofield, and Trey Anastasio as well as the entire Allman Brothers Band
9. Bob Weir & RatDog
10. All-Star Jam

That's just what took place on the main stage. In between, we had Tom Tom Club with the Dirty Dozen Brass Band (and various guest musicians) on the awards stage.

It is possible to look back on some of this on YouTube because we brought in cameras to shoot the night.

It was an expensive undertaking because venues typically require payment of what's known as an origination fee for any video shoots. These charges were costly, and it is why we could not afford to shoot every year of The Jammys unless we had an outlet confirmed in advance. That said, there may be a tape of the 2001 Jammys filmed from the corner of the balcony, and it's possible that in 2008, rather than making an official recording of the performances, we might have pointed a camera at the IMAG, the video that the venue projected onto the screens on either side of the stage. (A YouTube search for "SpottedStripers" could reveal some answers.)

While we do have video from portions of 2002, no one was shooting the awards stage, which meant we lost the Tom Tom Club / Dirty Dozen performances as well as some acceptance speeches (d'oh!). Trey won Tour of the Year Award for the Trey Anastasio Band summer 2002 outing during Phish's hiatus and enlisted TAB members Jennifer Hartswick and Cyro Baptista to rework the lyrics to *West Side Story*'s "Gee, Officer Krupke": "We've tested all your patience, yet you've been tried or true / You're sick of Pork Tornado, you're sick of Vida Blue / If I would just stop talking, you would get your wish / Stop this shit and give us back our Phish." A little while later, Bob Weir accepted a Lifetime Achievement Award on behalf of the Grateful Dead, delivering a thoughtful reflection that stressed the lineage of improvisation going back to Louis Armstrong.

When I say Bobby made his speech "a little while later," that may be an understatement. This is because after the Gov't Mule / Allman Brothers Band set, we experienced a technical setback that resulted in a forty-minute delay. It was during this time that Al Franken, who was on hand to give a Lifetime Achievement Award to the Dead, muttered something about a flight and walked out the side door. Dean chased him a few blocks up Fifty-Second Street to no avail.

Here's Al's recollection: "I did agree to present the Lifetime Achievement Award to the Dead (humbly, I am an enormous Deadhead), but I had told the organizers of the event that I

would have to get out by a certain time—I believe midnight—
because I had to get up at 4:30 the next morning to catch a plane.
I was assured that I would be out by then and was asked to come
around 10:30 or so. I arrived at 10:30 and happily listened to
music and went backstage and got to meet Leo Kottke, a hero of
mine. I told the organizers I really had to be out by midnight, and
they assured me that I would. As it became clear that the show
was running over—which shows do—I told them I'd try to hang
in till 12:30 or so, but I really had to leave then. At about 12:30,
it became clear that it was going to run longer, so I said I'd hang
till 1:00, but that was it. More assurance, et cetera, and I could tell
that these guys didn't have control of the show (it's The Jammys,
for god's sake), but that, of course, was the problem. It just kept
going on."

Well, it did, then it didn't, then it did.

Unfortunately, during the lull, we not only lost Al, we also lost
our film crew.

Eventually, though, we sorted everything out. Bobby accepted
the award (thankfully, we also had a video recording from Senator
Patrick Leahy), and then RatDog performed.

The night then finally concluded with an epic two-stage jam
that exceeded my wildest expectations. Yes, we were well past
curfew, but we were given a pass on this one, as everyone who
remained—and this was nearly everyone who attended—stuck it
out for what was described in a *New York Times* photo caption as
the "Jam of the Titans." Bobby, Trey, Warren, Popper, Rob Wasserman, moe. guitarist Al Schnier, and many others were on one stage,
collaborating across the room with Mike Gordon, Robert Randolph, and Tom Tom Club. Nobody in the audience quite knew
where to look. Heads were spinning.

I would almost end the story there, except people continue to
ask me why I don't bring back The Jammys, which ended its run
in 2008. There are a couple of answers.

One of them is that a few years after we began the show, we
received a legal notice from an organization that puts on an event
that rhymes with Jammy, telling us to cease and desist. Their contention was that only one awards show could possibly rhyme with
ammy, and it wasn't ours.

Can one organization shut down another due to a rhyming name? I was told the legal standard was whether there would be any confusion between the two, and I don't think anyone thought we were the Grammy Awards. Nonetheless, litigation is expensive, and we didn't start The Jammys to get into a fight with NARAS.

We went out in style, though. In 2008, we gave the Lifetime Achievement Award to Phish at a time when they had broken up. All four members of the band attended and accepted their trophies. This was the first time the four of them had appeared on a public stage together since their final show in 2004, giving fans hope that they might yet return, which they did the following year. For the record, while we knew that Page McConnell and Trey Anastasio would be there since they had agreed to perform, Mike Gordon and Jon Fishman were a surprise until the very end.

In addition, as I mentioned, free can still be expensive, and the cost of putting on The Jammys only increased over time. Plus, many other shows have followed in our wake with unique pairings (including that other *ammy* show). I also feel like we achieved what we set out to do, by shining a light on the scene.

The Jammys was a time and a place.

By 2008, the backstage scene had become a full-on party. *Rock Band* was a sponsor, and they set up the game on a giant monitor in a backstage lounge. I remember Mountain guitarist Leslie West (RIP) hanging out and schooling everyone on a version of his song "Mississippi Queen" before appearing onstage with Rose Hill Drive and schooling everyone on a version of his song "Mississippi Queen."

In that last year, we gave out *one thousand* backstage passes. It became so congested, particularly in the hallways, that there were moments when I could barely breathe.

Which brings me to a final memory from 2002. Randy Henner at SFX had allocated two hundred backstage passes and wouldn't allow us to have any more. Unfortunately, we knew we needed five hundred to do right by all the musicians and their guests, along with our own. We weren't quite sure how to resolve this until we cooked up a plan on the day of the show.

One of us went to Roseland to pick up our credentials, and then we sent a *Relix* intern to the local Kinko's to make three hundred copies of that laminate (we thought that sending the intern gave us some plausible deniability, although in retrospect, I question our definition of the term *plausible*). Again, I don't recommend this, and I wouldn't do it again (necessarily), but it did get us through the night with the number of passes that we actually needed.

It worked, at least until settlement. We were in a room with Randy, finalizing the financials after the show, when she noticed that my laminate seemed to be peeling. She became a bit flustered when she started to suspect what we had done.

I mean, what kind of a person would make a fake lammy to their own show?

17

INAUGURAL BLUES

John Kerry Presidential Inaugural Celebration
National Mall, Washington, DC
January 19, 2005

This was going to be a big one.

Imagine working with Quincy Jones on a presidential inauguration, collaborating on an epic event that blended a live music score from an all-star cast of artists with the images of America—my *American Road* idea finally realized in the most prestigious setting possible.

Well, I'm still imagining it.

For about an hour, I thought I had it, though.

This hurt.

Literally.

It was one of the few times in my life I can remember experiencing physical pain when something didn't happen.

I am usually pretty good about letting things go when they don't come to pass, but occasionally, something will get to me. For instance, I made a run at producing a 3D film of Phish's August 2004 Coventry Festival. It looked like these would be the band's final gigs, and I was aching to pull it off, knowing that the band's swan song would be a significant cultural moment. It would have cost over a couple of million dollars to shoot, though, and I hit a snag because the band wouldn't offer us permission to release whatever we'd filmed. They required approval after the weekend to ensure that the music met their high standards.

Ultimately, we could not justify the risk, so we passed. As it turned out, the band was so rattled by their impending breakup that their performances suffered and they never would have given me their permission. Missing out on that opportunity was so disheartening to me that I ended up taking a friend's offer and fleeing the country in mid-August to attend the Athens Olympics.

As for the inauguration, I had become friendly with Mark Ross, the head of Quincy Jones Productions. I pitched him on *American Road* as a project for Quincy. They were interested, but the way this eventually netted out was that it would happen as part of the John Kerry inaugural concert.

That sounded good to me!

We were going to score the music of America, set to the visuals of America on screens all along the National Mall. It would be the ultimate *American Road*.

This was during a time after Wetlands had closed and Brooklyn Bowl was a blip on the horizon. I was working with my brother Jon along with David and John Modell on 3D test footage for the NFL, but we were still a few months away from piecing together what would become *U2 3D*. *All Access* was a couple of years in the past, and my Verizon money had almost run out. I still had The Jammys, but I was scrambling to find a new project where I could stick the landing.

So this would be huge.

Something like this lasts for a while. It's got spray around it. Or to think of it another way, it's got really good drift.

There is drift in front of an event and after it takes place. When people first hear about something, that anticipation of the unknown can take on its own momentum. And then, if you're successful, there are reverberations as well.

Kerry was running against Bush 43, the incumbent, and by all accounts, it was going to be close. No one was sure what would happen, but as Election Day approached, a number of pollsters predicted that enough undecided voters would break for Kerry to put him over the top.

I was at home, pacing around our apartment on the evening of November 2, 2004, when the election returns started to roll in. Kerry was strong in his native New England, so it was no surprise that the initial results were in his favor. Then the focus turned to the battlegrounds of Florida and Ohio, where the TV networks pointed to early exit polling and suggested that Kerry was on track to win both states.

Around 11:00 p.m., I received a call from Mark, who was at a party in Los Angeles. He told me, "I'm with Quincy. I just talked to the guy who's going to be the chairman of the inaugural committee, and it looks like we got the gig. This is going to happen!"

Just three years after Wetlands closed, I would be working with Quincy Jones to produce an inaugural concert.

I could not believe it.

As it turned out, disbelief was the proper POV.

In retrospect, I was not the only one who had a painful reckoning that night. Based on the initial data, Kerry's friend and senior adviser Bob Shrum took him aside and asked, "Can I be the first to call you *Mr. President?*"

Shortly thereafter, John Kerry began work on his victory speech.

Then he lost Florida, lost Ohio, lost the election.

I lost the gig.

There was about an hour when I started to dream and scheme about what I would put together for this glorious moment on the National Mall.

Then it all evaporated.

Over the course of sixty minutes, I went from working with Quincy Jones on the inaugural to literally nothing. There was no consolation prize. George Bush was going to be president, and I was going to be watching his inaugural on TV.

By the fall of 2004, I had certainly come to understand that not all my ideas would achieve critical mass. I'd experienced that at Wetlands, The Jammys, Coventry, and even with *American Road* itself.

Nonetheless, when the networks called the election for Bush, I collapsed onto my bed, doubled over in pain.

I don't experience setbacks the same way anymore. I've come to internalize the idea that nos often lead to yeses. Still, I do have a touch of that PTSD, some of which I can attribute to Election Night 2004, which ended with me curled up on my bed, screaming into the pillow.

Four years later, though, I had another chance.

I was in consideration to produce We Are One, the event that took place on the National Mall two days prior to Barack Obama's inauguration.

I had produced the Earth Day celebration at the same location in April as part of the Green Apple Festival. We had free concerts in eight cities from coast to coast, but the National Mall was the flagship event. Unfortunately, that flagship capsized halfway through the day due to torrential rains.

Participating in President Obama's inaugural weekend would be something else entirely. Again, I returned to my *American Road* 2.0 template. I'd have footage from all the states, then a live musical score from people connected to the various regions would be showing on the screens. We'd have Willie Nelson performing "Texas," someone from Colorado singing "Rocky Mountain High," and so forth.

I was in play until the end, but they didn't pick me. Instead, they went with the team that produced the Kennedy Center Honors. It was tough to quibble with that selection, even if I was frustrated by another near miss.

They did offer me something of a consolation prize, however. They asked if I wanted to be involved in the video roll-ins that they would screen before the show. Since they expected a few hundred thousand people to be there, many of whom would arrive well in advance, they needed something to keep them entertained.

While I was disappointed with the way things had turned out, I wanted to be a part of the day, so I said yes.

As it turned out, I would make another contribution as well, albeit in a quieter way.

I was on-site a couple of days before the inaugural, sorting out logistics for the pregame videos that ran on the Mall, when I was handed the run of show for the main event.

As I looked at the schedule while sitting in the bathroom, I noticed that We Are One: The Obama Inaugural Celebration at the Lincoln Memorial was going to conclude with Bruce Springsteen singing "This Land Is Your Land."

As soon I saw this, the first thing that occurred to me was that Bruce should do it with Pete Seeger. I'm not sure why no one had thought of it, but I can say from experience that sometimes when you're in the middle of something, you can lack perspective. But while I sat there reading the run-through, it was obvious to me. (As the song goes, "Once in a while you get shown the light, in the strangest of places if you look at it right.")

Even though it was only a few days before the show, I suspected I could help facilitate this. At the time, Pete Seeger was managed by Michael Cohl along with my friend Mike Luba. So I called Luba and shared the idea. Everyone liked it, and the next thing I knew, Bruce had sent a plane to New York to pick up Pete.

I keep a photo in my office of the moment when they appeared together.

It's a quiet reminder to myself of something I was able to facilitate.

In 2009, when I became the publisher of *Relix*, part of the appeal was that I would inherit a much larger office than I ever would have selected for myself. I was able to fill my new space with posters, photos, and other mementos of my various projects. You can find a Jammys program, the *All Access* Verizon CD, a Wetlands schedule, and the first sketch of what Brooklyn Bowl would look like, which I made in an Italian restaurant on a napkin. I don't display those for other people; they are there for me. They help settle me when I have my doubts about whether I can do it all again.

As for major Washington political events, I would have a third bite at the apple in 2018, when I was invited to produce a celebration to commemorate the Democrats reclaiming the majority in the House of Representatives.

Thankfully, I didn't have to sweat out the competition. I was offered the gig directly via Mickey Hart and Nancy Pelosi.

It was a real honor.

And what could possibly go wrong . . .

18

BE THE LAST MAN STANDING ... OR THE FIRST TO LEAVE

Leonard Cohen and U2
The Slipper Room, New York, New York
May 19, 2005

One of the lessons I have learned is that sometimes it is smart to leave early.

It can be good strategery. This allows you to say goodbye, which is a good moment to let someone know that you want to connect on an idea or project.

This is what happened when U2 appeared at the Slipper Room on the afternoon of May 19, 2005, to perform a song with Leonard Cohen for the documentary *Leonard Cohen: I'm Your Man*.

I had arrived before the musicians so that I could greet everyone and show off the venue.

After I had poured Bono and myself a couple of Stellas, he went off about the club's vibe and décor, comparing it to a Victorian theater located in a red-light district, which was, of course, accurate.

Bono's description sounded like the pitch that had been made to me as a potential investor before the club opened in 1999. I had been at Wetlands a few years when I met Norman Gosney, a real downtown New York City legend. Owning music venues, particularly in NYC, you meet people. He introduced me to James Habacker, who had the vision for a vaudeville theater in the Lower East Side. James already had the space, but he needed investors. I liked his idea, so I was the first one to put money into the Slipper Room—thirty grand, which was almost everything I had available at the time, but it felt like the right thing to do.

While there wasn't much crossover between the artists who appeared at the Slipper Room and Wetlands, there was a similar energy. It was experiential in an analogous way. Very different from Wetlands but still church.

The Slipper Room contrasted with Wetlands when it came to my role at the club. It was a learning process for me to operate as an investor with far fewer day-to-day responsibilities. By 1999, I had become accustomed to my position at Wetlands as a benevolent dictator, an approach that still works best for me.

Although at one point, Larry had contemplated a three-person team to take over the club, he eventually changed his mind because decision by committee can lead to indecision. That is not the way to operate a music venue where you need to be quick and definitive with a clear chain of command.

In order for a benevolent dictatorship to be effective, you need to listen to your inner circle and be willing to take someone else's advice. But while you should be receptive to other ideas, everyone else on the team needs to accept that when you make a decision, it's the final word and time to move on.

For me, this works. I take into account the advice from all my senior people, along with trusted friends and colleagues. There are a lot of phone calls and caucusing. One good thing about where I am today is that people work for me in various time zones, so I can find someone whenever I want to talk through stuff.

My experience at the Slipper Room in 1999 was very different. James was the founder and artistic director, so I deferred to him, although I felt comfortable expressing my opinions, the way that someone in my circle would do with me.

When the Slipper Room first opened, there was a full-service menu because James wanted to have a restaurant. I wasn't convinced this was the perfect match for the vibe he was creating, so I raised my concerns, then let it go.

I became far more outspoken on the very first night of food service. I remember sitting there at the initial "friends and family dinner" when the bill was delivered to my table. That is when I definitively realized that we had to get rid of the restaurant. James was operating with limited funds, so he couldn't go around comping meals, which I suspected could become a problem since he was part of a tight-knit creative community. Plus, rather than overseeing the kitchen, he needed to prioritize his role as artistic director. I should also mention that although the bill that appeared at my table was discounted, even discounted can be expensive, since James had wanted a high-end dining experience.

It was shortly afterward that he got rid of the restaurant and placed all his energy on the burlesque of it all.

At times, working with James could be frustrating for me because I am happiest when I control a project, despite all the stress and responsibility that comes with it.

Still, I am proud of the Slipper Room, which became a Lower East Side institution. Lady Gaga is one of the alumni, along with Murray Hill, Dirty Martini, the Scissor Sisters, and plenty of others.

On occasion, I've hosted some events at the Slip. I held my engagement party there in 2002 for my friends who wouldn't be traveling to Chicago for my wedding. It's also where I celebrated my thirtieth birthday, and Mike Gordon showed up—I can still remember which booth Gordo sat in.

Even though I contributed a relatively small sum (albeit not so small to me), I know that it mattered. As I've pointed out, you always need a first person. Without a first person, you can't get a second. That applies equally to investors and artists.

Plus, I actually got my money back.

Having said that, I did not contribute the original $30,000 looking to earn multiples on my investment. That probably should not be your goal in situations like this. If your intent is to support a vision, that is the reason to buy the ticket and take a ride. Plus, it helps if you want to hang there.

You never know what will come out of the experience, though. In my case, it was the world's first digital 3D concert film.

In May 2005, James called me to let me know that U2 was going to be at the Slipper Room to film a song with Leonard Cohen.

As it turned out, I had been trying to connect with Paul McGuinness, U2's manager, to show him some of our test footage. I wanted him to see our multi-camera digital 3D shoot of an NFL game to demonstrate the full power of the medium. In addition, a single camera had captured U2 six weeks earlier in Anaheim, thanks to Catherine Owens, the band's creative director of screen imagery, as well as Willie Williams, the group's lighting designer.

I did not immediately approach Paul about any of this, opting to host and toast the band. The filming itself went well other than a moment when Leonard Cohen disappeared. Everyone was on a quick break, and then he was gone. At first, there was some mild curiosity as to what might have happened to him, and then some people began to panic. As it turned out, he was oblivious to the commotion while he sat across the street at an outdoor café, sipping a cup of coffee.

When order was restored, I had a gut feeling that it was a good time to exit. Sometimes you want the deep hang, which means you should be the last man standing. But you also need to know when you should be the first one to leave.

I sensed it was time for a tactical move, so I paused to speak with Paul on my way out. I explained that I had to go, but I had been attempting to reach him to share our 3D test and talk about an innovative idea I thought would be perfect for his band. He pulled out his black book and said, "Great. I'll be here next week. When do you want to meet?"

This is the importance of reading the moment and occasionally leaving early. I believe that if I had remained to watch the entire shoot, I would have missed my chance. If Paul had left before I had, I do not think he would have been looking to say goodbye to Pete Shapiro, so I would not have been able to mention the 3D footage. When you say goodbye, that can be an opportunity to drop a piece of knowledge or make a request because you will have a moment to connect, as I did with Paul McGuinness.

Which is how I was able to sit with him a week later to pitch *U2 3D*.

19

THE DAYS BETWEEN

Soul to Soul: A Central Park SummerStage Benefit
  for Hurricane Katrina
Central Park SummerStage, New York, New York
September 28, 2005

I am sometimes asked what is my favorite venue that I don't own. While I've been to a lot of amazing places, including Red Rocks and the Gorge, I don't hesitate to say Central Park SummerStage.

If you attend a show in any other 5,500-cap venue and you walk outside, there's a parking lot. Pick a facility with that capacity in the middle of Boston, Chicago, Atlanta, or San Francisco, and when you exit, you'll see cars.

Not at SummerStage.

On the right night, nothing tops it. You step out of the venue and you are in the middle of the best park on earth. There have been plenty of evenings when I would play Frisbee with Ryan from Guster in the Sheep Meadow and then walk over to see a show.

Ryan's a great fellow adventurer, and I've enjoyed moving through the world with friends like him. I don't separate my life into different buckets, and I don't recommend that. I have one life, one group of friends, and a lot of them overlap.

I met Ryan after a Trey Anastasio concert at the Palace Theatre in Albany, over twenty year ago. We were outside some hotel, peeing into a snowbank, which is an interesting place to meet someone. Ryan told me Guster would be playing Woodstock '99 that summer, and we decided they should perform at Wetlands on their way. We hatched that plan at two in the morning after the Trey show and we've stayed close ever since.

As for SummerStage, I am currently on the board of the City Parks Foundation, which oversees the venue, so it almost feels like one of my places. The board provides oversight for more than 750 other green spaces across New York's five boroughs. It is gratifying to be involved, particularly because so many shows and programs are free, thanks to donations and the support of sponsors. At this point in my career, with ten thousand shows under my belt, hopefully my survival instincts can be helpful.

In September 2005, I was on the Arts Committee of the City Parks Foundation. This was right after Hurricane Katrina, and I wanted to do my part to help all the displaced and struggling musicians.

The New Orleans sound and spirit has spoken to me ever since I attended Jazz Fest while in college. When we began thinking about Brooklyn Bowl, I wanted the environment to feel like late night after the festival. Before we opened, I would bring people in for a walkthrough, and I would say, "It's New Orleans, it's two in the morning after Jazz Fest, and Galactic's playing." I always used Galactic as the prototypical example in my head when thinking about who was onstage and envisioning what Brooklyn Bowl would be like. That ended up being the right atmosphere.

In 2017, I did a show with Phil Lesh & Friends at the Anthem in Washington, DC, with the Preservation Hall Jazz Band. They came out during the second set, and then Phil and his band yielded the stage to them. It was sort of like an old-school drums-and-space segment except this time it went to New Orleans.

I love the culture of New Orleans, and I love Preservation Hall. I continue to work with them on various projects, and I hope to do something with them in their home city when the timing is right.

On the subject of timing, in September 2005, I had a limited window to pull things together because the final announced show of the SummerStage season occurred on September 15 with Arcade Fire (and surprise guest David Bowie).

Thankfully, I had the energy to aggressively chuck ideas at the wall. Whenever I do this, it reveals little cracks, and you never know what's going to come out of there. It's well worth the effort.

Two all-star Katrina benefits were slated to take place in Manhattan on September 20, at MSG and Radio City, but so much of the New Orleans vibe is outdoors that it felt appropriate to have that component. Plus, given the way SummerStage operates, it would be a free show, drawing in some folks who otherwise hadn't experienced those sounds or that culture. Our goal was to raise proceeds for the New Orleans Musicians' Clinic, so we had a suggested donation of twenty-five dollars, but I also believed that we could welcome a new generation of NOLA enthusiasts.

Through the assistance of friends and colleagues who shared my passion, I was able to lock down September 28 for what became the *final*, final show of the 2005 SummerStage music calendar. This was the first time I had become so deeply involved with an event there, although I've been part of many shows since.

Having said that, in 2004, I produced the first TV program to present live performances from the venue. On six consecutive Saturday nights from July 24 through August 28 at 11:35 p.m., WABC-TV aired *Live from Central Park SummerStage*. Local weather anchor Sam Champion hosted the show, with my co-author contributing some off-camera interviews with the artists. The roster included Guster (which was fitting, given my time tossing Frisbees with Ryan Miller), Rufus Wainwright, Ben Folds, Devo, stellastarr*, and the Yeah Yeah Yeahs (who later inspired my lone stage diving experience at Brooklyn Bowl—stay tuned).

I took pride in being part of the first TV series to present music from the venue. Of course, as the saying goes, "That and a dollar will get you a dollar." This expression is particularly relevant because it was very expensive to shoot, about a hundred grand per day, with HD cameras, a mobile truck, and everything else that comes with capturing a performance in Central Park. We did our best to limit the costs on *Live from Central Park SummerStage* by shooting the six episodes over two days, using three-band bills in which each artist performed for close to an hour.

The SummerStage series came together during an era in which my brother Jon and I were very active with HD. We shot more live music for HDNet during its infancy than any other independent producers. (Yes, that and a dollar . . .) While it wasn't lucrative, given all the associated expenses, it was still a cool experience. We were on the cutting edge of HD television programming.

Jon and I had ramped up our HD initiatives following *All Access*. Our first project was Chick Corea's sixtieth birthday run in December 2001 at New York's legendary Blue Note. They thought I could bring something to the table because of what I had done at Wetlands. Chick played three weeks of acoustic shows with nine different combos, which yielded our ten-part series *Rendezvous in New York*.

I feel lucky that I got to do that project and create a relationship with Chick. He was welcoming to me and so pro throughout the entire eighteen-night, nine-band run. He always held it together, even though he took the music pretty far out there night after night. He later joined us at the 2006 Jammys, appearing with Zappa Plays Zappa, and the *New York Times Review* noted that Chick's "array of Moog and other synthesizers sounded weirdly perfect, and perfectly weird."

Rendezvous in New York aired on HDNet and resulted in a 2-CD set that included "Matrix," which won a Grammy for Best Jazz Instrumental Solo. Much later, a 10-DVD box set presented all the HDNet episodes.

We worked with director David Niles on the Chick release and a few projects that followed, including The Jammys and live concerts from Dion and Sheryl Crow. He was a real pioneer when it came to HD. It's smart to partner with those on the front edge when working with new technology.

My experience working on *Live from Central Park SummerStage* and my involvement with the arts committee helped me gain trust and ultimately a green light for the NOLA fundraiser.

Still, it was up to me to pull together the lineup, and I needed to move quickly. For the house band, I asked Soulive. That was an easy call, as they are so versatile and we had been friends going back to Wetlands.

At this time, Soulive was touring as a quintet, with Eric Krasno, Alan Evans, and Neal Evans joined by Rashawn Ross (who would later join Dave Matthews Band) and Ryan Zoidis (Lettuce, Rustic Overtones). In addition, James Corden's future *Late Late Show* band leader Reggie Watts appeared on multiple dates contributing vocals. All six musicians participated in Soul to Soul: Central Park SummerStage Benefit for Hurricane Katrina. Throughout the evening, they were joined by a variety of New Orleans legends and other performers who felt the same way that I did about NOLA.

As I look back on the lineup, I can see how it came together on such short notice, thanks to existing relationships. Relationships are key. I reached Dr. John via his manager Peter Himberger, whom I knew from The Jammys. Our connection to Lou Reed and Laurie Anderson came through their publicist Annie Ohayon via Rob Wasserman. The executive producer of SummerStage, Alexa Birdsong, knew Cassandra Wilson. Ivan Neville is someone I first met at Wetlands, who calls me *Petey* to this day. My friend Kevin Morris manages Drive-By Truckers and Angélique Kidjo. I first met Corey Glover and Vernon Reid via the Black Rock Coalition at Wetlands. J Mascis joined the lineup thanks to manager Brian Schwartz, with whom I also continue to do business. Dar Williams was managed by the Velour Music Group, founded by Jeff Krasno, Eric Krasno's brother. Hubert Sumlin and Bettye LaVette would both later appear at the 2006 Jammys, in part due to this event, but I'm pretty sure I had approached their teams in previous years.

I can't quite remember how we connected with Allen Toussaint. This was during a period of time when he had moved to New York after being displaced by Katrina, so any number of folks might have helped. I am proud to say that my wife, Rebecca, worked with him on a publicity campaign the next year when he recorded an album with her client Elvis Costello.

The night flew by in a bit of a blur, even though the show was allowed to run longer than other SummerStage concerts. The good shows usually do fly by. I recall that the food won some raves, as we raised additional money for the New Orleans Musicians' Clinic by offering cuisine from New Orleans favorite Jacques-Imo's as well as New York's Blue Ribbon (who would join me at Brooklyn Bowl a couple of years later). I remember that Lou Reed gave me the silent treatment—he was polite but uncommunicative, which I suppose was on brand. Still, his performance of "Baton Rouge" really brought the house down, as did Bettye LaVette's soulful, aching "When the Saints Go Marching In." Above all else, the moment that still gives me chills was watching Dr. John and Allen Toussaint walk onstage together before Allen settled in behind the grand piano, while Dr. John picked up a guitar out of respect for

Toussaint. The place went nuts, and Dr. John's manager told me that he hadn't yielded the piano to another musician like that for quite some time.

It was also a victory for Soulive. They were able to demonstrate for thousands of people something that I already knew—they are one of the greatest house bands out there. My experience with them on this evening later contributed to the realization that they could carry ten nights of Bowlive.

Soul to Soul remains a personal favorite because I was able to pull it off in a place that was so important to me, *for* a place that was so important to me.

20

U2 IN 3D

U2
River Plate Stadium, Buenos Aires, Argentina
March 2, 2006

Bono had one question.

We were seated inside a movie theater in downtown Manhattan having just screened the 3D test footage of U2 that we filmed a few weeks earlier. We had scheduled four individual screenings across the country to make things as convenient as possible for the band members to watch while on tour.

For our test shoot, we had utilized a single stationary camera set up near the lighting board at an arena in Anaheim, California. Our equipment was so new we didn't have a backup, which meant that when the camera began falling apart in the middle of the show, we borrowed bungee cords to tie it back together. Thankfully, we'd pulled it off thanks to Steve Schklair, the technical wizard with whom we had partnered in a new company called 3ality Digital.

"Will we be first?" Bono wanted to know.

We informed him that U2 would indeed be the initial band to appear in a live concert film featuring digital 3D technology.

That was all he needed to hear.

"Let's do it in South America," he added. "That is where the crowds are best."

We had hoped to shoot in Los Angeles, closer to the laboratory where we were developing the technology, although anywhere in the continental US would have been preferable from a budgetary standpoint.

Nonetheless, Bono understood that the energy of seventy-five thousand ardent fans at River Plate Stadium in Buenos Aires, Argentina, would lend compelling visuals.

It was conceptually and geographically far from our original idea, which had been to capture NFL football with 3D technology. However, I recognized that this was the route that would lead to creative satisfaction (and as it turned out, the seventh-best concert film of all time, per *USA Today*).

Things usually don't come together in a straight line.

It all began when my brother Jon and I decided to build on the momentum of *All Access* after we finally turned a profit thanks to the phone plan (allowing me to purchase what Rebecca and I refer to as *the Verizon ring*). While IMAX no longer seemed viable, we remained interested in visual spectacle. So we began to explore 3D digital, where we wouldn't have to deal with the camera loads necessitated by film (with IMAX, that had meant three minutes at a time).

While Jon and I were talking about this, he ran into his friend John Modell at a party and told him that we were developing digital 3D for our next project. John indicated that he might be interested in exploring this along with his brother, David.

Their father, Art Modell, was a self-made multimillionaire who bought the Cleveland Browns in 1961, moved the team to Baltimore thirty-five years later, and then sold it in 2004. Art Modell helped establish NFL Films and became the company's first chairman. He also spurred the creation of *Monday Night Football*—I can remember reading about him when I was a student at Northwestern.

So the Shapiro brothers partnered with the Modell brothers to form a digital technology company. In 2004, we began shooting portions of NFL games with the hope of eventually reaching home consumers and also creating a stand-alone 3D football film. The first live broadcast happened on December 4, 2008, when 3ality Digital beamed the San Diego Chargers–Oakland Raiders Thursday-night game into movie theaters in three cities as proof of concept.

Then things kind of fizzled, at least when it came to the home broadcasts of NFL games in 3D. There were a couple of reasons for this. Some of it was that companies like Samsung and Panasonic rushed into producing 3D TV units and actively promoted first-generation technology before it was ready for prime time. Also, people don't want to wear special glasses in their living rooms where so much of the TV experience is social. That's why I'm not bullish on VR—it'll be good for gaming, but most of the entertainment experience is communal (which I believe is true now more than ever).

Although our partnership in the digital 3D project with the Modells began with football, music is always on my mind. So as we began our NFL test shoots, we also started thinking about making a digital 3D concert film.

It was easy to figure out the title, the concept, and the artist: *U2 3D*.

All Access had taught me to focus on a single mega-band, not fifteen different groups. I learned from the multi-act approach that something for everyone is often something for no one.

The name *U2 3D* also drew on another lesson from *All Access*: say what it is. The title was direct, to the point, and frankly quite awesome.

Now all we had to do was get to the band.

My initial point of contact was Catherine Owens, the group's creative director of screen imagery for animation, film, and video. She was the force behind the visual content for all U2 world tours from 1992 to 2010 (Zoo TV to U2360°). Catherine was supportive, particularly due to our state-of-the-art technology. She connected me with Willie Williams, the band's longtime lighting designer, who allowed us to place a single camera near his station during U2's performance in Anaheim on April 2, 2005 (at the Arrowhead Pond, if that means anything to you—at the arena now called the Honda Center, if that means anything to you).

Still, to gain any traction, we needed to schedule a screening of our U2 footage (along with some more dynamic, multi-camera NFL footage) for the band's longtime manager, Paul McGuinness. That finally happened in mid-May thanks to U2's appearance at the Slipper Room for the Leonard Cohen documentary.

Paul then allowed us to move forward with screenings for the individual band members across the country. I can remember watching with Larry Mullen in the Boston Museum of Science's enormous domed theater. I recall that at another point, Edge mused, "What if we just make the whole movie one shot?" While this would have been very cool, it would not have allowed us to utilize the technology to its fullest effect, with some cameras onstage and others sweeping in from the rear of the venue.

The band was impressed with our technology and our team, although our *yes* answer to Bono's initial question probably sealed the deal. Catherine Owens signed on to codirect with Mark Pellington (*Arlington Road*) whose early work included a video for the U2 song "One."

Much of my role focused on being an emissary between the film and the tour.

U2's team was top-notch. Jake Berry, who served as production manager for the Vertigo Tour, was simultaneously performing the same function for the Rolling Stones' A Bigger Bang Tour, which says a lot right there.

It was a matter of balancing interests, in knowing when to ask for the film to be prioritized and when to let the production come first. This applied to a variety of subjects ranging from seat kills to artist access to stage access to catering.

I had a few memorable interactions with Paul McGuinness. One that jumps out took place at Estadio Azteca in Mexico City at the beginning of the tour. He invited the Shapiro and Modell brothers to a meeting inside a cavernous, nearly vacant, all-purpose room located inside the stadium. Paul was seated in the middle, behind a wooden desk, with an oxygen tank to his side (Estadio Azteca is 7,200 feet above sea level).

He peered into the little black book that he carried around for the purpose of all U2 business. Then, in a relatively friendly tone, he explained that the band hadn't received much in the way of profits from the *Rattle and Hum* film. With this prelude, he turned to the expenses that the group had been asked to bear for our movie, such as freight fees associated with our equipment. Then he asked for additional money to help defray those costs (and for general goodwill).

It felt like he was making us an offer that we couldn't refuse.

So we didn't.

We agreed to pony up the funds and then looked forward to the principal photography at River Plate Stadium two weeks later, when it would be midsummer in the Southern Hemisphere.

I had never experienced a show in Argentina, but everyone in the U2 camp assured me there was nothing like it.

That much became clear on the evening before the first performance, when Mark Pellington and I sat with Bono in the hotel restaurant for dinner. While Bono consumed a salad with his bare hands, a couple of hundred fans gathered just outside a window overlooking our table and began chanting, "Bo-no! Bo-no!" while waving flags enthusiastically. He was so nonchalant about it that it must have been par for the course.

That energy was translated onto the stage the next night and fully reciprocated. In fact, the audience response may have led Bono to push his vocal cords beyond their comfort zone, because the following afternoon, I discovered that he couldn't speak. But before I could worry about it too much, the band brought in a doctor. Bono's voice went from nothing to amazing in short order. I was impressed. It was varsity ball. Bono knew what was on the line and that we needed additional footage, so he delivered.

Of course, even that wasn't as easy as it should have been. Hamish Hamilton, who had directed a few previous U2 concert films, was working on a live broadcast for TV Globo in Brazil. We had to split up shot locations, staking out time and territory. It was exciting to be in the middle of that conversation.

That show represented the end of their tour, so there was a throwdown at the Four Seasons afterward for the crew and the band's extended family. Bono was a perfect host. At one point, he even switched T-shirts with a member of the hotel staff, which is a ritual in European soccer, where members of opposite teams swap jerseys at the end of a match. He remained to the very end, dancing with the hotel workers. I know this because I was there with him, inspired by his generosity of spirit.

Back in May 2005, I had helped kicked this project into gear by recognizing that I needed to be the first to leave. So it felt good on the final night of our South American shoot to acknowledge that sometimes, I can be one of the last men standing as well.

U2 3D captures a band at the peak of its creative output. It wowed audiences at Cannes and Sundance, then received positive press when it opened worldwide. I'm particularly proud of the rave from Chris Blackwell, who said in an interview that watching *U2 3D* at Brooklyn Bowl was "about the best U2 concert I've ever seen." The film was selected to play at the main theater at the Rock & Roll Hall of Fame and ran multiple times every day for years because Terry Stewart, the president of the Rock Hall, said it was the closest thing to being at a stadium concert.

Thanks to *U2 3D*, I even had another chance to work with Quincy Jones a few years after the Kerry inaugural fell apart. We screened the film for Quincy in LA because he was interested in producing a 3D movie about Carnival in Brazil. We met with him a few times, and although it didn't happen, I had some more Quincy time. He carries himself with a similar grace as Chris Blackwell. (That can be a nice part of projects that don't happen—you can still get in some greats hangs.)

The economics for *U2 3D* were challenging, though.

Not as many theaters were equipped to show digital 3D as we had anticipated. This would gradually change over the years to follow, and films such as *The Hobbit* trilogy and *The Amazing Spider-Man* used 3ality Digital equipment.

While there's a real rush that comes with being on the vanguard, from an economic standpoint, it often makes more sense to be second.

That said, I'm with Bono because what really gets me off is being first.

21

ROXY MUSIC

World Premiere: Wetlands Preserved: The Story of
an Activist Rock Club
Ziegfeld Theater, New York, New York
April 23, 2006

After Wetlands closed in September 2001, I explored the possibility of finding a new location for the club, which had been such an important part of my life.

As per my agreement with Larry, I could open a new Wetlands, as long as it maintained a social and environmental activism center funded at $100,000 per year.

Looking back on the sales contract, it included some additional interesting provisions.

For instance: "All retail, marketing, advertising and office activities will incorporate environmentally friendly materials, and all Wetlands clubs will incorporate recycling programs within its offices, including the recycling of paper, tin, aluminum, cardboard and glass. Containers for all juice, soda, liquor and beer will be recycled. All non-deadline promotional materials will be printed on 100% recycled paper or cardstock whenever possible."

Also: "All products for sale at any Wetlands club will meet the environmental and social justice standards set by the environmental director."

What's so impressive is not that Larry demanded this of me but that he placed these burdens on himself (mostly). Even today, it's a challenge to abide by such obligations. But to do so in 1989 while maintaining a for-profit orientation was revolutionary and righteous.

I kept all of this in mind after Wetlands closed and I began looking for a potential new home. But the more I visited available sites, the more I came to the conclusion that I wasn't going to build a new Wetlands. I came to appreciate that Wetlands was 161 Hudson Street. I wouldn't be able to replicate it by taking over an existing box and then painting it green and brown.

However, while I decided not to create a second Wetlands, I was still interested in opening another venue. In 2004, I identified two possible locations, both of which were Loews movie theaters in midtown Manhattan. At the time, the theater chain was experiencing some economic troubles, and both spaces were available. I was looking for a partner, so I mentioned one of these locations, at 1515 Broadway (on the corner of Forty-Fourth Street), to someone at AEG. They ended up taking over the space, which became known as Nokia Theatre Times Square and then Best Buy Theater and then PlayStation Theater (all of which made me further appreciate a venue called Wetlands Preserve). The theater closed in 2019.

My second site was a Loews located beneath a Virgin megastore at Forty-Fifth and Seventh, just a block from Times Square. By 2004, the Loews State 4 was no longer screening first-run films due to the construction of yet another Loews on Forty-Second between Seventh and Eighth. (I never quite understood why the same company put two movie theaters across the street from each other.)

I was pretty obsessed with both locations and would send people in to check on ticket sales. (I had been there so many times that they recognized me, and I didn't want to seem overeager.) I remember being in Chicago with Rebecca's family over Thanksgiving, calling the box office and asking how crowded the theater was, making some excuse about coming to see a movie.

On the subject of monitoring ticket sales, it's important to have a handle on how other shows in your market are doing. One way to do this is to sign up for emails and follow the socials of companies that sell discounted tickets (like Groupon). That way, you'll have a sense of how shows are doing—specifically, which shows are tanking. It can help you make decisions about future bookings and provide general insight on your own competing shows (plus, it's always good for some gossip with your friends and colleagues, like the time I saw discount Barbra Streisand tickets).

AEG soon took over the first theater, and I lost my enthusiasm for the second, in part because the entry point was through the Virgin megastore, which seemed a bit off to me. The expense certainly was a factor as well, as construction on the Nokia Theatre Times Square exceeded $20 million. It's tough to build in such a congested setting, and doing it during off-peak hours comes with overtime costs.

In the midst of doing all of this, my thoughts returned to Wetlands. I couldn't create another venue that would match everyone's memories of the original, but I could create a documentary film that would try just that. This was not going to be my story but rather Larry's. He didn't get his due. He not only talked the talk but he walked the walk. And when he was walking, he was doing it at his own pace and with a unique stride, reflecting an inscription on the wall just inside Wetlands: "We labor to birth our dance with the earth."

Larry taught me that you can be a good businessperson and still have a positive impact on the planet. While it can be frustrating when other people conduct themselves unethically and find some success, the real win isn't the short-term gain. Instead, the goal is to create magic and lift people.

Even so, I imagined that the film also would capture Larry's idiosyncratic side. He wouldn't want us to shy away from that.

My contract to purchase the club included the following provision: "Bloch shall also have the right to continue to promote at the Club an event based on the television program 'The Prisoner' in the same manner as has been his prior practice."

One of his favorite bands was Zen Tricksters, who were leading interpreters of Grateful Dead music (and they're still at it today). Another contract clause provided: "Bloch shall have the right to produce and shall furnish his services as producer of a live album by Zen Tricksters, to be recorded at the Club, currently entitled *Dead Dream*. In this connection Bloch may rent and use the Club, at its normal charges, for three consecutive days at a time mutually convenient to the parties. Bloch shall have full production control of such album."

Speaking of control, here's what Jeff Mattson of the Zen Tricksters (and now Dark Star Orchestra as well) had to say about his interactions with Larry, in the film that eventually became known as *Wetlands Preserved: The Story of an Activist Rock Club*: "Larry was pretty unique as a club owner. No other club owner would look at our set list and say, 'Do you really want to end the set with this song? I think the energy would be better if you ended with this song or that song.' And I'd be, 'What?!?'"

I set the film in motion, but I was mostly hands-off, particularly when it came to editorial decisions. Most of the work fell to two people. Dean Budnick, my coauthor, served as director and later made the paper edit that was executed by Jonathan Healey, who also served as cinematographer. The two of them went out on the shoots as a tandem and later sat side by side in Healey's studio on Fifty-Fourth Street (where in his day job at *National Lampoon*, he created a music magazine designed for college audiences). They both still work with me, Dean at *Relix* (and other projects) and Healey as my vice president of marketing and digital strategy (as I mentioned earlier, he also directs most of my livestreams, including those originating from the Cap and LOCKN' and really stepped things up with FANS.live).

While we had audio recordings from throughout the club's run, the biggest challenge in creating the film was the lack of archival video footage. However, through the club's two longtime house photographers, we had images that spanned its history. So we hired digital animators, who created unique sequences pairing images and audio. At the end of the day, I think the results better evoked the Wetlands experience than a collection of old videos. They felt three-dimensional rather than flat.

I think the finished film really captures the spirit of the club. I suspect it's for this very reason that we weren't invited to screen at the Tribeca Film Festival. There's a line in there that would always get a laugh about Larry selecting the neighborhood for Wetlands. Remy Chevalier, the original head of the Activism Center, observes, "There was nothing down there back then. It was all wannabe art galleries, there were no restaurants. Robert De Niro hadn't discovered Tribeca yet." It was a good line, but it might not be the most strategic way to name-drop the cofounder of the Tribeca Film Festival.

Nonetheless, *Wetlands Preserved* enjoyed a fair amount of success. It screened at SXSW, the Woodstock Film Festival, the Santa Barbara International Film Festival, and quite a few others, including events in the UK and Japan (it even won Best Documentary at the Asheville Film Festival). The Sundance Channel acquired TV rights, and First Run Features became the distributor, lining up theatrical openings in New York and LA. Eventually, First Run released it on DVD, and while it now streams online, I still recommend that you pick up a DVD—assuming you have the capacity to play a DVD—to check out the bonus features (Questlove's story about P. Diddy browbeating him in the band room while Questlove sat on a "dingy-ass couch" next to Q-Tip is worth the effort).

The key to selling a film typically involves enlisting a producer's representative. Here we had a brief working relationship with Jeff Dowd, better known as the Dude. He's the guy who inspired Jeff Bridges's character in *The Big Lebowski*. In real life, he's pretty close to the character in the film, which means he's an entertaining guy. On the other hand, we also came to realize that it might not be the wisest decision to entrust our two-years-in-the-making documentary to the Dude, which makes perfect sense to anyone who's seen *Lebowski* (perhaps I didn't think that one all the way through at the time). Not so surprisingly, the Dude was not always focused on the matter at hand, even if he was an epic hang. A month or two after paying him a retainer, we began to feel like we'd been "Duded," with no developments on the film front.

While we parted company on the Wetlands doc, it was still "hail, fellow, well met." He presented an award for us at The Jammys, and we continued to stay in touch. Then he resurfaced about fifteen years later and called me out of the blue, conferencing in AT&T so that we could pay his phone bill, which I gladly did before he disappeared into the Dude ether.

Around this time, we showed the film to Tom Bernard, the copresident of Sony Picture Classics in their screening room. Tom was supportive but didn't make an offer on the spot as we had hoped. Instead, he suggested that our most lucrative option would be to road show it ourselves. We shared a meal at one of Miloš Forman's favorite restaurants while we discussed our game plan, and Tom has since become a friend. He was later seated at a table with me when we won a *High Times* Stony Award for the documentary at B. B. King's in Times Square. (The trophy was a glass bong.)

After the Dude went Dude, it took us a number of months to land a producer's rep. Tenacity was key. We kept pushing forward, lining up opportunities to play the film for potential reps in theater settings. Sending out screeners (or sharing links) is fine, but your odds of success increase if you can engineer an opportunity to make a personal connection. Beyond that, having someone watch the film on a big screen with an audience was preferable for us because it played particularly well in front of a crowd.

We finally achieved our goal when *Wetlands Preserved* was shown at the Anthology Film Archives as part of the New Filmmakers series. We sent out a few invitations, received an RSVP, and our deals flowed from there.

In March 2006, we decided to launch *Wetlands Preserved* in style with a special sneak-peek world-premiere screening as part of the inaugural Green Apple Festival. Where better to do this than the Ziegfeld Theater, a true picture palace, with over 1,100 seats that had hosted many Hollywood premieres over the years, including *Apocalypse Now, Close Encounters of the Third Kind,* and *Tommy.* It cost us about ten grand, which we couldn't recoup through ticket sales (since we had so many comps), but I wanted Green Apple to go out in style. The film perfectly embodied the event's interlaced themes of music and activism.

The Ziegfeld premiere took place on April 23, 2006. It was a bit nerve-racking, not only because we would be debuting *Wetlands Preserved* in front of a thousand people (we blew out the room), but to show the film on such a massive screen, we needed to convert it to HD. We went through this process, but sound issues required some last-minute tweaks that went down to the wire.

Oh yes, and I've failed to mention that the intensity was compounded by the fact that Rebecca was nine months pregnant with our daughter.

So even though I was smiling while I stood outside the Ziegfeld and watched Larry and Laura roll up in a limo, leaning into the full premiere vibe, I was feeling the magnitude of everything in the air. This was further amplified by the experience of looking out at close to a thousand faces in the audience from the front of the Ziegfeld, while Dean and I gave our introductions. These people spanned my days growing up in the city through my years at Wetlands to the present—a journey that would be forever altered by the birth of my daughter.

Rebecca, who was at home, could begin labor at any moment. My phone was at the ready in case I received the call. Short of that, I was prepared to enjoy the world premiere of *Wetlands Preserved: The Story of an Activist Rock Club*.

Which is what I did for fifty-three seconds until the audio fell out of sync.

From three separate locations in the giant theater, Budnick, Healey, and I jumped out of our seats and charged up to the projection room. This was starting to feel like a disaster, and I wasn't sure we could fix it.

Finally, one of us, or maybe all of us, had the idea to stop the digital projector and reset it, with the hope that somehow this would resolve the issue.

So we turned it off and brought up the house lights.

We heard the murmurs below during the few agonizing minutes that passed as the projector rebooted. Meanwhile, we stared at the lights on the side of the machine, uncommunicative and lost in our own thoughts. It would be quite an anticlimactic turn of events if I needed to slink back to the front of theater just minutes after my glorious welcome speech to inform everyone that due to technical issues, the screening was canceled.

Then the projector reset itself, and we switched off the house lights.

The tension was overwhelming as we restarted the film.

Wetlands Preserved opens with a still image of quotes from the *Village Voice* and *New York Times* about the club's closing. This lasts for twenty seconds until our first sequence with sound (we'd animated a performance from September 10, 2001). At the

Ziegfeld, those excruciating twenty seconds seemed to unfold in super slo-mo as I waited on the moment of truth.

And then . . .

The film played just fine.

Actually, it played even better than we had hoped, garnering a ton of laughs and moments of spontaneous applause from the packed house, culminating in a rousing ovation at the end.

I shook a few hands, received some slaps on the back, and then I received the call.

Rebecca was in labor.

I rushed to the hospital, where our daughter took the slow route and was born twelve hours later, forever changing my life for the better.

We named our daughter Roxy. I figured if things didn't go so well for me, I would be able to rely on her to help.

I would book an artist named Roxy Shapiro any day of the week, especially if she were playing reggae.

I really would.

22

GREEN APPLES

Green Apple Earth Day Celebration
Speedway Meadow, Golden Gate Park,
San Francisco, California
April 22, 2007

L arry Bloch was a visionary.
The way he blended his love of music with a commitment to social activism remains with me to this day. A lot of my activism and advocacy in the years since September 2001 are a result of my Wetlands experience.

It's also worth noting that my grandfather Ezra Shapiro served as world chairman of the Keren Hayesod, the official fundraising organization for Israel. His son, Daniel, my father, was president of the Federation of Jewish Philanthropies and facilitated its merger with the United Jewish Appeal (UJA). I am also the great-grand-nephew of Joel Elias Spingarn, a former president of the NAACP, who worked closely with W. E. B. Du Bois.

Their decency and altruism have not only served as an inspiration, I also carry part of them in me, which I believe has propelled me in a certain direction.

So, too, did my tutelage at Wetlands.

While I was still at Wetlands, I founded a company with my brother Andrew. He attended Brown, then Yale Law School, and in 2000 was working as a senior adviser at the Markle Foundation, a nonprofit advocacy group then focused on using the internet to help Americans with issues such as health and economic security.

We called our new business GreenOrder because that was quite literally what we were hoping to facilitate.

It took us a little while to get there because, as I've said, things rarely develop in straight lines. Prior to GreenOrder, we were going to launch a lifestyle portal/aggregator called Kind.com ("Our mission is to make it easier to find Kind content, Kind products, Kind experiences and Kind people. Our vehicle is the internet"). The initial team also included the author David Shenk and my coauthor. When The Jammys debuted in 2000, we viewed it as a model for future KindMusic events. Our business plan contained the refrain "Are You Kind?" which worked on a few levels, including its nod to the Grateful Dead (Shenk's first book, written with Steve Silberman, was *Skeleton Key: A Dictionary for Deadheads*). The largest shareholder was to be a charitable fund called the Kind Trust, which would direct proceeds to causes selected by the site visitors (or as we called it, *user-assisted corporate philanthropy*).

However, the summer of 2000 was not so kind to us. This was not the ideal moment to be an internet start-up. The dot-com bubble burst, as did Pets.com, Webvan, Go.com, and, yes, Kind.com.

We then pivoted into a new business model prompted by my experience at Wetlands. I often struggled to purchase environmentally friendly cleaning products and suspected there were plenty of other folks who faced this challenge. So we created a Kind Products Portal to assist with the process.

However, while we were starting to gain traction, in our efforts to raise capital we found ourselves at the mercy of macro trends. So from there, we became a B2B marketplace called GreenOrder for a little while.

Ultimately, we settled in as a consulting firm that demonstrated to corporations how energy and environmental innovation could put them at a competitive advantage. By then, Andrew had brought on a new team, and I served on an advisory board while focusing on my other projects. One of GreenOrder's early successes was working with GE to develop its Ecomagination initiative, which led to other opportunities, such as advising GM on strategic issues, including the launch of the Chevrolet Volt and serving as the green adviser for 7 World Trade Center, NYC's first LEED-certified office tower. Andrew sold GreenOrder in 2008 and currently leads an investment group that works with clean energy and sustainable approaches to transportation.

GreenOrder was the first post-Wetlands project where I revisited some of the environmental concerns that had prompted Larry to found the club. However, I was eager to add a musical component to these efforts, which would play better to my strengths and also because it's what I love. That happened in 2006 with the Green Apple Festival.

Here's the mission statement: "The Green Apple Music & Arts Festival is an educational and socially responsible celebration of Earth Day committed to raising environmental awareness through mobilization of the arts."

The first year, we focused on New York City. Rather than building the event entirely from scratch, we used a tentpole that was already in place: The Jammys, cohosted that year by Mickey Hart and Bill Kreutzmann. It not only helped us gain recognition for what we were creating, but since we already had so many artists coming to town, we could recruit them for some of our Green Apple performances. We partnered with Earth Day New York and enlisted over thirty music venues (including the Canal Room, Carnegie Hall, CBGB, Coda, and the Cutting Room, just sticking with the letter C).

Green Apple opened on Thursday, April 20, at the Theater at Madison Square Garden with The Jammys and concluded on Sunday, April 23, at the Ziegfeld Theater with the world premiere screening of *Wetlands Preserved: The Story of An Activist Rock Club*. Dozens of bands participated and offered underplays, including Richie Havens at the Bitter End, Béla Fleck and the Flecktones at the B. B. King Blues Club, and Umphrey's McGee at CBGB.

We also set up a stage at New York's Earth Day Fair for two afternoons of free music outside Grand Central Station. The highlight was a set from Mickey Hart where he enlisted Mike Gordon, Steve Kimock, Baaba Maal, Angélique Kidjo, and special guest Walter Cronkite (?!?) for a performance that concluded with a percussion jam that led out into the crowd, New Orleans second-line style.

In 2007, we expanded to three cities: New York, Chicago, and San Francisco. I made it my mission to attend shows in all three of them, culminating with an indelible moment in Golden Gate Park.

We came to learn there were no significant coordinated Earth Day efforts across the country. While this local focus benefited some communities, the lack of an overarching communication or education strategy often proved limiting as well.

So I partnered with Earth Day Network, establishing a great rapport with Denis Hayes, who organized the very first Earth Day, and Kathleen Rogers, the former environmental attorney who has long served as president of EDN. Our goal was to coordinate messaging, starting with our three cities in 2007.

We cut back the number of participating clubs in New York because beyond tabling and signage, we asked the venues for a commitment to greening their venues during the event with the hope that there would be some lasting impact. We also hosted three major free outdoor events on Earth Day proper, which was Sunday, April 22. These took place at the Great Hill in Central Park (Laurie Berkner Band), Lincoln Park Zoo in Chicago (Umphrey's McGee and the Disco Biscuits), and Speedway Meadow in Golden Gate Park (Bob Weir and RatDog, Stephen Marley featuring Jr. Gong, the Greyboy Allstars).

Leading up to the Central Park show, we had two days of music on Vanderbilt Avenue outside Grand Central, like the previous year. That's where I began my Saturday, with a performance by Zero, the first time they had played NYC in a decade. I was also able to catch State Radio, the band led by Chad Stokes (of Dispatch, whom I had first met when his group was called One Fell Swoop), as well as my friend Reid Genauer's Assembly of Dust. Then it was off to Chicago to check out Umphrey's at the Vic, still a favorite venue going back to my college days.

My weekend peaked the next morning in San Francisco. It had rained heavily on Saturday, and the forecast was for more of the same on Sunday. When my plane landed at SFO, things were looking dicey for me and my wingman Josh Baron (always need one of those).

I had been warned a week or so earlier by longtime Grateful Dead publicist Dennis McNally that there was not much awareness of the event, so we had made a push to spread the good word. I had no idea what I would encounter at Golden Gate.

We hopped in a cab and made our way to the park. When we pulled up, I was in a daze. The sun had come out, the weather had turned, and everything was vivid.

The perfect weather for an outdoor show is a sunny day after a rainy one. The air is cleaner, which pops everything you see, as if the colors are from a Pixar movie.

From my perspective, it looked like hippie heaven in Speedway Meadow. There were vendors, Hula-Hoops, bubbles—a kaleidoscope of colors. Oh, and twenty-five thousand people on hand for some free RatDog with bonus guest Sammy Hagar. As I walked over to this big, beautiful gathering, it was one of those rare occasions when I said to myself, *Oh my God,* I'm *putting this on.*

Green Apple lasted two more years. In 2008, we went to eight cities, but I was so caught up in other things—like *U2 3D* and building Brooklyn Bowl—that I didn't attempt to smash my record from the prior year and pull an octofecta by visiting each of them. I'll take my victory and know when to walk off the field.

The same was true of Green Apple, which we retired in 2009.

Just like The Jammys, we got a cease and desist, this time from Apple (I told you this entrepreneur thing was hard).

I'm okay with something ending. I don't mind reinventing and trying a new thing. Green Apple had its time, as did The Jammys, as did Wetlands. They occupied so much of my head for a while, and I still carry them with me. I'm grateful for that, but I have a pretty good discipline about not getting too hung up in the past and recognizing when it's time to start thinking about what's in front of me.

Rather than revisiting the moment when I walked up to Speedway Meadow, I'm looking to create something new so I can experience the *feeling* when I walked up to Speedway Meadow.

23

ROCK. AND ROLL.

Dan Deacon / Deerhunter / No Age
Brooklyn Bowl, Brooklyn, New York
August 2, 2009

We were a few months into construction of Brooklyn Bowl when I invited my good friend New York concert promoter Ron Delsener to come check out our progress.

I hadn't yet divulged the full details of what I was planning because I preferred to show him in person.

I ushered him around the twenty-three-thousand-square-foot building that had once housed the Hecla Iron Works. We were still in the middle stages of the project, so we hadn't installed any of the features that would come to define the Bowl. At this point, it was mostly a cavernous space.

This project had consumed so much of my time over the previous eighteen months that it felt good to finally share it with Ron, an industry legend, who had worked with the Beatles at Shea Stadium.

I pointed out where the lanes would be located, then I walked him over to the spot we had designated for the stage.

At this point, Ron grabbed my arm and pulled me aside, intent on imparting some special wisdom wrought from a lifetime in the concert business.

He looked me square in the eye and asked, "Are you okay, kid? I'm worried about you."

Ron wasn't giving me shit; he legitimately thought I was crazy.

"You have a f-ing bowling alley next to the stage," he continued. "No one is going to play here."

He wasn't entirely wrong.

It would take an educational campaign and a bit of groveling to get artists into the room. But eventually, Brooklyn Bowl would be named the busiest venue in Manhattan and one of the ten most active clubs in the world.

And it all began with a Wetlands staff party.

Back in 2000, general manager Charley Ryan and I took our employees out to a local bowling alley so we could blow off some steam. Everyone seemed to enjoy themselves, even if they hadn't bowled in years (or ever). Charley and I discussed this the next day, and while we made no immediate plans, it did prompt some interesting conversations, particularly after Wetlands closed.

Translating that experience into a venue that offered awesome food and drinks, powerful live music, and colossal video screens in addition to bowling didn't happen in a single eureka moment. Instead, like many of the most successful ideas over the course of my career, the vision for Brooklyn Bowl was the product of ongoing discussions and iterations.

I don't believe that the first idea is the best idea. In fact, I think that's rarely the case. Too often, people have the tendency to cling to their original concepts, in part because they maintain a sense of ownership over that initial formulation. I think that cream rises over time, and the way to get there is to churn through some variations. I also prefer working with a partner, particularly someone who shares that philosophy and doesn't get too caught up in staking claims while seeking a collective goal.

Charley and I spent a few years together at Wetlands and had a strong working relationship, so we teamed up on what would become Brooklyn Bowl. Rather than have a real estate broker show us spaces, we walked around the streets ourselves, starting in Manhattan and then making our way out to Brooklyn in search of the ideal location. There's something to be said for that approach because you get a real feel for the neighborhood. Plus, if you're doing this without a broker, you have an opportunity to strengthen your position, as I'll explain.

In 2006, one of our walks led us to the former Hecla Iron Works foundry at 61 Wythe Avenue in Williamsburg. Built in 1882, it had thirty-five-foot ceilings and a footprint of over twenty thousand square feet. It was essentially an old brick-and-wood barn. I do not think we could have found that anywhere else in New York City.

While there's value to being on the fifty-yard line (this would particularly be true when it came to Brooklyn Bowl Vegas), it is not always about location. I'm also big on cubic space, and with 61 Wythe, it was all about that barn.

It took a while to get a deal. I began courting the owner, Jack Nastro, in mid-2006. He had bought the building in the late '80s for $1 million and had been thinking about selling it, but Mayor Mike Bloomberg helped me out with the New York City rezoning of 2005. It's one of many random things beyond my control that have assisted my career. As a result of the rezoning, 61 Wythe couldn't be transformed into a hotel or a residential building, even though this was permissible just one block away. It's almost as if some time traveler came back from the future to ensure that the city would carve out the perfect spot for Brooklyn Bowl (and if that's true and if the time traveler is reading this, thank you!).

Jack Nastro, on the other hand, was pissed. He was a warehouse guy who worked in the area and had anticipated the long-term value of his purchase. If the Williamsburg zoning had gone another way, he could have sold the building for millions. Eventually, he came to terms with this and was willing to lease it.

We did whatever we could to facilitate the deal. One tactic was to make his real estate broker our broker. There were other potential tenants circling, and this gave the broker incentive to push for us so she'd receive a full commission. That's a good tip for anyone in a similar situation, but if you do that, it's also important to have a skilled real estate lawyer. Mine is a longtime friend, Ian Lester, whom I've known since first grade and who also happens to be a great attorney.

It's important to have trust and a good relationship with a lawyer. Ian is one of my closest friends from growing up. My dad, Dan Shapiro, who passed away in 2016, helped me keep Wetlands open when the SLA wanted to shut it down. These days, Jordan Goldstein, who is an attorney, helps me run the legal and business side.

To close the deal with Jack, I also needed some financial assistance, and for that, I will thank the Verizon All Access phone plan. When Verizon purchased all those *All Access* soundtracks, it allowed me to pay back Arthur Cornfeld. Six years later, thanks to the support of his son, Alex, my fellow Northwestern grad and *American Road* cinematographer, Arthur was willing to take another chance with me.

As it turned out, Arthur's capital and Alex's friendship were essential at another key moment. Our original deal with Jack Nastro had only covered thirteen thousand square feet of the building. As we were finalizing construction plans in the late spring of 2007, Jack called to inform me that he'd made a deal with an art gallery for the remaining space.

In that moment, we knew that we needed the additional square footage. If we hadn't been able to secure it, our stage would have been smaller, our music capacity would have been two hundred (rather than eight hundred), and we would have had less room for food. The whole experience would have been different.

So I pleaded with Jack to let us have the entire building. He told me that he had shaken the other guy's hand, but that if I could make a commitment by evening, he'd let us have it. This was a super-brief window of time, but I made a frantic call to the Cornfelds, trying to persuade them that we needed the whole thing. Arthur was reluctant to increase his risk exposure, but he eventually relented. I made the call to Jack Nastro, who allowed us to lease the entire space. If he hadn't, I suspect my life would have been different.

I had been friendly with the Blue Ribbon brothers, Bruce and Eric Bromberg, for a while. They hadn't done anything other than a Blue Ribbon restaurant, which they control, so it was a big deal to get them to be part of the Bowl. But I had some great late nights with Bruce back in the Wetlands days, and their love of music tipped the scale. It also helped that we had known each other for about ten years.

As I've pointed out, relationships matter. This also impacted my decision to work with Ticketfly, our initial ticketing company. I was the first customer, and we made the deal before either of us was open to the public. What happened is that while we were in construction, I ran into Andrew Dreskin, the company's cofounder, while he was standing on the corner of the next block. He'd co-created TicketWeb back in the mid-'90s, and I'd known him for years.

Andrew hadn't seen the venue, and I didn't know his product, but we were comfortable with each other, so we came to an agreement. As it turned out, before we were formally open for business, we hosted our first party at the Bowl in celebration of his fortieth birthday. This was a tense experience because the guest list was out of control and we weren't technically supposed to be open (assuming any of this happened).

The challenge with Blue Ribbon and the Bromberg brothers was we needed to figure out how the economic model would work for all of us. I didn't want to rent to them, because it would feel like they had one side and we had the other. It was important to avoid a situation where someone said, "Don't buy your beer over there." So we struck a deal where it was all one business, and while they were compensated for their contribution, they also had a piece of the whole thing. That way, we were in alignment, which is always the goal. You want everyone to be rowing in the same direction.

This reminds me of a moment when we weren't aligned. We signed the deal with Jack Nastro on June 1, 2007, and while Arthur Cornfeld had real estate holdings, when the recession started to hit in 2008/09, he became illiquid. We started to run out of money at the Bowl, and I remember he asked, "Can we open without the kitchen? We'll just do hot dogs and hamburgers. None of this Blue Ribbon; it's too complex. We'll open, and if it goes well, then we can add the Blue Ribbon." But in this era when first impressions linger on the internet, we couldn't add it later. So I fought hard, and we kept it. But while we weren't in alignment there for a little while, to Arthur's credit, he had previously stepped up when we needed the extra space.

The scale of the Bowl is a key element to the experience. There's an article in which someone called me "the Rabbi of Brooklyn Bowl," and I think that says something about the room, not about me. It's like a synagogue or church—they tend to be vast, which helps them be impactful. In this era when people spend all day in front of a screen, we need places that will encourage people to be in each other's physical presence and interact directly. That was part of the Wetlands ethos, and I think given the impact of the coronavirus pandemic, it's something we can appreciate all the more.

The Bowl is a multisensory experience that operates on a grand scale. We have enormous high-definition projection screens at the end of the bowling lanes to help us create spectacle. Having said that, we don't want people to stand there idly, gazing at the visuals. Instead, we're using them as means of transport, taking everyone into a new environment where they can connect with fellow travelers. We're using our big screens to get you away from your little screens.

Brooklyn Bowl has become an iconic name, but there was also a brief moment when we considered naming it Rock'n'Bowl. So I called John Blancher, who created Rock'n'Bowl in New Orleans, to look into it. We have a different layout and vibe, but some of the spirit of the Bowl comes from Rock'n'Bowl, just as it comes from Asbury Lanes in Asbury Park and Fireside Bowl in Chicago.

John informed me that I could pay a license fee and open as Rock'n'Bowl. Ultimately, though, I decided we should be our own thing. So, returning to the idea of "say what it is," we're Brooklyn Bowl.

It ended up being a matter of right place, right time.

Taglines are still important, even if you have the perfect name. A good tagline offers another chance to define and describe your intent.

So we went with "Rock. And Roll."

It's direct and powerful in conveying who we are.

As we were in the planning stages in 2007, a bowling alley opened down the street in Williamsburg called the Gutter. Plenty of people said, "You're second. You missed it." But higher water can lift all boats, which is why gas stations do better next to each other. So we put our heads down to do the work. Cream rises.

While we were envisioning Brooklyn Bowl, Charley and I had Wetlands on our minds. Our intent was to keep the best of Wetlands and replace the stuff that wasn't ideal. At our core, we embraced the village aspect, with lots of areas to congregate. We also maintained the vibe, the energy, and the special staff touch

(Stephen Schwarz, our longtime general manager who formerly worked at the Knitting Factory, shared a similar mindset).

We have a lot of wood, a lot of brick, but really high ceilings, so it feels open. We have great sight lines, but you can still walk away from the music if you wish. We've got great food, which Wetlands didn't have (I've found that musicians *really* appreciate Blue Ribbon—we'll often get their food orders far in advance). We've got good air in here, which Wetlands didn't have. We've got LED lighting, which Wetlands didn't have (it had par cans that used to get sizzling hot).

We've certainly embraced the Wetlands ideals by becoming the first LEED (Leadership in Energy and Environmental Design) certified bowling alley in the United States. This means we met the standards of the world's most widely used green building rating system. For instance, our pinspotter machines utilize 75 percent less energy than comparable devices. They're able to do this because they operate through a system of strings rather than a mechanical device, which is not only energy efficient but also cuts down on noise (the clatter is further mitigated because our pins are hollow).

We made plenty of other decisions that cut back on waste and limit environmental impact. The floor of the concert stage was fashioned from recycled tires. We used reclaimed materials throughout the venue, including glass from the Brooklyn Navy Yard. I also maintained the Wetlands policy of selling beer on tap rather than in cans or bottles. Plus, our beer is local, which means it is fresh, and the delivery is less resource intensive. Similarly, we've made an effort to hire local skilled laborers and purchase furniture made in Brooklyn.

Larry Bloch visited Brooklyn Bowl early on and told me it was cool, which was high praise, indeed.

As for our neighborhood community, I did sense a bit of skepticism as we reached the summer of 2009 and prepared to open. Some people compared us to Dave & Buster's. There was a meme that circulated with the message "If they think they're going to bring the String Cheese Incident to Williamsburg . . ." above an image of a desert.

I understood this perspective. The general public had no idea of what we were doing. I had faith they would come around, though. These days, we're old-school Brooklyn, and a lot of those early naysayers are our regulars who will walk up to see Pigeons Playing Ping Pong or Zen Tricksters, which I count as a victory.

We started to win over our critics on what became our first night of music. Dan Deacon, Deerhunter, and No Age had been scheduled to open their Round Robin Tour, where all three would share the stage and trade off tunes, at East River State Park on the Williamsburg waterfront on Sunday, August 2, 2009. By 3:00 p.m. that day, the state parks department called it all off due to rain. Shortly afterward, the promoters, JellyNYC, announced that the event had been relocated to Brooklyn Bowl, where we hosted free early and late shows.

Sometimes you have to make your own luck. I had been paying attention to the weather and called Alex Kane at JellyNYC to let him know that we would be available if needed. They didn't show up at *our* door; we knocked on *their* door. The Bowl wasn't entirely ready for business, but we made some adjustments for these pop-up shows that would help introduce us to the community.

When we finally did open a few weeks later, we got hit harder than we had expected. There were so many people who wanted to check it out that we couldn't handle all the foot traffic. We did not have reservations (and except for parties, we still don't), so some folks put their names on a list, waited four hours, and then left without getting to bowl. They were rightfully pissed, and a number of them emailed the info@brooklynbowl account.

At that time, I was getting the info@brooklynbowl emails, and if someone sent us a complaint on a Saturday morning, I would often bounce back a response in less than a minute. I'd introduce myself and encourage them to give me a call. Then, when we spoke, I would apologize, explain the situation, and make sure that we took care of them next time. I think this helped our reputation, and it also set a tone for our staff, since I was the one putting in the time to do that. Plus, it just bugged me if someone went to the Bowl but couldn't enjoy the experience.

While we were winning over the local community, one person who remained a doubter for quite some time was Ron Delsener. After we'd completed construction, I invited him back so that I could demonstrate that the bowling would not detract from the music. He conceded the point (sort of), but then he took issue with our business model.

Two of the most important decisions we made at the Bowl—and they are interrelated—involved how much we were going to charge at the door and what percentage of those proceeds we were going to pay the band.

We decided that for most shows, fifteen dollars would be ideal. At that price point, people would still be willing to come in, watch the show and maybe bowl, have a bite, and get something to drink.

We also determined that we would pay the bands close to 100 percent of the door proceeds. We further incentivized them to perform at the Bowl by allowing them to keep 100 percent of their merch sales—most venues keep 20 percent. The bands also recognized that since we were maintaining a relatively low entry fee, there would be more walk-up. If you're managing a band, you want them to be seen by new people. If it's thirty dollars at Irving Plaza, there likely won't be any walk-up, but with fifteen or twenty dollars at Brooklyn Bowl, there is.

Ron thought that what we were doing was bad business. He believed that I was initiating a price war that made no sense for us and certainly wasn't helping him over at Irving.

But as I explained, "I have got this huge restaurant with a lot of bowling lanes, and now I've got Galactic playing and helping me fill it for free."

That's how I looked at it. Galactic helped me fill my restaurant, and then they'd collect all the proceeds from the door and merch. Plus, they would have an opportunity to play in front of new potential fans.

And that is exactly what happened.

Brooklyn Bowl worked from the start, which is a rarity.

Our initial skeptics eventually seemed to come around—maybe even Ron.

(Maybe.)

24

BOWLIVE
(SO MANY MEMORIES
I DON'T REMEMBER)

Soulive
Brooklyn Bowl, Brooklyn, New York
March 2, 2010

O ur ten-night run with Soulive in March 2010 was a key
moment for the Bowl becoming the Bowl.

When we announced Bowlive, people thought we were crazy.
Soulive had just come off two nights at the Music Hall of Williamsburg, where the tickets didn't go fully clean. Nonetheless,
we were moving forward with two weeks of shows, from Tuesday
through Saturday on March 2–6 and then again on March 9–13.
We revealed that the band would have guests throughout the residency, but we didn't identify all of them in advance.

How do you know if something is going to work? You don't
know until you try.

Sometimes you have to put your finger in the air and feel it.

You need to remind yourself to stop running the numbers and
start working on making the numbers better.

When it came to that first Bowlive, we had no idea what the
numbers would be. We had just opened Brooklyn Bowl and we
needed to do special shows. I realized, "This thing is seven nights
a week." Wetlands had been closed since 2001, so I had forgotten about that steady pressure to deliver. It's somewhat unique

because most music venues go dark for at least a few evenings each week. Not us.

When you're working on a film or a play or even a book, that process can be ongoing for months or even years. When you're working at a concert venue like Brooklyn Bowl, you put everything into a show, and then there is typically a show the very next day (and for me, with multiple venues, there's several shows).

I find the creative pressure that comes with this both nerve-racking and exhilarating.

One day in early 2010, I was riffing and it came to me. The idea originated with Wetlands Power Jams and The Jammys.

I believe that events like Bowlive become stories. Those stories help make the event bigger than itself.

It's also easier to promote a weekly residency or a run of shows.

If something starts working, my preference is to keep it going. I'm not concerned that we might burn it out.

Sometimes when we want to test out a concept, I'll say, "Okay, but we've got to do it every Wednesday for a month and promote it." Trying it once isn't enough.

Once you go to a residency, then you can leverage the promotional efforts so that people will say, "Oh yeah. I heard about this concept at the Bowl or Garcia's every Wednesday in July. I'm going to make one of those." The alternative is one event on July 8, where it can be tougher to get people to commit, particularly for something new. Also, once you go into multiples, you can deploy additional resources and amortize the marketing costs across those shows.

So we went for it.

I believed so much in Bowlive that I can recall exactly where I was when I pitched it to Jeff Krasno (Eric Krasno's brother), who was managing Soulive at the time along with Sean Hoess. I was at Fifty-Seventh Street and Park Avenue on the northwest corner at the Citibank. I can recall going to the ATM and being on the phone, explaining it to them.

Sometimes people will say to me, "You're selling." I take issue with that, though. I am not selling; I am expressing a belief in an idea. I would prefer to call it a *pitch* or *conveying a vision*. It can bum me out when someone tells me I'm selling. That is not what's happening inside my head. I believe in what I say.

I have had a pretty good run, but my belief does not always guarantee success. In 2019, we tried six nights of Drive-By Truckers at the Bowl, but it was during the summer when our business is more challenging. I still think booking a six-night run with DBT was the right thing to do, and you have to lean into what you believe in, even though that comes with risks. Especially these days.

A lot of my faith in Bowlive came from the structure of the event and the model with the guests. If you go to MSG and see Justin Timberlake, it's going to be the same show he's played across the country in every single Verizon Center. It's dancers, it's pyro, it's choreographed. It's awesome, but we aspire to offer something different every night. It's about artists figuring things out on the fly and exploring.

That's the glory of improvisation. Sometimes when you're taking those chances, it doesn't always work. But when it does, that's what the audience is there for, those magic moments—just like Ken Kesey said to me on my birthday in 1993.

Plus, I'll roll the dice on Soulive any day of the week.

In a brief film that was made about Bowlive, Neal Evans explains, "Just imagine you have this incredible show the first night of Bowlive and you're like, 'Oh, that was so killing,' and then you have to do it again, but you have nine shows ahead of you. And you're just kind of going, 'Yo, how we gonna top that? How can you *even* top that?' Then the next night would happen and you were like, 'I can't believe it, that was so insane,' and then it was the next night and the next night. So there's something about that kind of kinetic state of energy, and when it's released, it's magical."

The guest musicians help with that. Some of them we lock down in advance, but not all of them. In that same film, Eric Krasno recalls, "It just kind of snowballed. It was the sort of thing where we invited a certain amount of guests, and all of a sudden, this person would show up, and that person would show up. All of a sudden, they'd be like, 'Derek Trucks is at the book door,' and we'd be like, 'Cool, bring him up here,' and we would talk through what we were going to do onstage."

So many styles of music are represented in a given run. A short list of Bowlive guests over the years includes Questlove, Bernie Worrell, John Scofield, Warren Haynes, Talib Kweli, Aaron Neville, George Porter Jr., Leo Nocentelli, Oteil Burbridge, Susan Tedeschi, Vernon Reid, Chris Robinson, Robert Randolph, Charles Bradley, Ivan Neville, Marcus King, Citizen Cope, Allen Stone, Nicki Bluhm, Luther Dickinson, Jennifer Hartswick, Anders Osborne, and Alecia Chakour.

Back to Kraz: "Bowlive is really unique in that, in the same night, you could hear DMC and Talib Kweli but also hear John Scofield, and you get the same crowd going wild for both . . . My generation has had access to so much great music on our phones and on our computers that you have people who love all that music. And I think that Bowlive is a place for them to gather."

When it comes to assembling the guests each year, I like adding to the list, but I also enjoy having the old faithfuls, like George, Oteil, and Sco. That never gets old for me.

People occasionally ask me to name my all-time favorite night of Bowlive, but I can't pick one. It all feels like one big night.

I have so many memories I don't remember (ha!).

Over the years, I've tried to help build the Bowlive story by making special presentations. In 2011, I opened Bowlive with a toast to the band. Then I explained that I had previously done this on an earlier occasion, and I wanted to step up a level, so we kicked off Bowlive 2012 by handing out six hundred tequila shots to the audience. You have got to be careful about that type of stuff, so like my stage dive at a Yeah Yeah Yeahs show (more to come), while it was awesome, it was a onetime thing.

There have been other moments as well. Bowlive 2013 ended with the band's fortieth show at the Bowl, so we gave T-shirts to everyone in the house, with the Bowlive logo on the front and the number 40 on the back.

I have done similar things outside Bowlive as well. I enjoy the opportunity to lift the show. You cannot go over the line, but sometimes you want to get to the line, and I am willing to go there.

It does not necessarily add to the bottom line (certainly not in the short term), but another number that is important to me is how many epic memories I can generate for the band and the audience, even if I cannot always remember them.

Before the final set by Bob Weir & Wolf Bros at LOCKN' in 2019, I gave Bobby a trophy commemorating the most sets played at the fest since its launch in 2013.

The first musicians to play all three original Brooklyn Bowls were Neal Evans and Eric Krasno. However, the first full band to complete the trifecta was Galactic. So before their encore on the final night of a four-show run in July 2014, I handed them a trophy that proclaimed, "First Place Brooklyn Bowl World Tour." I've also awarded trophies to Umphrey's McGee and the Tedeschi Trucks Band. Who doesn't enjoy a good trophy?

On March 26, 2016, at the close of Joe Russo's Almost Dead's three-night stand, I gave JRAD a sword with the date of the band's debut gig at the Bowl engraved on it. Then I used the sword to knight all five musicians (this was a riff on a prank that originated at Wetlands in 2001, when Jake Szufnarowski first "revealed" that Prince Charles had given Joe the title of Sir Joe Russo, loyal servant of the British crown—check out sirjoerusso.com for the details). The crowd joined me, as we declared, "We, the freaks of Brooklyn Bowl, hereby anoint Dave, Scott, Tommy, Marco, and Sir Joe Russo as Knights, Birthed at the Bowl, and dedicated to Rock and Fucking Roll."

I have delivered plenty of cakes onstage, particularly to Phil Lesh on his birthday. Speaking of Phil, before a SummerStage show in 2014, I gave out T-shirts to audience members in an array of colors to offer him the vision of a loving rainbow.

Back to Bowlive, the band's concluding show in 2015 represented their sixty-first gig at the venue, which is located at 61 Wythe Avenue. In celebration, I gave each of them a diamond chain necklace in the shape of a *61*. In 2019, we opened the run with a double celebration of the band's twentieth anniversary and the tenth anniversary of the Bowl. In commemoration, I presented the three musicians with individual keys to the Bowl. And yes, they work.

There's plenty more of that to come.

I'm probably not doing the six-hundred-shots thing again, though.

Looking back, Bowlive became bigger than itself, which helped Brooklyn Bowl become bigger than itself.

Bowlive is a communal feedback loop. There is no start or end; it just keeps going from the band to the fans to the venue to the staff to the band to the fans . . . and there probably also is some fried chicken in there.

25

NEARLY FLAMING OUT
AND THE ROOTS REDEEMED

The Climate Rally
The National Mall, Washington, DC
April 25, 2010

The National Park Service was adamant about one thing: "He cannot go in the bubble."

I was informed of this prior to the appearance of Wayne Coyne and the Flaming Lips at Earth Day on the National Mall in 2009. This was the second straight year I was executive producer of the event in conjunction with the Green Apple Festival.

"We've researched this Flaming Lips band," the park rep explained, "and we know what he normally does. But this is different. We have our own rules, and he will have to abide by them. It is a security issue because we are right in front of the US Capitol. If he gets into his plastic bubble, he is going to be arrested, and *you* are going to be arrested also."

I understood and I was genuinely appreciative that they even allowed us to be here. It is rare to have an event that's free and non-ticketed so close to where Congress meets. Most free concerts occur in places with fewer national security concerns. But even a free show in Central Park typically requires advance ticketing so that it's easier to gauge and control the crowd.

Before Wayne took the stage, we explained what the Park Service had told us, and thankfully, he refrained from entering the bubble.

For one song.

The Lips opened with "Ta! Da!" but before the band performed their next tune, they paused while four crew members dressed as construction workers helped Wayne inside a deflated plastic ball and then filled it up with air.

I watched it happen, knowing there was nothing I could do.

As the Lips began "Race for the Prize," Wayne raised his arms in triumph, and then he was off, rolling on top of the crowd . . .

There is an iconic photo of that moment, as the jubilant musician gestures to the audience with the Capitol Building behind him. Google "Wayne Coyne National Mall" and you'll see it.

I had moved into the middle of the crowd at this point to enjoy the Lips' epic set. I turned my eyes to the side of the stage to see if our head of production, Jon Dindas, was being led into a paddy wagon. Thankfully, he appeared to be okay, so I let out a nervous laugh, resigned to the situation.

That is why we love these artists so much; they have their own creative visions and the courage of their convictions.

In this case, I suppose Wayne had the courage of my conviction as well, but it ended up turning out okay.

Just another white-knuckle moment in front of a hundred thousand people.

At least it was sunny.

Unlike the prior year, I experienced another dicey situation, not because I feared arrest, but because I had some concerns about electrocution.

After our success in three cities with Green Apple 2007, my relationship with Denis Hayes and Kathleen Rogers of the Earth Day Network continued to flourish. We agreed that in 2008, Green Apple would expand to eight cities, each of which would host mega-events. We returned to Central Park, Golden Gate Park, and Lincoln Park Zoo, then added Bicentennial Park in Miami, Fair Park in Dallas, Santa Monica Pier in Los Angeles, and City Park in Denver.

The big one, though, would be the National Mall. By this point, I had a solid team in place to work with me on the technical aspects and logistics (including the aforementioned, nearly incarcerated Jon Dindas), while I ran point on programming.

We had landed an impressive array of artists to appear at Earth Day 2008 on the Mall. The performances would build from the DC Boys Choir, Umphrey's McGee, O.A.R., Warren Haynes, Thievery Corporation, Gov't Mule, Toots and the Maytals, and finally, The Roots. We confirmed passionate, thoughtful speakers, including Thomas Friedman, Ed Begley Jr., and Earth Day Network board member Jayni Chase and her husband, Chevy. Unfortunately, we never made it to the full Mule. Torrential rains and lightning shut us down in the middle of the afternoon. My lasting memory of that day is Edward Norton delivering inspiring, eloquent remarks in the middle of a deluge.

My lasting memory of the next day is Chevy Chase offering me twenty dollars to valet his car. Chevy and I had shared some pretty intense moments up on the metal staging during the event. Then the next morning, we happened to check out of the hotel at the same time, and as we said our goodbyes, he commented, "Great working with you. Can you get my car for me?" Then he handed me a twenty. I felt like I was in the movie *Fletch*. There have been a couple of times over the years when I have had similar experiences. There are few things that fire the synapses the same way as when you feel like you're inside a movie—whether it's a real movie like *Fletch* or a movie flickering in your head. I have felt like that when I first stood in the middle of Phil Lesh's preshow huddle with everyone doing vocal exercises. So, too, when I helped Phil find some sparkle before he enjoyed an evening of entertainment in Manhattan (at age seventy-eight, bless his heart . . . if that happened).

As for Chevy, shortly after he asked me to fetch his car, I asked him to appear at The Jammys. Chevy played piano and accompanied guitarist Keller Williams for a version of "(You Make Me Feel Like) a Natural Woman." The two of them bonded offstage, and when Keller took home the Song of the Year Award for "Cadillac," Chevy walked out *as* Keller, accepting the Jammy and observing, "Wow, this is so much lighter than I thought it would be." Then Chevy delivered Keller's speech: "I'd like to thank my wife, Emily, and my manager, Nadia"—both accurate—"my record company, Blow Me Records"—less accurate, and added, "Clive Davis, for no particular reason." After this, he gestured at the award, which was a Gibson guitar neck mounted onto a base, and concluded, "This is so, so out of tune, man, I mean, wow," before he wandered off. I'm not sure if Chevy was in Keller's movie or if Keller was in Chevy's movie at that moment. They both received a standing ovation, though. I can vouch for that.

Chevy was back with us on the National Mall in 2009. Beyond the Flaming Lips, we had moe., Los Lobos, US Secretary of Labor Hilda Solis, Representative Edward Markey, Matthew Modine, and much drier weather.

We also did a cool thing with the Green Apple Festival that year, where we placed an emphasis on environmental volunteerism that reflected President Obama's Call to Service. We encouraged folks to give back to their local communities, and we hosted free thank-you concerts for people who participated. Each of these shows featured a headlining act joined by "Friends"—guest musicians to underscore the collaborative nature of what we were encouraging. We had Galactic & Friends at Variety Playhouse in Atlanta, Bassnectar & Friends at Slim's in San Francisco, Ivan Neville's Dumpstaphunk & Friends at Cervantes' Masterpiece in Denver, and Soulive & Friends at Paradise Rock Club in Boston, among others.

This became the last year of Green Apple, which had become difficult to manage from an administrative standpoint with our limited staff. In 2008, Chase (the bank, not the actor) had given us a lot of sponsorship money, and we spent it on the shows. Then, in 2009, following the financial crisis, we had nothing in the coffers, and Chase wasn't sponsoring Earth Day concerts anymore.

I returned to the National Mall the next year, though, to serve as executive producer for the Climate Rally.

As I've envisioned these events, I have never let myself believe that by having an Earth Day concert, we are going to solve the problem of climate change.

However, I do feel strongly about combining the power of community and music.

If a show can encourage my community to connect with a larger community, then maybe we can work together to help transform public policy and address the crisis before it's too late.

The Climate Rally marked the fortieth anniversary of Earth Day, and we used the occasion to marshal some prominent voices for the cause, including President Barack Obama, who addressed the crowd via a taped message. The roster of speakers included EPA head Lisa Jackson, Rev. Jesse Jackson, James Cameron, Margaret Atwood, and Dhani Jones. On the musical side, I enlisted The Roots, who had been rained out in 2008, to be our house band. They backed an all-star collection of artists over the course of the day: Bob Weir, Mavis Staples, Sting, John Legend, Booker T. Jones, Joss Stone, and Robert Randolph. It was an incredible afternoon, and thankfully, the weather cooperated this time, as projected showers failed to materialize.

When I first took over Wetlands in 1997, I had no expectation that, thirteen years later, I would be the executive producer of the official Earth Day 40 celebration. I also could not have guessed that the house band for Wetlands' Black Lily residency would be the house band on the National Mall, playing to over 100,000 people.

Another cool thing about the three consecutive years that I ran Earth Day on the National Mall was how many Wetlands artists participated.

I am proud to say that we never forgot our Roots.

26

BOWL TRAIN

Questlove
Brooklyn Bowl, Brooklyn, New York
September 8, 2011

O ne of the first people who understood what I was trying to do at Brooklyn Bowl was Questlove.

Having said that, it took a minute to get going.

When we opened the Bowl, we built it so that the monitors could be run from the soundboard. The monitor system allows musicians to get a proper sound mix while they are performing. Typically, adjustments are made at the beginning of a set once the music starts. When you see musicians looking over to the side of the stage to communicate with some unseen figure and then raising or lowering their index fingers, that's an attempt to alter the monitor mix.

Before the Bowl opened, we were sold a system with some new technology that allowed the monitors to be run from a port in front of the soundboard. We were told that our main soundman, whose job is to mix for the room, could also mix for the band. That is cost effective for a venue. Except when it's not.

The Roots played the Bowl shortly after we installed our new monitor system, and what we learned was that the musicians onstage want to be able to turn to their side and have the monitor guy be about sixteen feet from them. It is hard to communicate with someone who is at the other end of the room. Plus, all of this was compounded by the fact that as Questlove has already pointed out, The Roots play *loud*.

I was there when The Roots walked offstage, complaining that there was no monitor guy. This was embarrassing for me, so we bought a traditional monitor board the next day.

This situation with The Roots was difficult because I knew that they had been doing me a favor. I faced a lot of resistance early on when I was trying to get bands to give Brooklyn Bowl a shot. I'd tell them about it, and they'd say, "Pete, your new bowling alley concert venue sounds awesome. We're already routed for the rest of this year, but maybe we'll come by next year." There were plenty of doubters. Thankfully, I had earned some pretty good pay-it-forward moments. I had built relationships with the talent, the agents, and the managers, so I felt comfortable saying, "Actually, I need you to do the gig now."

Toots and the Maytals was our first big ticketed show. Bob Weir made an early appearance with Rob Wasserman and Jay Lane (echoing Wetlands's tenth anniversary). I also convinced the Biscuits, Soulive, and Galactic. I remain appreciative of all their support.

Gov't Mule was another group who performed an early date. I have been friends with manager Stefani Scamardo (who is also Warren Haynes's wife and an occasional tennis partner), ever since the Wetlands days, along with Chris Tetzeli, Jon Topper, Mike Luba, Kevin Morris, Bob Kennedy, Erik Newson, Dalton Sim, Vince Iwinski, and other key members of the community, like the Annabel Lukinses of the world.

Unfortunately, the Mule gig had a couple of problems. We only sold six hundred tickets, forgetting that some people just don't show up, so it didn't feel quite full. Also, keyboard player Danny Louis took me aside and told me he thought the room was slightly off-kilter. It's tough when you call in a favor and things don't quite turn out the way you had hoped.

Although booking typically involves negotiating with agents, since I have developed friendships with so many musicians and managers over the years, I can occasionally contact them directly about potential gigs. I have a little room to maneuver, unlike a booker at one of my venues, who needs to communicate directly with the agent. Knowing when to paper an agreement versus doing it via a handshake is a good skill to develop. There is a nuance and balance to it, with pros and cons to each path.

I'll also occasionally help an artist land a private gig when someone with a budget approaches me looking for a suggestion. Those gigs pay pretty well, so they can be a nice thank-you to a particular artist. That can even come back around when it places the band in proximity to one of my clubs with travel expenses already covered. So sometimes I'll get a public next to the private.

Sticking with the topic of charities, I've found that the best gift I can give to an auction is four tickets to any show, including sold-out shows. The great thing with a sold-out show in a GA venue is there's always a little extra room for house comps. I'll also keep a few in my back pocket for non-charity cases, although I limit that to pairs.

Back to 2009, I wanted to get Questlove to come back for a DJ set. That took a while, though. He had been doing a residency at (Le) Poisson Rouge, and I needed to sell him on Brooklyn because he was focused on Manhattan. The problem is you get one ask. I'd already used it with The Roots, and the monitor thing had been a bit of a disaster. Plus, he had his doubts about how a DJ set would work with the bowling lanes.

I believed in this, though, so I was persistent but also respectful. Eventually, I worked it out with Shawn Gee, his manager, who shared duties with Richard Nichols. I also had a text thing going on directly with Questlove, but I'm not entirely sure how I finally won him over. In an interview once, he mentioned his love of Brooklyn Bowl fried chicken.

Whatever it was, when Questlove finally returned in 2010, he got it immediately. He used the screens in an interactive and powerful way that no other artist had done yet. He knew Don Cornelius, the creator of *Soul Train*, so he had all this archival video that became part of the show.

Brooklyn Bowl was designed to be a multisensory experience. All those screens at the end of the bowling lanes are part of the canvas. At first, some people were dismissive and compared the Bowl to Epcot, but I didn't take that as an insult. The visual component has always been a big part of what I do, from *All Access* to *U2 3D* to the dome at the Cap.

A couple of years later when we were putting screens into Bowl Vegas, I had a choice. Our budget would allow us to get Samsung

LED screens with a twelve-millimeter pixel pitch (which means twelve millimeters from the center of one pixel to the center of the next pixel). Or I could buy screens from a new company with a five-millimeter pixel pitch. The lower number meant higher pixel density and thus better resolution. The danger was that if something broke, it might be more challenging to fix. So what do you do? It's the same price. Do you pick better or safer? I went with better, and as it turns out, not only has the resolution been superior but there haven't been any problems.

When Questlove started his Thursday night party, it wasn't called Bowl Train. That was something that MC Yameen Allworld said on that very first night: "Ladies and gentlemen . . . Welcome to the bowwwwwlll traaaain!" I was standing there, and it hit me in that moment. I mentioned it the next morning to Justin Bolognino, our founding media and marketing director, who had heard the same thing. That speaks to the value of showing up and paying attention. So I texted Questlove, and we had our official name. He has since hosted over three hundred Bowl Train parties at the venue. He calls it his woodshed.

Here's what Questlove said about Bowl Train in 2013: "This is where you can chow down on Blue Ribbon's finest cuisine, watch the finest musicians, and talk smack about your 225 bowling prowess. Between co-owner Pete Shapiro and me, we aim to attract the hippest of the hip and the brightest of the bright. I'll say that the coolest element is the fact that many a celeb has frequented our parties unscathed (I usually wait until after the night is over to thank whatever notable figurehead has paid us a visit). It's here that you often find *SNL* currents and alumnae having gutter contests or jamband heroes like the cats in Phish, or gods like Todd Rundgren or starlets like Alison Brie or Janet Jackson even (!) getting their bowl on. Even Alicia & Swizz have many a date night here. The music is quality, and my seven-hundred-plus *Soul Train* episodes keep people amused and boogying."

Once he became a regular presence at the club and had a feel for it, he'd start texting me with ideas. He wouldn't always give me the details, he'd just say, "What are you doing at the Bowl next

Monday?" Or he'd give me a specific date, and I would respond really quickly and try to find the avail.

John Legend with The Roots is a show that came together like this. On June 17, 2010, they appeared at the Bowl to celebrate his *Wake Up* album release. Maya Rudolph was another one where Questlove contacted me, and we made it happen on super-short notice. She debuted her Prince tribute project with her longtime friend Gretchen Lieberum and some help from The Roots. It was awesome.

I have been told multiple times there is an energy in the Bowl that is conducive to creating musical magic. I think some of that is a product of the layout, along with the warmth of the wood and the hundred-plus-year-old brick.

Sometimes it all explodes in unexpected ways. On November 7, 2012, Gary Clark Jr. was onstage during the moment that CNN projected Barack Obama's reelection. Gary couldn't see the screens, but the audience went nuts, and he built off their energy, which they then reciprocated, for a climatic final guitar solo that Bowl regulars and staff still talk about.

The venue's vibe begins early in the day with all the activity, particularly when Questlove is performing a late-night set. By the time Maya Rudolph walks in, there's something in the air that's a product of the staff touch, the general kindness, and the enthusiasm of the attendees. It's a chemistry equation, and you need the right ingredients. Then once you have it, you can bring Maya Rudolph in to do Prince, and everyone in the room feels it. You have that circle, that living organism. Of course, it always helps when the band is The Roots.

Another key show was D'Angelo. He hadn't performed a US club gig in about a dozen years until Questlove joined him for a duo performance on March 4, 2013. It was just the two of them, keyboards and drums, stripped down and incredibly powerful.

It was either at this show or JRAD where we created a new configuration for the venue. We move all the couches toward the bowlers' foul line. This allows us to open things up, so we can go to a thousand capacity. We've done this with Robert Plant, Jane's Addiction, Guns N' Roses, and a couple of other big shows. It is not something we figured out until after we had been open a while, but that is how we've approached big shows at the other Bowls from the very start. Although we tweaked this slightly after Jane's because we blocked the box. It was the most crowded of the shows, yet it had the smallest bar.

Since we're open seven nights, we also have the ability to pivot and program quickly. When Prince died on a Thursday, we hosted a shiva that night with Questlove spinning. When Phish's festival at Watkins Glen was canceled due to weather, we had six hundred people show up, and we played video from one of their prior festivals. We cranked it up on the PA, and with the quality of our sound system, it became experiential—it felt like a festival in its own right.

These two shows also demonstrate how important it is to pay attention and react. In February 2010, a snowstorm postponed Galactic's performance at the 9:30 Club in Washington, DC, on the day before their hometown football team, the New Orleans Saints, were set to play in Super Bowl XLIV. Galactic had appeared at NYC's Terminal 5 on Friday, so I figured they would be in the area, and I invited them to play a postgame party at the Bowl. We all watched on the big screens, and when the Saints came from behind in the fourth quarter to win their first-ever NFL title, it made for another epic evening.

One more last-minute gig that Questlove orchestrated was with Usher. They came to rehearse for The Roots Picnic in Philly. Usher's a giant pop star, but their show had a Wetlands feel along with that late-night New Orleans vibe. It was super impressive.

Questlove's comfort level in the Bowl translates to his guests. It feels like *his* room, too.

He'll text me with all sorts of questions or looking for suggestions. It might be a recommendation for a rooftop club where a friend can celebrate her birthday. Or it could be assistance reserving a bowling lane for a bandmate and his kids. If he texts me, then the pressure's on, and I'll try to oblige whether it's an Elvis show or a bowling lane for Annabella Sciorra.

One additional benefit of Bowl Train is that it's always the second show of the night. We'll have a band earlier in the evening before Questlove goes late. This quickly turned Thursday into a weekend and had a significant impact on the bowl's reputation and financial strength.

It became a competitive advantage when we were booking acts if we could offer a band a slot before Questlove's Bowl Train party. Not only would you have the opportunity to perform for some new people, but if Questlove liked you, he'd tweet about it—he's *that* important, and he's continued to grow in importance over the years (plus, he's a great documentary filmmaker—see *Summer of Soul*).

We have also had some artists invite Questlove onstage. In 2011, he guested with Bustle In Your Hedgerow, which is the Led Zeppelin alter ego of Joe Russo's Almost Dead. Questlove also did a cool sit-in with JRAD when Bowl Train followed their show—he joined them on turntables from his DJ booth during the "Not Fade Away" encore.

Something else that's happened over the years is Questlove occasionally will have another artist sub in for him if he can't make it. Then, if Questlove is cool with it, I'll pitch *that* musician on performing with the earlier band.

This is what took place on September 8, 2011, when Umphrey's McGee performed the third of four shows at the Bowl. The night before had been my birthday, so I consumed a few beverages with them while riffing on musical ideas involving the artist whom Questlove had tapped to appear the next evening as the guest Bowl Train DJ.

Which is how I ended up onstage following Umphrey's second set to announce: "Last night, we were having a cocktail or a couple of cocktails, and Brendan said, 'Did you make a wish?' I said, 'You know I did. I want to see you guys play some Steve Miller Band . . . with Biz Markie!'"

It was time for "The Joker."

Followed immediately by . . .

"Ladies and gentlemen . . . Welcome to the Bowwwwwlll Traaaain!"

27

GOOGAMOOGA

The Great GoogaMooga
Prospect Park, Brooklyn, New York
May 19, 2012

The Great GoogaMooga is an example of something that did not work because it worked *too* well.

GoogaMooga was the first time I deployed significant capital into something that wasn't mine. I had recently raised funds through an investor for my company Dayglo, so when I saw an opportunity, I decided to pursue it.

Food festivals are hard to figure out. People had done smaller things, but the Superfly guys who created Bonnaroo had bigger goals in mind. They were going to treat food similarly to how they treated music (except there would be music as well). I believed they knew what they were doing and could deliver the ultimate food fest. So I contributed funds with the assumption that if it succeeded in Prospect Park, we could scale it and bring it around the country (Chicago's Lincoln Park was the next targeted destination).

GoogaMooga kicked off at 11:00 a.m. on May 19, 2012. Over seventy-five food vendors, thirty-five brewers, and thirty winemakers were spread out across the Nethermead section of the park with a design aesthetic that matched the tagline "An Amusement Park of Food, Drink & Music." The roster of chefs included Anthony Bourdain, David Chang, Danny Meyer, Masaharu Morimoto, Tom Colicchio, April Bloomfield, Marcus Samuelsson, Michael Symon, Ruth Reichl, Amanda Freitag, and Pat LaFrieda.

Over twenty bands provided the musical pairings, such as Daryl Hall and John Oates, the Preservation Hall Jazz Band, Fitz and the Tantrums, Charles Bradley and His Extraordinaires, and Lucius.

Entry was free, although the event was ticketed to ensure that the park wasn't overrun. Two months before GoogaMooga, all forty thousand tickets disappeared within a couple of hours, which reflected the level of enthusiasm.

Still, I was unprepared for what I saw when we opened the gates. It was like being in an eighteenth-century war and watching the troops called to the battlefield. The weather had broken the right way, and the waves of people never seemed to stop.

Once everyone made it inside, they lined up in front of an incredible roster of food vendors. This was when a major problem revealed itself. People would wait until they were at the front of the line and *then* start thinking about their eight choices. This slowed down the entire process, as did the preparation of so many different menu items. In retrospect, limiting each station to only two options would have been preferable.

Another mistake was to go cashless in the beer and wine pavilions. Purchases had to be made via GoogaMoola cards, which were available at the box office, and then funds could be added at kiosks around the site. So you had to wait in a line to get your digital money and then get in another line for your drink. On top of that, there were some technical problems with the cashless system, which stopped functioning altogether at one point.

I wasn't a fan of digital currency ideas in 2012, but I wasn't in control. Around that time, a number of people had pitched me on various "send your friend a drink" apps for at the Bowl or the Capitol. How many worked? Not many. The problem was you had to pull up the app at the bar, which slowed things down because everyone else was using cash or credit cards.

Another time when food service went awry was my junior year at Northwestern. I thought it was important to try out different jobs, so I became a Chinese food delivery guy using my scooter that I had painted in the Kesey bus colors.

I worked at Yin-Yangs, which was located in Evanston, Illinois, right under the train tracks. On Saint Patrick's Day, the owner decided to use food coloring to make the sweet-and-sour chicken green instead of orange. So I had to deliver this green food to people. The owner had done it as a surprise, but it wasn't the right kind of surprise. When people got their food and saw that it was green, they freaked out and yelled at me. Was it my fault? No. Did I take it? Yes. What was I going to do? I was on the front lines.

At the Bowl these days, I try to handle it differently if things go wrong, although the end result is the same as when I was delivering green chicken for Yin-Yangs: I get yelled at. If something goes wrong at the Bowl, it's on me, whether I was there or not.

My staff is fully enabled to make decisions, but if something goes awry, I take the heat. Our record is pretty good, although we have occasional lapses. For instance, as the owner of Brooklyn Bowl, I probably should have refrained from stage diving during the Yeah Yeah Yeahs show. I'm not allowed to do that again, but it was an incredible performance, and I felt like I was in twelfth grade at a Jane's Addiction concert.

This was during a benefit for Jonathan Toubin, the DJ who was asleep in a hotel in Portland, Oregon, when an errant taxi crashed into his room and ran him over. He was a Bowl regular, so we hosted a night to help with his medical bills.

A couple of other people were stage diving, and I got caught up in the moment, so I decided to go for it. When you own a venue, you're not supposed to stage dive. I landed on someone, and he was annoyed but he wasn't injured, so I'm thankful for that. I'm glad I did it, but I won't do it again.

As I've said, there's nothing like putting in the time and gaining the experience from the ten thousand hours (or in my case, shows). In the live music business, experience may be the single most important ingredient to being good at what you do.

How did I apply *my* experience to the Great GoogaMooga? Selectively.

I had some input, but there were limits because I was involved as the investor.

One lesson I took away from GoogaMooga is I don't enjoy being limited to the investor role, and I have not really done it again.

Still, there was some great food and amazing moments at GoogaMooga 2012. Marcus Samuelsson's Harlem Renaissance

Party inside the Boathouse stands out. James Murphy deejayed a full-on rave at dusk around the Big Gay Ice Cream truck in an area of Prospect Park that feels like you're in the woods. Things were going off in a way that sometimes happens in the LOCKN' forest but I had never seen in New York City before (or since).

The festival returned in 2013, expanded to three days, and addressed some of the problems from the prior year. However, Sunday was canceled by the parks department over concerns that intense rain would damage the meadow (this created some exasperation from the chefs because GoogaMooga had been billed as a rain-or-shine event, and many of them had planned accordingly, prepping food they couldn't sell). Then in October the parks department assistant commissioner announced that GoogaMooga could not return to Prospect Park because of the potential impact to the land.

We haven't done it since.

I still believe in GoogaMooga. We were just never able to execute on the concept in an optimal manner. I still understand why I had bet on it even if things didn't quite go as planned.

Plus, I was able to experience something that was a major success in certain ways, yet that same success took it down.

Again, this all remains a learning process.

On the Friday night in 2013 when the Yeah Yeah Yeahs closed out the music on day one of GoogaMooga, I maintained a respectful distance to suppress any urge to jump from the stage.

I also refrained from telling the Blue Ribbon guys not to serve green chicken. They have ten thousand hours of their own.

Took this of Ken Kesey with one of those cardboard box cameras at his farm in Oregon on my twenty-first birthday. Peak moment!

I went to Timothy Leary's house to interview him for *And Miles to Go*. When he looked at me, I could feel him seeing inside me. It was pretty cray.

With the Originator, George Clinton, in the basement of Wetlands.

"Hey, Derek, we are going to be doing this for a long time..."

(Below) Hanging with Perry, the lead singer of my favorite band in high school.

B.B. & Trey. Best sandwich ever.

Helping place a piano with Chick Corea.

Landing in Las Vegas with The Roots for the opening of
Brooklyn Bowl. I mostly remember that plane ride.

Sometimes you have to leave it all on the field.

My one stage dive at Brooklyn Bowl. At the Yeah Yeah Yeahs. I got caught up in the moment. It felt like the right thing to do, although I probably won't ever do it again. I'm glad I did it, but sorry to whomever I landed on!

Having lunch with Stevie Van Zandt at Minetta Tavern in the Village. We go back and forth with ideas. He has as many as anybody, so it's kind of like a sport where we are boinging back and forth.

Wayne in the bubble on the National Mall. Thankfully no arrests were made.

People talk about the GD50 Rainbow but this came first. The rainbow saved us because otherwise people would be talking about the peace sign skywriting miss. D'oh!

My Dad could not believe Bill Walton was at Fare Thee Well.
He was even more shocked when Bill not only knew my name
and who I was, but also expressed affection for me. My Dad passed away
a few months later, so this moment stands strong for me.

The Garcia women: Annabelle, Sunshine, Trixie,
and Mountain Girl. They each evoke Jerry in a
unique way and have amazing personalities.

"Should we pull a prank
on Mickey?"

(Above Left) Acid Warfare (aka Fare Thee Well at Soldier Field).

(Above Right) Standing with Robert Plant on the deck at Brooklyn Bowl in Las Vegas. I should have asked him to go on the Ferris wheel with me.

(Above) Hanging with Cheech and Chong at the Capitol. That is a cigarette I'm smoking. Just sayin'.

(Left) Bono wondering how we beat U2's attendance record at Soldier Field. He wasn't too pleased about that one. Sorry. Not sorry.

Roxy Shapiro singing "Happy" onstage with Pharrell at Bowl London.

When Bob Weir plays your office… 🙄

Working the valet stand with Ronnie Delsener.

Backstage at Wetlands with Mickey Hart and Baba Olatunji.

With Mickey twenty years later at Lockn'.

My favorite spot to watch a show is often at the back of the room. It is the best place to take in visuals, whether lights or wall projections. That is why I like sitting upstairs.

Hanging with my brothers, Jon and Andrew, and our fourth brother, Sting Shapiro.

It turned out Phil's seventy-ninth birthday fell on his seventy-ninth show at the Capitol Theatre. That is the Grateful Dead.

Doing the Hora with Matisyahu at Congregation Bowl.

Kissing Mavis Staples. She went for the lips, so I did too. Respekt!

Lifting a toast for 600 shots of tequila at Brooklyn Bowl for Bowlive.

Happy eightieth birthday, Del McCoury! Birthday cakes never get old. Everyone loves to sing "Happy Birthday."

I love giving out trophies.

Swords are fun to give out, too.

With the family at Lockn'.

Larry King is the witness as I sign a joint venture deal with Live Nation to create new Brooklyn Bowls.

In Jamaica with Chris Blackwell. He is showing me a new video by Koffee, an emerging reggae act. He still has his finger on the pulse. And on the screen.

At the opening of the Fillmore in New Orleans. I love going to shows that are not my own, especially when they are in New Orleans with friends like Trombone Shorty and Ivan Neville.

Neil Young FaceTiming with Paul McCartney.

Ladies and gentlemen, John Popper.

At the opening of the Bowl in Nashville with my Preservation Hall brother, Ben Jaffe. He showed up on a whim, which is pretty much how we both do it. Not many people understand the life I live, but Ben lives the same life so . . . we are buddies!

Jimmy Fallon is the most naturally talented performer I've ever seen. Whether on his back at the Capitol . . .

. . . Or on my couch at Relix.

Our first "Be in the Stream" from the Bowl in Nashville. This has to be Jason Isbell's youngest virtual fan, beamed in live from the maternity ward.

"Come on, Chuck, we need more help!"

Billy Strings and Carlos Santana listening to Coltrane in Kauai.

When I look at this photo, I see my friend Billy. If you told that to young Peter, he would not have believed it.

Checking out the Lockn' schedule with Jon Batiste.

Anders Lee of the New York Islanders asked to meet Billy Idol, who was playing the Capitol. Simon Shapiro asked to meet Anders Lee. This became my first double meet & greet.

"Hi, Rick!" FaceTiming from the Capitol with Marcus King to Goose at the Bowl in Nashville.

Why I do what I do.

28

THE OBVIOUS IS OBVIOUS
(UNTIL YOU MISS IT)

Fishbone (Noon Family Show)
Brooklyn Bowl, Brooklyn, New York
July 8, 2012

L ooking back, I am still not sure how I missed this one.

I was searching for a location to host a special series of workshops and performances for kids. So I decided to build one.

It became a challenge due to a handful of people in Gowanus, Brooklyn, who caught NIMBY fever and decided they weren't quite bound by the facts.

So I decided to cut bait, at which point I realized that I didn't need to build a venue at all because it turns out I already had a few of my own . . .

The moment when I first envisioned what the Rock and Roll Playhouse could be was in July 2012 when I had Fishbone at the Bowl for a Sunday show. At the time my daughter, Roxy, was six, and my son, Simon, was two and a half, so I had children's music on my mind.

In particular, I was thinking about live music. Kids respond to music, and they *really* respond to the energy of live music. There is energy at a concert you cannot find anywhere else. However, live shows are mostly unavailable to kids. I wanted to change that.

This led me to ask Fishbone if they wanted to play a special early show for families. It makes sense for a band. That is incremental money because they are already there. Rather than a sound check, they can play a forty-minute set and take home more pay for the additional gig.

Fishbone was into it, and I had a feeling it would work based on my experiences at the Bowl. When we first opened, there was a question about what would happen on Saturday afternoons when bands came in to sound check. Some people thought the musicians would be perturbed by all the kids running around. It turned out that they loved the energy, the kids dug it, and the parents got a free mini-show.

We had also done something like this with Soulive a couple of months earlier, but I figured if we could do it with Fishbone, we could do it with anybody. I told them to play a little easier, a little lighter, a little softer.

The place went bonkers.

Somehow my takeaway from this was that I should build a new venue called the Rock and Roll Playhouse. I was looking to do something a bit more than concerts for kids. We created developmentally appropriate programming for four different age groups. Our physical layout would incorporate an outdoor garden and an indoor space with high-end playground equipment.

My wingmate on the Playhouse was Amy Striem. She was a certified early childhood and elementary teacher who was working as an administrator at my kids' nursery school. Amy developed the programming for RRPH while we moved forward with plans to begin construction in a vacant building—it had previously functioned as a plumbing supply company—at 280 Bond Street in the Gowanus section of Brooklyn.

On April 18, 2013, we gave neighbors official notice regarding the renovations that would begin the following month.

That's when the problems began.

The section of Brooklyn where we intended to locate the Playhouse was in an industrial zone named after the Gowanus Canal, a polluted waterway that the federal government had recently designated for Superfund cleanup. Gowanus had not experienced gentrification like the neighboring Carroll Gardens and Park Slope, although some homeowners were hoping this would change. So even though our intended use of the building had been approved by the New York City Board of Standards and Appeals, a few residents of the nearby brownstones took issue with it.

There were a number of young families in the area who would have appreciated the Playhouse, just Not in My Backyard.

When I took over Wetlands, I'd had to address similar issues. Larry Bloch had not been sympathetic to the NIMBY crowd living near the club because the area was zoned as a mixed-use neighborhood. I had acknowledged the neighbors' concerns and eventually won them over.

I attempted to do the same in Gowanus. I made the rounds, explaining our goals for the Playhouse while pledging to work in partnership with the community. However, unlike Wetlands, this time nobody called me a "good boy" (although admittedly, I was forty, not twenty-four).

A few people became loud in opposition, which is easy to do in the social media age. Calling themselves We Are Gowanus, they initiated a campaign of half-truths. Their core misrepresentation was that I didn't care about children's programming, but instead, I was trying to use the RRPH as a "Trojan horse" (their words) to open a nightclub for adults, claiming that our building plans didn't even include children's bathrooms. That was beyond absurd.

We Are Gowanus established a "Defend the 'hood" GoFundMe campaign (raising $2,505 of a $20,000 goal). In conjunction with this, they created an animated video titled "The Rock and Roll Playhouse Impact," which showed a thousand hipsters standing inside a rendering of our venue while Muse slammed into "Stockholm Syndrome" (or a version of Muse with a phantom sax player, and as for their song selection, I'm not quite sure if they were attempting to send a message and, if so, to whom). They also presented an "acoustic amphitheater impact zone" map, which looked pro, but there was one major problem: we weren't building an amphitheater.

Looking back, I suppose it is slightly amusing, but I cannot say I was amused.

Their next move was to rely on a series of procedural mechanisms to appeal the original ruling by the Board of Standards and Appeals.

This continued through the fall of 2014, at which point, my perspective changed. On December 28, we hosted a Grateful Rocks children's music workshop with special guest Phil Lesh at

Brooklyn Bowl. It was a huge success that also provided my light bulb moment.

The obvious is obvious until you miss it.

I didn't need to build a venue; I already had a venue. In fact, I had a few of them. So we began hosting shows at Brooklyn Bowl and then Garcia's, starting with the Music of the Grateful Dead for Kids. As we described it, "Using the songs created by the most iconic musicians in rock history, the Rock and Roll Playhouse offers its core audience of babies and kids games, movement, and stories and an opportunity to rock out. The Rock and Roll Playhouse is an early and often first introduction to a child's lifelong journey with live music and rock and roll."

Then we expanded into the music of the Beatles, Phish, the Rolling Stones, Tom Petty, Bob Marley, and Dave Matthews Band. We found that we were most successful when we focused on specific acts. When we did general tributes to classic rock or funk or reggae or the '80s, they had less appeal.

Each show paired our trained staff members with a cover band, typically a Grateful Dead cover band. As we began scaling up into weekly events, it became a lot harder to land artists like Soulive, Fishbone, or Phil Lesh.

Frankly, sometimes you don't want to rely on big-name talent. Nonprofits often ask me, "Can you help us get a famous artist for our gala?" I'll typically respond, "You're better off if you can pull off the gala without that. Make it about the event, the organization, not the artist. Plus, you're going to overpay. So do it without them, if you can."

After our success at Brooklyn Bowl and Garcia's, we decided to expand into additional cities. Most venues are otherwise closed on a Saturday or Sunday at noon, so they're happy to have us there.

When we go into a new market, we reach out to the local Grateful Dead cover band. I swear, every town's got a Dead cover band, and those musicians tend to be easygoing people and skilled players who know plenty of additional classic rock songs.

We also utilize the venue's email lists and socials to reach their regular patrons. That's an important piece of the puzzle.

The venues appreciate the Playhouse, because aside from creating goodwill and making some extra money, parents will notice the concert calendar and realize, "Oh, Drive-By Truckers are going to be here next month."

We've established reputation and scale, which makes it easier for us to recruit venues and staff. I suppose a club could attempt to do this for itself, but it's not worth the effort. You have to pay everyone involved and be sure to hire someone who knows how it works, including the parachute—the staple of the Playhouse shows is the colored parachute that the kids get inside while it drifts up and down.

Rock and Roll Playhouse is successful because it's targeted to an age group that is not self-aware. When two- to five-year-olds dance, they go nuts. After they get older, say eight or nine, they are far more concerned about looking like a cool kid. But you'll see these three-year-old dancers who are totally free with their limbs flying around. What they give you is real and in the moment. When I'm watching them, it feels like I'm at a Dead show, or sometimes a Slayer show.

We have done more than one thousand RRPH performances at more than forty rock clubs, including the Boulder Theater, First Avenue, the Showbox, Antone's, Sweetwater, and the Sinclair, and sold them out regularly. We had a Playhouse at Wrigley Field in 2019 and would have done it at every MLB park in 2020 but for the pandemic.

In retrospect, I nearly missed it.

I was caught up in trying to build a venue when I should have realized that it wasn't necessary. But I try to focus on what's in front of me and not look back too much.

In golf, the second shot is the critical one. That has been true of my career as well. I have found that long-term success comes from your response when things go awry. The initial idea is important, but what's more crucial is how you maneuver and adjust. Nothing is a pure straight line.

And if you're feeling stressed, then go dance inside a colored parachute that is floating over you.

It's inspiring.

And surprisingly psychedelic.

29

THE ORIGINAL ROCK PALACE

Bob Dylan
The Capitol Theatre, Port Chester, New York
September 4, 2012

"Peetah, the concerts are too hard . . ."

This is what Marvin Ravikoff said to me while explaining why he had pivoted away from producing live music at the Capitol Theatre.

The Cap had opened in grand style on August 18, 1926, with a sold-out house of two thousand and hundreds more turned away from the doors of the Port Chester, New York, venue. Those who had been able to secure tickets were treated to a performance by a ten-piece orchestra, which also supplied the soundtrack to the movie *The Sea Wolf* (this was during the silent film era). Renowned architect Thomas Lamb designed the Capitol Theatre, which was one of the hundred "picture palaces" he worked on across the globe from the US to India.

What's remarkable is that Thomas Lamb built most of them in the 1910s and 1920s when today it would take years and nine figures to build just one. He is the Michael Jordan of architects. It's not just that he could work quickly, the theaters themselves were special. The Cap has got these rounded edges and an intimate feel.

Over the years, musicians like Jeff Beck, Brandi Carlile, and Wayne Coyne have come off the stage raving about the energy of the audience. Some of this is because the venue attracts varsity concertgoers, who know all the words and are game to participate. When Robert Plant first played the Cap, he was thrown off a little by how loud the kickback was with the sing-alongs. However, it's also due to the curvature of the venue, the rounded edges that support and enhance the acoustics, which is why Jerry Garcia loved the Capitol Theatre so much.

By the time Marvin acquired the venue in 1984, however, the building was in disrepair. Marvin told me that when he first walked in, he could see the sunlight coming through the roof: "It was just me and the pigeons." He renovated the theater and did occasional shows but ultimately decided they were too much hassle, so he mostly used the space as a banquet hall.

"I don't know why you want to do the concerts," he continued as we walked through the venue together in late 2011. "I have one employee, Jim, and when we get a bar mitzvah, we hire caterers. It's a great business."

While I'm always up for a good chair dance or some quality hora action, I had other plans for the Cap.

When I stepped into the venue with Marvin, I looked up at the ceiling and instantly saw it as a planetarium. I noticed the round form and began thinking about how I could use it as a canvas. Eventually, that vision would extend to the walls as well, thanks to the ten projectors that we would install.

I also had a feeling that the Cap wasn't just a local venue. I knew it could pull in people from New York City, since it's directly on the Metro North train and a mile from I-95. I figured that with the right programming, we could reach beyond Westchester into Connecticut, western Massachusetts, and possibly the entire Eastern Seaboard. People will travel to see their favorite band at their favorite venue, and I had a feeling that the Cap could become their new favorite venue. (And it's worked, with Billy Strings and Ween runs in February 2022, each drawing audience members from forty-seven states.)

The Capitol Theatre had a brief, glorious run in the early '70s before it fell into disuse. When you walk inside, you can sense you're in a room that has had history with the Stones, Janis, Floyd,

Bowie, and the Dead. In October 1970, Jerry Garcia said, "See, there's only two theaters, man, they are the only two places that are set up pretty groovy all around for music and for smooth stage changes, good lighting and all that—the Fillmore [East] and The Capitol Theatre. The rest of the places we play are sort of anonymous halls and auditoriums and gymnasiums."

Air matters, and the Capitol has good air. It's a place you can breathe the magic from all those great shows.

Artists can sense that, and it becomes good kindling. They still have to make the fire, but the Cap becomes a catalyst and supplies that kindling.

I had experienced this myself during the one show I'd seen at the venue: an evening with Strangefolk in December 1998.

By the time I finished walking through the venue with Marvin, I was on board. I just needed to convince him.

After we opened Brooklyn Bowl, I began getting phone calls offering various opportunities. That's how I learned that Marvin was showcasing the Cap. He had promised his wife, Norma, that after he turned seventy-five, he would turn over the venue to someone else.

Marvin had a secret, though. He didn't want to turn over the venue to someone else.

He enjoyed working with the caterers and event planners.

Marvin was a real estate developer and self-made millionaire who liked to keep himself busy.

But Norma told him that enough was enough. They were spending more of their time in Florida, so he had to stop dealing with all the *mishegas* that came with owning and operating the Capitol Theatre.

To fulfill his promise to Norma, he took a series of meetings with interested parties.

Marvin didn't need to sell the Cap. He had no responsibility to shareholders or investors, and he'd paid off his mortgage. It would have minimal financial impact on his life.

So I had to win him over.

My pitch was that the time was right to bring music back to the Capitol Theatre, and I was the guy who could make that happen. Some of our conversations reminded me of the time I had spent with Larry, just building trust. Marvin had to buy into the idea of giving me his baby (or at least lending it to me because initially we were only talking about a lease).

Our negotiations stretched over a year. I'd get to the one-yard line but then something would happen and I'd get pushed back to the thirty-three. He'd say, "Peetah, you're a good kid, but the deal's off. It's dead." If it had been a normal venue, a normal building, I would have walked away on day 3 out of 470, but there was no other rock palace within thirty miles of New York City.

Eventually, we worked it out.

Not without some last-minute drama, though. He pulled the same thing on me that he had done with everyone else. After we'd agreed to terms and I came in to close, he raised the price.

Twice.

I wasn't even looking to buy the venue; we were just negotiating the lease.

Both times, I said, "You know, Marvin, it's really not right, just on principle. But I want the theater. I want the Capitol. That is more important to me, so I'll pay the money."

That is what I agreed to do . . . and then that's what I agreed to do a second time.

It was a bit like *Groundhog Day*, which is somewhat ironic because the Capitol Theatre mascot is actually a squirrel (no joke, when Thomas Lamb designed the Cap, he included 271 plaster squirrels in various locations throughout the building).

Marvin later suggested that at least some of his behavior had been prompted by motivation to find someone who wanted the theater enough that they would pay more, even if the guy in the middle of the deal changed the deal twice.

So that is how I took over the Capitol Theatre.

Then the problems started.

The issue was handicapped bathrooms. The Cap didn't have any, and we needed them.

When I mentioned this to Marvin, he told me that the large stall in the women's room should suffice. He explained that it could accommodate female patrons with disabilities and that we could clear out the women's room for any men.

Marvin was concerned that if we made too many renovations, we were going to screw up the grandfather status of the theater.

I told him his idea would not work, and eventually, we came up with a solution. There was an empty storefront adjacent to the theater that had previously been a stationery shop. We rented that additional space as well, which would allow us to create four handicapped bathrooms.

Then I began thinking about installing a bar and transforming the room into a depressurized zone for people to get a drink during the show. From there, knowing how much Jerry Garcia loved the Cap, I had the idea to develop what became known as Garcia's.

I spoke with Coran Capshaw and Marc Allan, who were overseeing the Garcia estate on behalf of the family. Then I began working with Jerry's daughter Trixie to create the right vibe. She thought it made sense because Jerry's parents had once run a bar in San Francisco.

Trixie helped with the visual design, and the family contributed a lot of the items we display—we now have one of Jerry's banjos, a gold record of *Terrapin Station*, quite a few of his guitar picks, a briefcase that Fender made for him, and the collection is ongoing.

The situation now reminds me of landing the extra square footage at 61 Wythe for Brooklyn Bowl. The ability to convert the adjoining space into Garcia's was a similar crucial moment.

Beyond serving drinks on show nights, Garcia's soon became a performance space in its own right. My old friend Reid Genauer of Strangefolk kicked things off with three dates in May 2013—a nod to the first show I had attended at the venue.

There are not a lot of two-thousand-capacity theaters in the country that have a great three-hundred-cap venue inside them. This also helped make the theater economically viable, since the big room was dark so many nights a week.

When it came to the layout of Garcia's, we brought in a roll of tape and went to work. I am not great at sitting down with a piece of paper and drawing the details—Charley Ryan, my partner at Brooklyn Bowl, is the most talented person I've ever met at visualizing a space on paper before it's built. What I find helpful when building a new venue or revamping an existing one is to go in and lay out my plans in tape. Sometimes I will paint the floor, but that's a little harder to edit. If you tape out the space, you can move things around and get a feel for your options.

I am a believer in testing things out in a room whenever possible. The mezzanine in the Cap has a lot of black and gold—I was going for the classic rock palace vibe. Some people said, "I don't think that's going to work. The black and gold will feel too much like the New Orleans Saints." But the key word there is *think*. It's easy to think that the colors won't work, but my approach is to *try*. See what it looks like, and then make a decision.

We did the same thing inside the theater, where we painted three shades of tan on the walls. We even had seats made with multiple red hues and tested them out. If you can do that, it's a real benefit to see what things will look like in practice rather than theory (design assist to Tristam Strindberg, who also worked on Brooklyn Bowl).

On the subject of design, I should also point out that the most impactful and cost-effective addition I've made to any of my rooms is placing Christmas lights behind the bar. I first did this at Wetlands in 1997. I put up multicolored lights in late November, and we all enjoyed them for a few weeks until we decided it was time to take them down in early January. As soon as we did, the energy in the room changed. It didn't take me very long to put them back up. They're cheap, and they don't use much power. They have been up at every venue I have ever done since then. It's a minimal spend for maximum impact.

When it comes to maintaining the proper atmosphere, I also find some people in venue management are too quick to turn up the house lights after a show ends. If they remain low, it helps to keep the vibe going.

To achieve our larger goals for the new room, we needed to cut a hole in the Cap lobby to connect it with Garcia's. Otherwise, the handicapped bathrooms were of no use. Marvin was well aware of this, and I told him that we'd fill the hole at the end of the lease if he wanted us to do so. We'd restore it to the condition in which we found it.

However, Marvin ran his real estate business with his son, who didn't approve of the idea. He sent us a letter indicating we were in default on the lease because we didn't have full approval to connect the two rooms.

The first few months of 2012 were filled with tension. Marvin was aware of these issues, as we had become close. So he had his son on one side and me on the other. I think he had this conflict on his mind when I ran into him a block from the theater in early April on the afternoon before Passover.

After exchanging pleasantries, he said to me, "I'm going to sell the building."

My ears perked up.

"How much?" I asked him.

"Eleven and a half million."

At this point, I already had the lease, and I was aiming to open in September.

People may not realize this, but I pretty much still operate paycheck to paycheck. I own things but my desire to keep control has placed a limit on the amount of money I have on hand. I would rather own more and have less money (although that spread is starting to tighten as I near 50).

April 2012 was an exception. At that moment in my career, I had partnered with an investor, my friend Daniel Ziff. As part of this arrangement, I created Dayglo and put all my entities together in one company. It also meant that I had an account with some funds in it. There have been plenty of moments when I've been unable to tap any additional resources. However, at this specific time, I had a little over $1 million available to me.

I knew that Marvin would be going home over the weekend for Passover, where he would see his son. I suspected that if I ran into Marvin on Monday, he'd tell me that after further family discussion, he was no longer selling the building.

I realized the current moment was fleeting.

So in that split second after Marvin named his price, I said to him, "Well, I am going to buy it."

He seemed slightly thrown off, yet I suspect that part of him knew that this was the best way out of his problem.

I said to Marvin, "I'm going to walk over to the bank, get a million-dollar bank check, and meet you at your office in an hour. Give me six months to close, and I'll buy it as is. Right now. Nonrefundable."

"You're telling me that you're going to get a million dollars right now?"

"Yup."

Was $11.5 million the right price? It was hard to know how to value it. There are no theaters left like that. It had pedigree. I also knew the bones were good because I'd already done the environmental and structural work for the lease. What was I going to do, have a consultant tell me the actual value was $14.2 or $9.8 or $17.6? I was aware that the Kings Theatre in Brooklyn had been renovated for $90 million around this same time. I knew that the cost to build the Cap from scratch would be many times $11.5 million, and assuming you could clear all the paperwork hurdles, it would take forever.

That is how I came to own the Capitol Theatre, while I was standing on the corner of Westchester Avenue and Broad Street in Port Chester. It was similar to how I'd made the Ticketfly deal on the corner of North Eleventh and Wythe.

Except there were complications.

My next problem was that I couldn't get a mortgage. Marvin had been running the theater as this little business with a focus on weddings and bar mitzvahs, so the Cap didn't have sufficient economic history as a music venue to convince a commercial bank of its worth.

I had put down my nonrefundable deposit with a closing date of December 31, 2012, but I couldn't get a bank loan. If I failed to close on that date, I would forfeit the $1 million along with the right to purchase the Cap. I was fairly certain that Marvin's son would not grant me any forbearance (which he later acknowledged to my attorney).

So with time running out, I got in touch with Ray Dalio, who runs one of the world's biggest macroeconomics hedge funds. When his plane lands in India, the treasury minister meets him at the airport because when he makes a macroeconomics call, it moves markets. I met Ray through Ken Hays, creator of the Gathering of the Vibes, who produced Ray's China Care event. Ray loves live music—a lot of people like music, it can level the playing field in many respects—and there aren't many individuals who do what I do, so he was friendly with me. Ray appreciated my plans for the Cap, and he agreed to loan me the $10 million to buy the building.

When you're working with billionaires, even if they are nice people, they live in a different world. He told me that he was going to charge me the same interest rate that he charges himself when he borrows money from himself, which was 6 percent. That's the sort of comment I'd never heard before, but when it came from Ray Dalio, it kind of made sense.

Then, just when it seemed like everything was back on track, the end of December was fast approaching, and I couldn't reach Ray. I was unable to get him on the phone, and I wasn't sure what was going on. I was told he was traveling, that he'd made the deal and not to worry, but when late December arrived, I was starting to worry.

He finally called me while I was driving to the closing. By that point, the Cap had been open for three months, and we were operating under the lease. Ray informed me that he had changed his mind because there was too much risk.

This meant I needed to convince him to help me close the deal while I was in the car on the way to close the deal.

I was sweating that one for twenty or thirty minutes until he finally agreed to loan me the money (again), and I was able to buy the Capitol Theatre.

Opening night was a throwback for me. During my first year at Northwestern, I had volunteered for the Arts Alliance, the student-run organization that programmed a variety of events. As part of this, on November 4, 1991, I worked a Bob Dylan show at the basketball gymnasium. My role involved backstage hospitality—I remember carrying ice to Bob's dressing room before he got to the venue—but I had no interaction with him.

Cap booker Anthony Makes and I originally pitched Dylan on the 2012/13 New Year's Eve show. He'd previously rehearsed at the Cap, and we were told he liked it. When New Year's didn't happen, his agent came back to us and asked about opening night. So we confirmed September 4, 2012, as the debut of the refurbished Capitol Theatre.

A few weeks prior to the show, I prepared for what was to come with a sleepover at the Capitol. I do that at all my venues. It allows me to become one with the room, which helps me later when shit goes sideways (and shit is always going sideways). At

Wetlands, I slept in the basement on a couch. In the Bowl, I slept in the green room, and in the Cap, I did the same. (Later, in Vegas, it would be on a couch by the bowling lanes; in London, I opted for the green room; in Nashville, it was a couch again; then in Philly, another green room.)

When I took over the Cap, a paranormal expert called me and said, "There's a ghost in your place." We all joked about it until we saw a photo of an apparition that looked like Bob Weir in a cowboy hat. Now I'm not afraid of ghosts, but just to be safe, I brought Brett Fairbrother with me on my sleepover. He freaked out at one point and fled, but I made it through to the next morning.

As these things go, opening night was more complicated than we would have liked. We didn't receive our temporary certificate of occupancy until 4:00 p.m. that same afternoon. Also, while we had done a run-through of logistics, we hadn't anticipated the bottleneck that we experienced at the box office. The staff was stressed.

Bob was scheduled to take the stage at 8:00, at which point we still had a line that stretched up the block. I made an appeal to Jeff Kramer, his manager, asking if we could wait a little while.

"Sorry," he told me. "Bob goes on when Bob goes on."

Which is what he did, at 8:04.

The rock palace was officially reborn.

But it wasn't full for another twenty minutes.

We got a great review from Jon Pareles of the *New York Times*, who noted, "The Capitol's interior is once again resplendent in red brocade and gilded painted reliefs; many of the exit signs have Art Nouveau panache . . . a rock theater that looks and sounds as good as the Capitol is something to celebrate."

He also singled out "one bad practice: waitresses soliciting drink orders from concertgoers during songs, an intrusion."

He was right, and after reading the review, we made an adjustment.

You never know where good advice will come from, and you should always be open to it.

30

CHOOSE YOUR OWN ADVENTURE

Jazz & Colors
Central Park, New York, New York
November 10, 2012

Jazz & Colors was inspired by my experience at Lollapalooza in Chicago's Grant Park. Not the music but how they used the park, spreading out everywhere across the green space. There were eight stages, and I enjoyed moving around to all of them.

That same year, I was involved with the 3D filming of the Black Eyed Peas in Central Park on the Great Lawn. What struck me was how many fences and barriers had been brought in. It almost felt like the park was overtaken by steel. The concert was free, but everyone needed a ticket to enter, so it was access-limited. Free ticketed is definitely different from *free* free, where you can wander wherever you want.

So the idea I had was to create an event without barricades, which would allow the music and the natural environment to complement each other. It would take place during the fall, when the leaves were changing colors, and we would utilize all of Central Park.

I love Central Park. It is a magical place, and it's been a constant throughout my life. It is an oasis in the middle of New York City.

It is real. It is dense. It is deep.

When I was younger, I'd play Frisbee there, and many years later, I'd wander around taking calls and figuring stuff out.

I had been involved with the City Parks Foundation through SummerStage, so I pitched Adrian Benepe, the parks commissioner, for a free event in which thirty different bands would perform the same set list in their own styles, at various locations. When I met with him, I brought in a hardcover pitch book that I had made to demonstrate what this would look like. I had taken photos at the different places in the park where I hoped to present music, then photoshopped bands into each setting. I still have that book today.

It's important to come in proper, prepared for this type of meeting. It lets everyone know that you are playing varsity ball. You want to be able to demonstrate to the people on the other side of the table that you'll be attentive, detail-oriented, and can execute.

If you are delivering a presentation, then I recommend practicing whatever it is you're going to say. Ideally, you should do it in front of someone who can provide feedback, but even a run-through out loud by yourself is better than nothing. Don't go in cold. Remember, things get better with each iteration.

The idea for the event was to use the whole park with no tickets, no stages, no fences, no barriers, no boundaries. Live music in every direction. I brought in Brice Rosenbloom, the music director of (Le) Poisson Rouge and founder of Winter Jazzfest, to help with the programming.

My kids were little at the time, so I viewed it as a real-life Choose Your Own Adventure. This was an opportunity to share jazz with younger people, since jazz is typically played late at night in rooms that are twenty-one-plus.

The Gates was also an inspiration. The art installation by Christo and Jeanne-Claude covered twenty-three miles of paths through Central Park in February 2005. I had been there with John Perry Barlow a few days before the official opening. We arrived there at 6:00 a.m., shortly after sunrise. It was snowing lightly, the park was open, and there were no security guards keeping people away so early in the morning, particularly given the weather. The experience was memorable and meaningful to me. For a little while, I contemplated making a 3D film of *The Gates*, but I couldn't pull it together on such short notice. At least I have some footage I shot on my phone of Barlow (RIP) taking a few moments to dance in the park.

Most people know John Perry Barlow as Bob Weir's song-writing collaborator, and many others know him for his work as cofounder of the Electronic Frontier Foundation (EFF), the non-profit that fights for online civil liberties. I will always think of him as the ultimate explorer, someone who was prepared to go deep at a moment's notice, whether through psychedelics or ideas.

After our exploration of *The Gates*, he called me "Sweet Pete," because I had seen him at a party the night before, and although a lot of people promised to stay awake and join him at the opening, I was the only one who had stuck it out. Barlow was an adventurer's adventurer, and I like to learn from the best, so it was a no-brainer for me.

In that same spirit, jumping ahead thirteen years, I had plans to see him in February 2018, when I was visiting San Francisco. A few days earlier, I had texted my plans to him, and he told me, "For you, my amigo, we can make most anything work." This was a promise his family honored even though he died a day before I arrived.

Barlow and I first connected when I interviewed him in 1993 for *And Miles to Go*. We had an immediate connection because I had attended the Skinner Brothers Outdoor Wilderness Camp in his home state of Wyoming. He couldn't believe I'd been there at age twelve, which happened somewhat randomly (and perhaps ill-advisedly in the pre-internet age).

I had met someone in the city who had just returned from Skinner Brothers and informed me that I couldn't handle it. So I sent for the brochure, which somehow failed to mention that all the other campers were sent there to correct behavioral issues. It was a reform camp that culminated with four days in the woods where we were permitted a shotgun, a few matches, and no food. My fishing rod was made out of the hair from my horse. I built my own structure to sleep in, and we had to keep a fire going in shifts. The one indulgence we were permitted was you could have as much salt and pepper as you wanted if you ate squirrel.

I applied my experience with Barlow at *The Gates* to Jazz & Colors, which I saw as an opportunity to release the kinetic energy of a large-format event, where you're breaking the glass of the fourth wall. In this case, you have the music plus the visuals offered by the full-on majesty of the park. *U2 3D* is a version of this concept; so are the walls at the Cap, the four IMAG (image magnification) screens that we originally had at LOCKN', and the scoreboards that we used for video at Fare Thee Well. All these large-format visual presentations complemented and enhanced the live performances. It's great to do intimate shows, and I continue to produce plenty of them, but in the age of phones and people sitting at home in front of computers, there's something to be said for these oversize, experiential events.

Once I had permission from the city, the other major complication was money. Jazz & Colors wasn't sponsor-friendly because sponsors want access. In this case, there was no such thing as a backstage, because there were no stages. Chase helped underwrite the Black Eyed Peas on the Great Lawn because Chase could then leverage the event with tickets (and tiered VIP access) for staff and clients.

That is fine, but it is not what I hoped to achieve with Jazz & Colors. I wanted to create an intimacy between the artists and the audience, whether someone made an effort to seek out a particular performer or was just walking through the park and happened upon these world-class musicians, most of whom were playing with battery-powered amplifiers.

Eventually, since I believed so much in the idea and all it represented, I funded it myself, tapping Brooklyn Bowl as the sponsor. I took the funds out of the marketing budgets for New York, Vegas, and London, and I covered the difference personally (D'oh!). Sometimes, if you really want something to happen, you have to reach into your own pocket. This was also the beginning of my efforts to utilize social media outlets from all my different properties to support an event.

I will say this, though—while there were a lot of moving parts involved with presenting thirty bands in thirty different locations, there was one particularly liberating aspect of putting on a truly free show in Central Park: no guest list!

Sometimes I suspect the one thing that will finally do me in and get me to walk away won't be the challenges of the shows, per se, it will be the handling of the incoming. One of the most time-consuming aspects of my life is dealing with guest list requests. I have multiple shows going on simultaneously, and people hit me up all the time. The problem is that after putting on shows in New

York for over twenty-five years, it turns out I know more people than I know.

In certain respects, technology has made putting on shows easier. That is true for placing tickets on sale and spreading the word to people who might want to attend. When I'm watching a stream at home, I can offer feedback on the lighting when the venue is on the other side of the country. I can also add someone to the guest list while I'm in the corridor of a Phish show or an airport lounge. I can even give one of my venue managers the photo of a special guest who is in the house to offer that person a free drink and tour.

But sometimes I'll think about what it was like for Ron Delsener, who was operating without a cell phone in '67, '77, '87, and '97 (and, yes, even '07). When Ron or even Bill Graham had a megashow, they didn't have to deal with the incoming. No phone calls, no emails, no texts. It's a matter of accessibility.

My wife occasionally asks whether I can delegate this task to an employee, but what am I supposed to do when someone calls or texts me? If they have my number, then they have my number. I just can't ignore them; that would be rude. It's particularly hard with texts. When you send a text, there is an assumption that the person on the other side has read it.

I will admit, though, that I may not have an entirely healthy relationship with my phone. If I have not responded to all my texts or emails, then it is hard for me relax. I typically don't go to sleep at night without clearing the decks (this began in my BlackBerry days, later leading me to purchase a clip-on keyboard for my first iPhone). I can do certain things without looking at my phone, like playing some tennis or a round of golf (well, nine holes), but I cannot last three hours. Frankly, I often can't go twenty minutes. I know that's not necessarily an ideal way to live, but it is the way for me to be the best at what I do.

Thankfully, Jazz & Colors didn't come with guest list distractions, which allowed me to bike through the park and experience all these different bands working from a common set list. The participants included the J. D. Allen Quartet, the Jazz at Lincoln Center All-Stars, the Jason Marshall Quartet with Hilary Gardner, the Yes! Trio, the Doug Wamble Quartet, the Joel Harrison Quintet, and the Klezmatics.

Nate Chinen reviewed the event and really seemed to get what we were doing. He described cornet player Kirk Knuffke performing the song "Skating in Central Park" with his band by the water, while someone sketched him: "It was a moment both delectable and ephemeral, one of the many made possible by Jazz & Colors, which featured 30 groups interpreting the same two sets of standards, at the same time, throughout Central Park. A large-scale performance piece made up of countless small-scale impressions, it was physically impossible to take in as a whole . . . But its overriding success was in creating an atmosphere of festive and serendipitous discovery and making jazz accessible in every sense of the word."

My favorite moment from that first year was ELEW performing solo piano from a standing position on the road near the Jacqueline Kennedy Onassis Reservoir.

We brought it back in 2013, with an additional act from outside formal jazz circles. My friend Eric Krasno had been asking me about doing something with Phil Lesh, and since Phil was on the East Coast, I put that in motion. He has been a friend of Phil's ever since. The two of them were joined by another familiar face from the Wetlands days: Joe Russo.

Ben Ratliff covered it that year for the *Times*, and when it came to Phil's set, he wrote, "Maybe 50 people watched, on a strip just east of the Sheep Meadow called, coincidentally, Dead Road. Among them were a few who weren't holding a Jazz and Colors map, seemed unaware of the event and agnostic about improvised music per se, but who had happened upon a musician they knew and loved, playing through a battery-powered practice amp with his feet on the ground. Their facial expressions came as a series: recognition, shock, bewildered gratitude."

After taking a year off, I transformed the experience in 2015. We moved indoors to the Metropolitan Museum of Art, which hosted "the Masterworks Edition" in January, followed by "the Full Spectrum Edition" in April. Both of those were experiential celebrations in a different way. Later that summer, we moved to Chicago's Field Museum and morphed the concept yet again for Jazz & Colors: Wave That Flag, which featured jazz musicians performing Dead songs throughout the museum.

While Jazz & Colors is a challenge economically, I love it from a creative standpoint. I intend to revisit it again, ideally at a point in the future when I can fund it myself without worrying about revenue. (I wonder what that will feel like . . . probably nice!)

It is an adventure I looking forward to choosing.

31

GARCIA + WEIR = POW!

Furthur
The Capitol Theatre, Port Chester, New York
April 25, 2013

I love multi-night runs.

Along with the music, there's also the experience of seeking out something that's collectively inspiring. I have fond memories of road tripping to San Francisco in April 1999 to see Phil Lesh at the Warfield with Trey Anastasio, Page McConnell, Steve Kimock, and John Molo.

Multi-nighters also make sense for a venue like the Capitol Theatre, where we grow the geographic origins of the audience with each show that we add. One night isn't going to motivate people to travel very far, but for three nights of Dylan at the Cap, we start to get people from Europe.

There are other advantages as well because three shows are far easier on the band and your own staff. On the first day, there is load-in but no load-out. On the second, there is no load-in or -out. Then on the third day, there is only a load-out. That has material impact. It is good for the artist's crew, and it's good for your house crew.

Once you move to multiple nights, the whole thing becomes bigger than itself. It becomes a happening. That is also good for marketing, because if you are going to take out an ad, there is no additional cost to market three nights. Not only that, but it is a more impactful ad at three nights rather than one.

If you are crunching numbers, for a two-night run, it's not $1 + 1 = 2$. It's more like $1 + 1 = 2.4$. Then when you get to three nights, it becomes $1 + 1 + 1 = 3.8$ because you get a bonus bump.

Those are my standard calculations for three shows, but in April 2013, we hosted nine evenings of Furthur at the Cap.

Now that's some high-level math.

It also required some high-level strategery.

In the fall of 2009, Phil Lesh and Bob Weir debuted Furthur, naming the band after the bus that Ken Kesey and the Merry Pranksters painted Day-Glo colors and drove across the country in 1964. Phil and Bob selected John Kadlecik as their guitar player, who at that point was best known for taking on the Jerry role in the Dead tribute band Dark Star Orchestra. Jeff Chimenti, who had been a member of RatDog with Bobby and would later be part of Fare Thee Well, was on keys. The drummer was Joe Russo, who had first met Phil when they played together at the 2005 Jammys, so it was a real victory for the home team (RatDog drummer Jay Lane also was on board for the first six months but then left to tour with Primus).

By the spring of 2013, the Cap had already become the East Coast home for the Dead scene. So we made an aggressive offer and the band decided to play nine nights with us rather than go to Boston, Philly, and DC for one or two nights apiece. As I mentioned, three nights in a row makes things easier on the crew, but once you up that number to nine, life is far sweeter, with everyone based in one place for about two weeks. Plus, there is no need for tour buses, so the economics can be favorable, too.

Port Chester has been supportive of the Capitol and the Deadhead community, although not unanimously, and the relationship has developed over time.

In April 2013, just seven months after we'd reopened for music, nine nights of Furthur was risky. The thing is, you can't do nine nights of Furthur without doing nine nights of Furthur. We would be bringing magic to the Cap, but we would also be bringing the circus to town. That's two weeks of Deadheads who want to camp out and hang out. I understood this, but we were also proud to be part of the scene, which is an event scene. And doing nine nights of the band closest to the Grateful Dead at my venue is why I do what I do.

We were engaged in conversations with the local authorities from the start. One thing we did was to rent the parking lot across the street so that Deadheads would have a place of their own. Then we worked with the police to play zone defense rather than man-to-man. The goal was to keep things contained to protect the safety of everyone—that's an approach I would later take to Chicago for Fare Thee Well.

The village of Port Chester embraced that spirit by closing the nearby MTA train lot, resulting in a spontaneous, near-instantaneous Shakedown. It was a sight to behold.

Another thing we did was to open the doors on the side of the theater during the shows. This enabled the Deadheads who were over in the parking lot to hear the music. We were trying to maintain a welcoming vibe, although there's a trade-off, because when you do that, you're also encouraging people to come and hang out.

For the sake of community issues, we held back some tickets so that we could *sweep the sidewalks*. The idea there is to release additional tickets shortly after the show starts to pull people off the street and into the venue. Now that's got pros and cons, too, because if you do it too much, everybody knows it's coming, and it can increase the number of ticketless fans. But if there are forty or fifty people with fingers in the air, you want to sweep the sidewalks.

What we will often do is wait a few songs into the first set to see what it looks like outside while we assess the situation inside to make sure we won't upset the equilibrium with any additional people. The number varies from show to show and band to band. You want to keep things just below capacity, to the point where it's swelling but not bursting.

It is important to have a feel for how many people have yet to arrive because no-shows can vary due to many factors, such as the weather. In addition, the longer something has been on sale, the higher the no-show rate.

The StubHub listings also can be useful to help gauge demand for a particular show. Our box office manager will monitor these for intel, because if there are a lot of tickets listed for sale and the prices are low, this suggests that the attendance will be less than initially projected.

Of course with any live event, there are some things you just can't anticipate, which is what happened a few hours before the first night of Furthur on April 15.

I was still in the city when I received a call from Scott Raved, our director of operations, around 6:00 p.m. He told me that one of the Port Chester police officers had called a county-wide emergency code and that police were pouring in from all over Westchester. Apparently, this officer was freaked out by the prevalence of Wooks and dogs (I have no idea which of these was more terrifying). I held my breath that we'd make it through, and by the time I arrived, most of the officers had dispersed. Apparently, the Port Chester officer—who no longer works for the force—took some heat for that because although there were plenty of hairy mammals outside the venue, it wasn't an emergency situation.

The final night of the run on April 25 did present what looked to be an emergency situation. This one took place on the stage, though.

Before any of that happened, Trixie Garcia had a special announcement. We had yet to reveal that we were teaming with Jerry's family to create our new venue inside the venue. So we flew Trixie in from the West Coast to share the news about Garcia's.

She made a few remarks before Furthur took the stage, and it felt like a homecoming.

It was a big deal to have Trixie there, and I remember the fans were so excited to meet her. She evokes the spirit of her father. She's gregarious and funny and smiles a lot. People wanted to say hi to her and hug her, and there was a real halo effect.

Perhaps more of a halo effect than we had originally intended.

First off, though, given what was to happen, it's important to acknowledge that Furthur had an incredible run. They played 132 unique songs during the nine sold-out nights. They didn't repeat a single tune during the first six shows, debuted three new covers, and delivered three bust-outs they hadn't performed in a few years, including a version of the Clash's "Train in Vain" with Bobby on lead vocals.

Still, the set list for the final show of the run comes with an asterisk because Bob was led offstage with four songs to go. During the second set, he started teetering a bit, and then he collapsed to the floor at the beginning of "Unbroken Chain." His crew, led by longtime road manager Chris Charucki (who passed away in 2018; RIP, Chris), brought a chair out for him. Bobby remained there through the end of the song before his guys walked him offstage. Footage of the incident found its way onto TMZ the next day.

Here's my take on it . . .

Bobby had been in good form the previous nights, but he was having a shoulder issue. I remember he had been feeling so much pain that he had been playing with a lighter guitar to address this. Eventually, it required surgery.

When he arrived at the venue on April 25, I only saw him briefly, but it looked like he'd had a long night. Maybe he'd been celebrating the run. What I do know, or at least what I've been told, is that at some point before the show, he took an Ambien by accident. It might have even been his second Ambien. If you're looking to remain awake for over four hours in that situation, it's gonna be quite a battle.

I was standing next to Trixie on the side of the stage watching Bobby struggling with the Ambien, trying not to fall asleep. When the footage aired on TMZ, it was easy to view it as a strange, terrible moment. From my vantage point, though, I saw great strength in the way he fought to keep playing and remain standing. Even when he was in the chair, he still had that Bob Weir fight in him.

Once a show is underway, I typically limit myself to issues with the venue itself. If it has to do with talent, it's best to play a supporting role. In this instance, I think I texted Capitol Theatre general manager and all-around venue savant Tom Bailey to ask if he could get more oxygen on the stage. I must have meant fresh air.

Furthur played the inaugural installment of my LOCKN' festival that September in Virginia, but the band ended not too long afterward. Phil needed to go play with some younger guys, including his son Grahame, and teach them the ways of the Dead—he sometimes referred to it as psychedelic Dixieland. Bobby needed to rest and get healthy. He soon found himself in a good headspace. Then in June 2015, the two of them shared a big stage together again at Fare Thee Well.

One more thought about the night: Trixie had flown in to open Garcia's, and there was an energy in the room. We all could feel it, and maybe it was just a bit too strong for Bobby.

I don't really know.

I do know that he had been out late, he was in physical pain, and I think he took the wrong pill. But, maybe the Garcia DNA in proximity to the Weir DNA just kept building and building this reciprocal energy until it all became too much and it knocked him over.

When my time comes and I go upstairs, I plan on seeking out Jerry and asking him if he felt it, too.

32

VIVA LAS VEGAS

The Roots
Brooklyn Bowl, Las Vegas, Nevada
March 14, 2014

I was feeling it.

I had flown across the country on a private jet with The Roots, and while we were in midair, I had a few flashbacks to similar hangs in the Wetlands band room. The vibe was the same, along with some of the jokes, although thankfully the couches on the plane were an upgrade.

When we landed, I lost my bearings for a moment before I realized we were headed to my new venue on the center of the Las Vegas Strip with a police escort to celebrate opening night.

The energy in the room was electrifying.

It was shaping up to be an epic night.

I enjoyed this feeling for approximately eight minutes.

That is when I spotted my friend Jason Strauss, who I have known since high school. He started the TAO, LAVO, and Marquee nightclubs in Las Vegas.

I called out his name and went over to give him a hug.

He smiled, then pulled me aside.

"I want to chat with you," he said. "You do not know how fucked you are. I love you, and I'm saying this because I love you, but you do not know how fucked you are. No one does a venue in Las Vegas that is not in a casino. No one in Vegas raises the money and tries to own the club; you get a casino to pay for it, and you get a management deal. No one does live music; you do DJs who attract bottle service. If you were from Vegas, you never would have done this."

As it turned out, he was slightly wrong but mostly right.

We were in for a battle.

When the original Brooklyn Bowl opened in Williamsburg in July 2009, it crushed from the very start. We hit a cultural zeitgeist or whatever it was that led people to go and keep coming back. It was profitable from the beginning, which is rare for a music venue.

As a result, we were approached almost immediately about opening new Bowls. We received multiple inquiries from Las Vegas, which made sense because part of that environment is about re-creating other places, whether it's Paris or New York. It seems like most everything that works culturally gets reinvented in Vegas. So a number of people came to us, including the Tropicana, New York–New York, and the Cosmopolitan, offering the type of deals that Jason described. None of that appealed to me, because I didn't want to license the name or the concept—that didn't feel right (although Chris White, who was advising the Cosmo, *did* feel right to me and now helps run the Brooklyn Bowl business).

If I were to open a Brooklyn Bowl in Las Vegas, it would need to be the real deal, owned and operated by us, where I could make the creative decisions.

That opportunity came my way in 2012. A developer named Rick Caruso had created the Grove, an outdoor retail/entertainment space in LA. It was successful, and Caesars Palace brought him in to design the LINQ, with a similar open-air model in the center of the strip across from Caesars.

We were offered the opportunity to become the anchor tenant at the LINQ, which was being built on the former tennis courts behind the Flamingo hotel. Caesars was willing to put up a chunk of the money as the landlord, but we would remain the principal owners and decision-makers.

Jim Woods, who was helping me run the business side of things at the time, said, "This is a once-in-a-lifetime opportunity to build your own giant, dream live-music venue on the center of the Strip."

We would be on the fifty-yard line provided we could raise millions of dollars to match Caesars' financial commitment as the landlord.

A week after I was presented with this opportunity, Jim Dolan, the head of Madison Square Garden, came to *Relix* with his band, JD & the Straight Shot, to film a performance for our live music series. If most anyone else was going to meet Jim Dolan, he would say, "Great. Come to my office at Penn Plaza." But in this case, he came to *my* office, because that's where they recorded their session.

Jim had been to Brooklyn Bowl, and I knew he was a fan of Vegas. So I told him that I had an opportunity to do a Brooklyn Bowl in Las Vegas, and he asked to see the plans. I had them right there, so after his performance, I pulled them out and showed him. He looked them over, took a puff off his electronic cigarette, and said, "I'm going to do this. How much do you need?"

I informed him that I needed a lot of money.

He responded without hesitation, "I'm gonna do it. The company has a lot of money."

A few hours later, I sent an email to thank him.

He wrote back and cc'd his president of entertainment to make introductions.

This was an instance in which things were in alignment. If he hadn't come in to *Relix* that day to perform with his band and said, "I'm going to do this," I do not think it would have happened.

Jim agreed that there was room for a stand-alone 2,000-capacity live music venue in the center of Las Vegas. He believed that in the current climate, companies would rather have parties—in the industry, they're called *privates*, and they are a key part of the ecosystem—at Brooklyn Bowl than at some of the high-end restaurants or dance clubs.

One key decision we made was to use the architecture firm already working with Caesars. We were allowed to make our own selection, but it made sense to go with their architects. If something had gone wrong, the people from the LINQ might have said, "That's your fault. Your architect made a mistake. You're paying the overage." On the other hand, if things went sideways, we could always point out, "We picked *your* architect." That came with risk exposure, because we weren't using someone we'd worked with before, but since we were the little guy operating on their turf, it made sense. As it turned out, we never had a problem.

An important change that came late in the process was the addition of a second level. Originally, Brooklyn Bowl Las Vegas was going to be one level with a high ceiling. Caesars did not want a double-decker, but I told them that we would pay for it. In exchange, they agreed not to factor in the additional square footage when determining the base rent.

The thing is, you can't go up if you can't go up.

That second level brought us from fifty-five thousand to eighty thousand square feet. We only need it a dozen times a year, but it makes all the difference. Our ten biggest events carry the business, and we wouldn't have been able to host them without that second floor. So we always have that as an option, but we can also scale things down and shut it off. That way, the room works with 500 people and it works with 2,500 people. But without those big parties, we'd be toast.

We've been able to land those parties thanks to the live music. When it comes to paying the bills in Vegas, you don't make the money on the concerts; however, you don't get the private stuff without the concerts. The way I think about it is the whole cake is the private events, and the concerts are the sprinkles. No one wants the cake without the sprinkles. That's how we've been able to land some big events that otherwise would have taken place at a hotel ballroom. If someone wants to have a concert at a ballroom, they need to bring in the audio and the production. Not us. We're a turnkey operation, with all those elements and incredible food.

That's also true outside of Vegas. The Brooklyn Public Library came to us recently and said, "Mike Bloomberg told us to call you about our gala." Then after we'd hosted it, they said, "We've always had it at the library. By the time we hired the caterer and the production company to put in the sound and the lights, it cost more for us to do our gala event at the library than it did at the Bowl." So we do a lot of that stuff and adjust our prices accordingly for the nonprofits. Then I try to hit the corporates for a little more so they can help underwrite it.

Okay, now let's talk sprinkles.

As I've pointed out, my inspiration for Brooklyn Bowl was late night during Jazz Fest with Galactic. So when I opened up the new venue, I wanted to find out if I could make that New Orleans vibe work in Vegas. But rather than just the spirit of Galactic, this time

I booked the actual band. I didn't think I could test it out with just one night, so I booked twelve nights in late March and early April.

I discovered that it didn't work, at least not during that stage of our existence. As I would soon come to learn, though, we launched in Vegas without the right email list or the right social numbers, so I might give it a go again one day.

In addition to Galactic, I wanted to bring a number of the artists to Vegas who were a big part of the Bowl's success. The initial schedule included a midweek soft launch with Soulive, as well as Karl Denson's Tiny Universe, Robert Randolph & the Family Band, and Phil Lesh & Friends.

For opening weekend, The Roots played three nights, two of them with Elvis Costello.

At this point, The Roots are the home team. On that Friday, they were recording *The Tonight Show*, so I asked Caesars if they could send a plane to pick them up.

Here is a tip—use your asks well. You need to be strategic because you only get so many, and once you do, be prepared for the other side to ask for something in return. It all swings back and forth, and you do not want to go too far out of equilibrium.

In this case, I hadn't asked much of Caesars—plus, I told them I would try to get Jimmy Fallon on the plane. It turned out he couldn't join us, but he did Tweet about it, and that kept Caesars happy.

So on our big opening Friday night, we left Rockefeller Center, headed to Teterboro, flew west, gained three hours, and landed in Vegas around 11:30 p.m., where we received a police escort to Brooklyn Bowl in time for the show.

Now since I mentioned sprinkles, I should probably talk about Sprinkles as well.

Someone else who came out to see the new venue was Jim Dolan.

When Jim walked up to the venue on the LINQ, he saw that our big, beautiful Brooklyn Bowl sign that had cost us six figures was being blocked by a Sprinkles Cupcakes sign.

The developer of the LINQ's friend had opened a Sprinkles Cupcakes shop, and they had blocked our sign.

Jim hollered, "What the fuck is that?"

33

UNBROKEN CHAIN

Phil Lesh & Friends
The Capitol Theatre, Port Chester, New York
April 2, 2014

A few days prior to Phil Lesh's 2019 birthday run at the Cap, that Grateful Dead kismet surfaced once again.

In looking back over his prior appearances at the venue ever since we'd reopened, it turned out that his seventy-ninth show would take place on March 15, the day of his seventy-ninth birthday.

I immediately called Phil and his wife, Jill, to explain what we'd discovered.

Phil started laughing. Then he said, "It's like the rainbow. Keep doing what you're doing."

I responded, "I don't even know how I did this."

Jill added, "Yeah, Phil, how is he going to keep doing that? It just happened."

Phil paused, then said, "Exactly!"

So I have kept my head down and kept doing what I had been doing.

I suppose the idea is to put in the work and let the magic come to you.

That's been true of my relationship with Phil from the start.

We first met on April 26, 2005, at The Jammys. Phil not only hosted the event, he performed in three different collaborative settings. First, he joined Buddy Guy, John Mayer, and Questlove for "I'm a Man," "Stormy Monday," and "Rock Me Baby." A little while later, he appeared with Ryan Adams for "Wharf Rat," which segued into "Bird Song." Finally, he anchored a bass summit with Mike Gordon and Les Claypool, alongside Marco Benevento, Joe Russo, and Gabby La La on "Dee's Diner." In between all of that, he handed out awards and introduced acts. Like everything Phil does, once he commits, he *commits*.

That's certainly true of our relationship. Beyond those seventy-nine shows at the Cap (and the number has continued to increase), he's played just as many at my other venues and events.

Phil first set foot in the Capitol Theatre on March 20, 1970, with the Grateful Dead. He performed three separate runs with the Dead through February 24, 1971. Phil has said, "It was at these February 1971 shows where we premiered several iconic Grateful Dead songs: 'Bertha,' 'Loser,' 'Greatest Story Ever Told,' 'Wharf Rat,' 'Bird Song,' 'Deal,' and 'Playin' in the Band.' It was at that moment that the Capitol Theatre became completely entwined in our history."

I was eager for the venue to be entwined in *his* history as well. While we wanted to book him as close to the opening as we could, at the time, he was focusing a lot of his energy on his own venue, Terrapin Crossroads, which opened earlier that spring. When he finally came east again, we confirmed four nights from November 15 to November 18.

I spoke with Jill that very first night, and I could tell that she felt the same way that I did about the venue. It always helps to be there and breathe it in. This also happens at the Bowl, where occasionally I'll talk to someone who has never been there and can't quite conceptualize how the various elements complement each other: music, bowling, and food. But when they finally set foot in the venue, they'll be like, "Ahh, I get it."

I think that's true of the Cap, particularly when it comes to the full show experience with the visuals on the walls and the ceiling. That's why I believe the best two seats in the house are up in the balcony, two rows from the back, right in the center.

Those first four nights at the Cap left such a positive impression on the Leshes that we went to nine the next time around when Phil appeared with Bob Weir and their Furthur project for that April 2013 run.

The next time Phil played the room prompted an escalation of our relationship. In July, I scheduled Phil & Friends' triumphant return to the Cap for two days after an East Coast Furthur tour. Phil had a great lineup (four mighty Js: John Scofield, John Medeski, Joe Russo, and John Kadlecik), but our shows were on a Monday and Tuesday following all those Furthur dates, which had dented Deadhead budgets. So our tickets sales were steady, but we didn't immediately blow out both nights.

Then Phil announced a concert cruise in Manhattan. However, his Cap shows still hadn't gone clean, and I was unhappy that his performance on the boat would siphon our ticket sales. I explained this to Jonathan Levine, his agent, and shortly afterward, I received a call from Jill.

She was direct and fair, trying to address the situation: "Jonathan says you're not happy."

I told her, "We're doing these big shows and they haven't sold out, but you've gone ahead and announced something else."

In her defense, the show on the Infinity Yacht featured a different lineup from our dates. Rather than Phil Lesh & Friends it was Phil & the Terrapin Family Band (his house band from Terrapin Crossroads, which at the time included both of his sons, Grahame and Brian). Even so, I would have preferred a heads-up and ideally a delayed announcement.

There was nothing we could do about the yacht gig at that point, but we agreed to talk when Phil came to the Cap in July.

That is when Jill and I sat in catering and discussed Phil's future plans.

She explained how much he loved the Cap and that he was comfortable with me. She acknowledged our commitment to top-notch production with the sound and the lights. She also recognized that we were not a local venue; we were a regional one.

Then she informed me, "Phil is getting to a place where he's not going to want to tour as much, and we're looking for a partner."

It all started there.

We eventually agreed upon a forty-five-show exclusive contract for Phil to play the Cap and my other venues. It guaranteed him a set amount of money, and then I got everything else: ticket revenue, merch, and streaming. Jill cut a good, strong deal that required us to blow out every show to make it work, but the thing is, we did blow out every show, so it *did* work. It was a 360 deal akin to the ones that Live Nation signed with Madonna and Jay-Z, with a major difference. The point of those deals was to deliver big up-front payments to the artists, typically half of the grand total. In Phil's case, that would have been a few million dollars, but I didn't have that kind of money available. So they were willing to trust in me and take zero. No deposit, nothing up front. I'll forever be appreciative to Phil and Jill for that.

We signed the deal on Phil's bus at the very first LOCKN' in 2013. My daughter, Roxy, was there as a witness. Not a legal witness, mind you, because she was seven years old, but she observed the proceedings alongside my wife, Rebecca. That was a memorable one for me.

We announced the deal in November just after Phil wrapped up four nights at the Cap. As Phil said at that time, "I'm done with one-nighters. I've been on the road now for forty-six years, and I've gotten to a point where I'm jealous of all the time that I waste on buses and sitting around waiting to go on."

When Phil returned to Port Chester in April 2013, he demonstrated the extent to which he was eager to move past one-nighters, by performing eight shows. Not only that, but following the Cap run, he went to the Brooklyn Academy of Music for two dates. Then it was off to Vegas for three gigs at Brooklyn Bowl. All told, we kicked off the deal with thirteen performances from April 2 to April 20, 2014.

Eight shows might have seemed like a lot, but I think the fact that we'd sold out the nine Furthur dates at the Cap the previous year helped us with the Phil run. Here's a simple lesson I've learned over the course of my career: You can't sell out a show without selling out a show. Once people come to understand that tickets won't be available on the night of the performance, this prompts them to purchase advance tickets. This, in turn, helps fuel the excitement for subsequent announcements and onsales.

In April 2014, we broke the Phil & Friends residency into four-night stands and announced separate lineups for each. This contributed to the anticipation and reminded everyone that something singular and special would happen at every performance. Of course, Phil's penchant for exploration was the key to it all and ultimately the reason that tickets went clean well in advance. Every show felt like an event, which has always been my goal.

When Phil took the stage with John Kadlecik, Larry Campbell, Teresa Williams, Jeff Chimenti, and Joe Russo on April 2, the room was electric. Phil always gives as good as he gets, adding another layer of reciprocal magic to the Cap.

Jill Lesh's faith that we were not just a local venue was borne out during Phil's fall 2015 run. The zip reports (which list the zip codes from credit card charges for advance ticket sales) reflected all forty-eight continental US states.

Port Chester has embraced the relationship as well. Before Phil's 2017 Halloween show, Mayor Luis Marino presented Phil with a ceremonial key to Port Chester. On March 15, 2018, Phil's seventy-eighth birthday, the Port Chester Fire Department named him an honorary member and gave him a custom helmet. The local Hilton has long become known as the Philton because so many Deadheads stay there during the shows.

Phil & Friends' April 2 gig marked another significant milestone in the history of the Cap, as it was the first time we offered livestreams for sale to the public. We'd installed the cameras and editing equipment during construction, but up until that point, we'd only used the video to allow people to watch the music from various spots inside the theater, including the dressing rooms and catering as well as the bars and Garcia's (initially, we'd installed only four robotic cameras, although we now have over a dozen). I had been thinking about the potential for webcasts from the moment I took over the Cap, but it was my contract with the Leshes granting me streaming rights that finally made it happen.

I had my video director in place, as Jonathan Healey, who first worked with me at The Jammys and then on the Wetlands film, had been part of the Cap team from the outset. The system allowed him to cut the video live while watching the feed through multiple monitor views.

I had no distribution platform of my own at the time to deliver the streams. It didn't seem like it was worth the energy and expense to create (COVID would eventually lead me to reconsider this assessment). So I teamed with Brad Serling and Nugs .net on the tech side, offering individual shows, as well as passes for multiple nights.

We announced this after the Phil & Friends run had sold out, but even so, some folks advised me that the webcasts would diminish interest in future ticket sales because people would stay home and watch the streams. I disagreed. As a live music fan myself, I understood that the in-person live experience is unique and unparalleled. This is all the more so with an artist like Phil Lesh, who is feeding off the audience and creating in the moment. I suspected that if anything, the webcasts would build the reputation of Phil's Cap residencies because people could witness the magic coming off the stage as well as the full immersive environment with projections on the walls and ceilings. That's precisely how it played out in the end.

Once we started webcasting, it also gave me a new way to add my own touch from afar. If I can't be at a given performance, I'll often check out the stream and text my feedback. If I see something on the wall I really like, I'll take a screenshot and send that to the person responsible for the projections. Then they'll bring back that look later in the show.

Of course, most of the time when Phil was at the Capitol, I made sure I was there. I have really enjoyed building our relationship and watching the music that's at the heart of it. After we completed the original deal, we extended it informally, at times calling an audible to land on terms that felt fair to all of us.

We've now done over two hundred shows together as part of a deal that was going to be forty-five, spanning five thousand miles, from London to Nashville to Las Vegas.

On November 1, 2018, I joined Phil onstage to deliver the "donor rap." Back in December 1998, after living with hepatitis C for many years, Phil received the liver of a young man named Cody in an operation at the Mayo Clinic in Jacksonville. Every night prior to the encore, Phil honors Cody and encourages everyone to become an organ donor. I took the stage with him that evening to make the speech because it was my first Phil show since I had corneal transplant surgery to correct my eye disease, keratoconus. It was a powerful moment for me and intensified my connection with Phil.

At one point, we even discussed advancing our relationship so that I would take on a role at Terrapin Crossroads. I loved what they had done there, including their outdoor expansion. However, the pandemic forced me to step back and rethink my involvement due to the challenges of air travel and commitments to my family and my existing venues.

It was actually the second time I had to say no to Phil due to COVID.

We had scheduled a very special three-night run from March 13 to 15, 2020. The third night was to culminate in Phil's eightieth birthday. We billed it as a "surprise birthday party," although the surprise was somewhat in reverse. Rather than Phil being unaware, the audience would remain in the dark regarding the identity of Phil's Friends until the musicians walked onstage.

I had been planning it for about a year, and it was going to be quite a mix of collaborators old and new. However, by March 11, I no longer felt comfortable putting on the shows. Phil was already in the city, and he's always a gamer, so he wanted to see it happen. However, there had been a spike of COVID cases in New Rochelle, and I didn't want to put anyone's health at risk, least of all the birthday boy's.

I want to credit Stef May, our marketing director and one of Phil's biggest fans, who always has her finger on the pulse of our community.

The Capitol Theatre community is vast. Stef is responsible for creating the Squirrel Squad, our street team. She created the Cap Cares program, in which music fans can donate time to charitable projects and earn free concert tickets in exchange for their hard work. We also have ninety volunteer ushers who help out with the shows.

Stef let me know that folks were getting nervous about the potential impact of COVID.

So on March 11, we postponed the shows until the summer (and then eventually the fall . . . of the following year).

All in good time.

It is an honor to have Phil play the Capitol, whatever the date.

34

THE FARAWAY END OF
THE FAR AWAY

Ms. Lauryn Hill
Brooklyn Bowl London, London, UK
September 28, 2014

There is a certain amount of pressure that comes with being a live music entrepreneur. It is not only making sure that I can keep the lights on and continue to support my employees. I also feel a responsibility to explore whatever is next, which is why I think I became an entrepreneur in the first place.

That does not always mean big projects; it also refers to individual shows. During the day, I am blocking and tackling, dealing with administrative matters, logistics, and the like. Finally, at night, some of the space in my head is cleared out so I can brainstorm. That's when I allow myself to get creative rather than just handling whatever comes flying at me.

I don't watch too much TV because I don't have brain space to follow it when I have so much else to figure out.

When I was on Eric Krasno's podcast, he reminded me of something that I had once said to him: "When some people get home, they turn on Netflix. My Netflix is my head, staring at the ceiling and thinking through all the amazing things I'd like to do."

I do not get to read as many books as I would like to, either, although I look forward to the day when I can ease up on the throttle and kick back with a *Billions* marathon or dig into something by Doris Kearns Goodwin.

This does not mean I do not read, though. I am reading all day; I'm just not really reading books, but I am consuming information, mostly from the major news and entertainment outlets. That's essential for me to be able to play at the level I'm playing.

In this age, you need to be aware of business, media, tech, politics, sports, and contemporary happenings in general. I am not learned in the sense that I don't know a lot about the Greek philosophers or the Spanish-American War, but I have a pretty strong sense of what's going on in the world right now. That's important when I speak with all the different people I communicate with on a daily basis. I suppose this can be exhausting, but it doesn't feel that way until the end of the evening, when my eyes sometimes get tired (all the hours I spend walking around reading on my phone probably does not help).

Another live music entrepreneur once told me, "Sometimes I would rather stay home and break even." I understand the sentiment, but when you own the venues, you have got to fill the rooms. A big boat needs gas, which means I cannot stop putting on shows, so that my team can remain busy.

I am not someone who likes to sit on his hands. The impulse is to keep pushing and trying something new. I get a real buzz from that.

When it comes to economics, it is not always best to be first. It can offer adrenaline and excitement—you're on the moon! But it is also harder, because then you look around and realize that not everyone has caught up with you yet.

What a ride, though. Plus, you are on the moon!

I experienced some of that during the process of expanding Brooklyn Bowl to London.

Around the same time I was approached about Brooklyn Bowl Vegas, I received an opportunity to create a London Bowl out by the O2 arena in Greenwich.

I had a few misgivings because the location was somewhat desolate. People weren't heading out there unless they were otherwise headed to the O2. I would have preferred to be someplace like Camden or Shoreditch, which are more active, vibrant neighborhoods akin to where we now are in Williamsburg (Brooklyn), Germantown (Nashville), and Fishtown (Philadelphia). The problem is that there wasn't available real estate to create a thirty-thousand-square-foot venue in those areas; plus, the politics makes it challenging to get approval from the borough councils, which is why most London venues are so old.

However, I was made two promises that made me feel better about the situation: (1) there was going to be a twenty-four-hour train running out to the area, and (2) they were building other businesses out there so that we were going to be in the middle of the O2 entertainment district, a bustling area with shops and restaurants.

We opened in January 2014, and the venue *felt* like Brooklyn Bowl. However, there was no twenty-four-hour train. Also, the construction of the entertainment district stopped with us. This meant we were at the end of the O2, which was already at the end of the borough next to the river Thames. So on a Saturday afternoon at 5:00 p.m., a time when a Bowl should be bustling with walk-ups, we weren't getting much business.

I don't believe that AEG was malicious about anything; it's just that things got delayed, which had a material impact on how we were able to do business.

The lack of a late-night train hurt us because running the Bowl is expensive. To break even, we basically need to crush. The way we're able to crush in New York is we'll do a late show every weekend. A late show gives you two at bats, something we never had at Wetlands but has been instrumental to the Bowl's successful financial model. However, that wasn't an option in London.

Another thing I quickly realized is that all my neighbors at the O2 were associated with larger UK companies that enabled them to share resources. Some belonged to a restaurant group, and others were part of a chain, whether it was Nando's, TGI Fridays, or whatever. Scale is important so you can share HR and marketing expenses. It's all the more true in the UK, where there's a 20 percent sales tax (VAT) paid directly to the government by the seller.

One final complication was that our relationship with AEG changed. After my deal closed, they sold half the real estate around the O2 to a private equity firm. So they weren't as motivated to get involved and potentially change the lease terms. Still, AEG had paid for most of our construction costs, and the delay in late-night train service wasn't their fault, so I'm not looking to give them too much grief.

During my London experience, I also learned that the UK's live music industry operates differently from the US's. It's an open system where artists can play in any venue and work with any promoter. In New York, if you're a band doing shows with Bowery Presents or Live Nation, you only appear in their venues. It's a closed system. But in London, the venues are not exclusive to a given promoter. In fact, during the three years that Brooklyn Bowl was there, I'm pretty sure Live Nation did more shows at the O2 than AEG, even though AEG owned the arena. That was true of the smaller venues as well. If artists, promoters, and venues in the UK were more closely aligned like in the US, then perhaps AEG could have directed more bands to play the London Bowl.

On a related note, unlike the United States, where companies like Ticketmaster strike exclusivity deals with venues, in the UK, there's an open distribution system. The clubs sell tickets through multiple ticketing agents, and they are not allowed to sign contracts with a single partner. In the US, when ticketing companies strike exclusivity deals, they typically provide signing bonuses and advance funds against future sales (it's how I was able to get seed money for my Garcia's jazz room in Chicago). If we had been able to pursue this in London, it would have given us more cash on hand so we could ride things out while we were building awareness.

Our opening run on January 16–18, 2014, featured three nights of what we dubbed the Brooklyn Bowl All-Stars. We drew together members of Antibalas, Lettuce, and Soulive. I always try to kick things off at a new venue with the home team.

The goal from the start was to bring the Brooklyn Bowl *vibe* to London, not just bring Brooklyn Bowl to London. In July 2014, Phil Lesh & the Terrapin Family Band played two dates, and Grahame Lesh proposed to his longtime girlfriend, Claire. Gov't Mule, Umphrey's McGee, Galactic, and the Preservation Hall Jazz Band all made early appearances.

We also had shows from Lady Antebellum, Pharrell Williams, Conor Maynard, Fun Lovin' Criminals, We Are Scientists, and Dinosaur Jr.

What we didn't have was walk-up. This is why we eventually shut the doors in January 2017, after three years of operations. It is hard to build momentum once you don't have any.

We still experienced a fair number of evenings that popped where it felt like Brooklyn Bowl. One of the memorable shows was with Ms. Lauryn Hill, who's one of the most powerful live performers I've ever seen. She is a really detail-oriented person and a band leader in the classic James Brown mold.

One thing that's notable about her shows is I've seen grandparents and their grandchildren, both backstage and in the audience. It feels like a family reunion.

She is also open to new creative ideas. A lot of artists come into the Cap and ask us to turn off the projections on the walls. They'll say, "That's cool, but I have my own show." You might think Lauryn would have said that, but instead, she asked us to turn it all up.

At the end of the night in London, I felt proud because she doesn't suffer fools gladly. She was particular with sound, lights, and all the production specs, but there was nothing arbitrary about her requirements. We delivered, she delivered, and the audience responded.

She's an amazing artist in her right, but I should acknowledge that I'm also a fan of the Fugees. In late 2015, following Fare Thee Well, I began speaking with Wyclef about a reunion. He's another incredible performer, whose shows touch on the Fugees material along with so much more, including the songs he's written for people like Shakira. He's also able to freestyle and improvise in a way that aligns with the jam music that I love. He stopped by the *Relix* office and later invited me to his house in New Jersey as we discussed the Fugees, but it just wasn't the right time (that would have to wait until September 2021 when they played seven songs at New York's Pier 17 in partnership with Global Citizen Live). Still, he's performed tremendous shows at the Capitol, Bowl New York, and Bowl Vegas.

As for Bowl London, our nights with Ms. Lauryn Hill had all the right energy and demonstrated what the venue could be.

Unfortunately, not every night was like that.

I discovered that the audiences in England approach their live music differently. People like to drink, but they don't necessarily like to party. Before a show on a big night out, friends might meet at the pub after work, then have a few pints and come to the venue. Once they're there, they will have a few more pints, but they don't like to do tequila shots. They're a bit sedater than in America, sipping their beer rather than cutting loose.

Aside from the shows, I had the travel dialed in. I would fly from New York to London on the red-eye. So I'd leave at 10:00 p.m. on a Thursday and land on Friday morning. Then I'd do all day Friday and leave on Saturday night at 7:00 p.m. for Vegas. I would land at 9:00 p.m. because it is a ten-hour flight, but you gain eight hours. Then I would spend Saturday night and all day Sunday in Vegas before getting on the midnight red-eye back to New York. I was home on Monday morning to take my kids to school. That might seem like a lot, but it's doable because I did it.

What I could not do, unfortunately, was make Brooklyn Bowl London work given all the challenges.

Ultimately, we were just too far away from everything. We were at the faraway end of the far away.

35

THE MORE I PRACTICE, THE LUCKIER I GET

Robert Plant and the Sensational Space Shifters
Brooklyn Bowl, Brooklyn, New York
October 9, 2014

To succeed in the concert business (and pretty much any business), you cannot stand idle.

There's a quote I really like: "The more I practice, the luckier I get."

That has been true for my career.

You have to put in the ten thousand hours—or in my case, ten thousand shows—which then places you in a position to get lucky.

Some of it is about persistence. I think back to *And Miles to Go* when I was relentlessly trying to land additional interviews. That approach has continued in all my ventures, from Wetlands through *All Access*, The Jammys, and on to the present, when it comes to booking an artist.

You also need to develop field vision so you are aware of far more than what is directly in front of you.

This is how I was able to convince Robert Plant to perform a midnight show at Brooklyn Bowl on October 9, 2014.

That and a brown bag containing $50,000 in cash.

In September 2014, Robert embarked on a seven-date North American tour to support his new album, *lullaby and . . . The Ceaseless Roar*. He opened at the Capitol Theatre on September 25, but prior to that performance, he also rehearsed at the venue for a few days. The Cap is conducive to this given the size of the stage, the sound in the room, the vibe of the space, and the location of the theater (it's relatively easy to get here without becoming ensnarled in NYC traffic).

During a break in Robert's rehearsal, I walked up to him and introduced myself. He's got a very electric personality, and he's curious by nature: "Tell me about you. Who are you?" We became comfortable with each other after a few interactions.

In the process of hanging out, I learned through his publicist Ken Weinstein that after their tour concluded on October 7, they were going to fly back to New York for a performance on *The Late Show with Stephen Colbert*. I also discovered that rather than staying in Manhattan, they would be at the Wythe Hotel, which is across the street from Brooklyn Bowl.

So I decided to get him to play a midnight show on the night of *Colbert*. The logistics would be quite easy, given where they were staying. I'd offer him $100,000, which might be less than his normal fee, but it's good money for a last-minute club show.

I already had an act booked on the night of October 9, but in a case like this, I can usually work it out. I offer to pay the band their full fee and then allow them to watch the show from the lanes. I say, "I owe you one," and I take that pledge very seriously.

The next step was to make an offer to Robert.

Rather than go through his agent, I decided to do so directly.

B. B. King once said to me, "If you really want something, you bring cash."

So I went to the bank and withdrew $50,000 from the Capitol Theatre's account. It was five wraps of hundred-dollar bills, with one hundred bills in each wrap. They were each about an inch thick, maybe slightly less.

I placed the money in a paper bag, then I went over to the Cap and found Robert in his dressing room.

I said to him, "Here's a fifty-thousand-dollar deposit for you to play a midnight show at Brooklyn Bowl on the night you play *Colbert*. Your full honorarium will be a hundred grand. It will help with your hotel bill."

I like using that term, *honorarium*.

Then I handed the bag to him, and he looked inside.

"Is there any paperwork?" he asked.

"Nope."

He handed the bag to his tour manager, we shook hands, and it was on.

The band that originally scheduled to perform that night was happy to make a deal so that Robert and the Sensational Space Shifters could crush it at the Bowl. We also comped them a lane for the night.

I enjoy Robert's company, and he has incredible presence both on and off the stage. So it felt great to plan that out and then see it come to pass.

Things don't always work out, though, even when you *have* set yourself up for success.

In 2015, I did two nights of Robert and the Sensational Space Shifters at LOCKN'. They don't typically get hired for two shows at a festival. But aside from the fact that he's an incredible artist, I also figured I'd have some hang time with him after the first night.

I was trying to put myself in a position to get lucky, and what I had in mind was a moon shot. I wanted to make my pitch for a reunion of the mighty Led Zeppelin. This was two months after Fare Thee Well, and I figured I'd go for another epic event.

As it turned out, Robert did hang out with us at LOCKN', so my instincts were correct. However, there were so many other people around, the proper moment didn't present itself. This was okay because I knew I had one more chance a few days later, since I'd also booked him at the Cap.

Even though I may be the only guy to ever book a double with Robert Plant and the Sensational Space Shifters at a festival, he made the most of it. We made a gentle suggestion that people would love to see two different sets, and that's pretty much what happened. He played "Black Dog" on both Saturday and Sunday (no one quibbled), and he also did two versions of "Little Maggie" and "Rainbow" from his new album. Plus, I thought that worlds might well collide when I tried to pair him with Bob Weir during the Saturday show. Unfortunately, we all weren't quite in alignment. Maybe next time around.

We had another near miss on Saturday just prior to dusk during "Rainbow." This was months after Fare Thee Well, and all this rainbow talk was still going on. We see a fair share of rainbows at LOCKN', and toward the end of the song, I started to feel it. There was moisture in the air, and I thought we were going to pull a full-on freaking rainbow during "Rainbow." I looked out on the horizon, thinking, *It could pull, it could pull* . . . We didn't quite get there, but it would have been ridiculous.

Five days after LOCKN', Robert was standing next to me in my office cave at the Cap. It is a special room designed just for me, and I have Ray Dalio to thank for it. The venue had been open about eighteen months, and Ray was coming out to a show one night when he asked, "Peter, you've got a room we can hang out in, right?" The sad truth was I did not. We had multiple band rooms and a catering room but nothing of my own. The obvious is obvious until you miss it.

So I called Scott Raved, who helmed the renovation of the theater, and I said, "I think we forgot something when we did all that work on the Capitol. We forgot to build a room for me to hang out in!"

We remedied this shortly afterward, creating a sweet space where I could hang with musicians, managers, agents, and other folks, before, during, and after the shows. We have a direct feed from the soundboard, some cool lighting, a fish tank, Twizzlers, and a lot of gummy bears—all of which provides a great opportunity for human interaction in the age of phones.

In 2018, I booked Cheech and Chong for two shows on 4/20 at the Capitol, scheduling both early and late performances. This meant the two of them would be around to join me for some hang time in my cave. It was another one of those moments when it felt like I was inside a movie.

Three years earlier, I had a memorable interaction with Robert Plant in the very same spot. We were standing there looking at fish and talking about life. I knew he did not want to hear about Led Zeppelin. I knew that even mentioning it could put our relationship in jeopardy, but just like Fred Flintstone has that little guy buzzing in his ear, I started having a conversation with a little guy buzzing in my own ear. I was having two simultaneous discussions: one *with* Robert in real life and one *about* Robert in my head. I was standing there talking with him while also debating with myself about whether or not to mention Zeppelin.

Eventually, I decided to go for it, but it just was not there. I backed off because I did not want to jeopardize my relationship with Robert. Sometimes you get it, and sometimes you don't.

Over the years, I have found that I cannot get an artist excited without sharing my own excitement. But it's important to moderate that feeling and convey it without going overboard. You have to know when to pull back. Even getting a no with the right tone is important so that you don't go backward. You may not have gone forward, but you need to be able to stay neutral.

Phil Lesh didn't feel a need to do Fare Thee Well. He believed it was time to start educating younger musicians about the ways of the Dead, and he enjoyed doing that. However, I knew what it would mean to so many people, which is why I kept my foot down on the gas.

When I was alone with Robert, although I had my idea for how to do a Zeppelin reunion, I was prepared to ease off the pedal pretty quickly. I said to him, "You do it as one show so you can put it to rest." That's what Fare Thee Well would be for Phil. I told Robert that this way whenever he did an interview about new music, he would not have to answer the inevitable question about the Zeppelin reunion. I went with the angle of "Do it to end it."

I tried, but it wasn't there.

At least I got the chance.

Hanging out with Robert Plant and shooting the shit in my cave was pretty satisfying in its own right.

Even if I didn't pull it off, I still enjoyed the practice and look forward to getting lucky when I try again.

Sorry, Robert, but I'm probably coming at you one more time . . .

36

DOUBLING DOWN

NetApp Private Party
Brooklyn Bowl, Las Vegas, Nevada
May 13, 2015

In late June 1994, I traveled to Las Vegas for three Grateful Dead shows at Sam Boyd Stadium.

An enduring memory of those shows (beyond a red ant attack) was watching Deadheads in action on the Strip. There were drum circles on Las Vegas Boulevard, and Circus Circus was transformed into Shakedown Street, now that the actual circus had come to town. It was a different era, but Vegas was cray cray then, and it's still cray cray now.

Before I explain the quiet role the city played in Fare Thee Well, let me get to the red ant story. I was standing outside Sam Boyd Stadium wearing sandals when I was bitten by a fire ant on my foot and had a severe allergic reaction. My entire body started tingling, and when I began experiencing discomfort in my arm from the bite on my foot, I knew I was in trouble. Thankfully, Rock Med was at the shows, and given my familiarity with a Grateful Dead parking lot, I knew exactly where they were located. This became important because I was starting to feel woozy. As it turned out, I needed to go to the hospital, where I received a couple of shots of histamine. A few hours later, I was fine.

I never had another experience like that until Outside Lands 2019 at Golden Gate Park, when a wasp flew inside my sunglasses. As I reached in to remove it, the wasp stung me. I had an immediate reaction, and my eye swelled shut. I was there with Becca, who walked me over to Rock Med, and they were my saviors again.

A quick PSA: Since I have discovered that I am prone to allergic reactions, I carry a couple of Benadryl pills in my wallet as a matter of practice. If you're like me, I recommend that you do the same.

Las Vegas also had a hand in the making of Fare Thee Well.

By late October 2014, I had begun discussions with the Grateful Dead guys about coming back together one more time to celebrate their fiftieth anniversary. Finding a suitable guitar player with Jerry's otherworldly skill set, temperament, and passion, as well as the ability to navigate the internal politics of the band members, led me to one man: Ernest Joseph Anastasio III. And over Halloween weekend 2014, I knew where to find him.

Most importantly, I knew where to find his manager. That was the proper way to approach this. There are instances where one can run an idea past an artist, at least to gauge interest. (I may have done this once before with Trey, although I can neither confirm nor deny.) But this was of such magnitude that I went directly to Coran Capshaw, who has been managing Trey ever since 2005.

My relationship with Coran goes back to Agents of Good Roots at Wetlands. We have continued to do business together as he has expanded his company, Red Light, and I knew he would give me a clear read on the situation. Since he is a former Deadhead (although all former Deadheads are current Deadheads), I also suspected he would see the long-term positive impact of what I had in mind. In general, I find it is always easier if someone is a Head because they usually get it.

So I let Coran know that I wanted to chat with him, and he invited me to stop by at set break during the Phish show at the MGM Grand on November 1, 2014. This was the second night of their run after they had performed an amazing multisensory interpretation on Halloween of the 1964 Disney album *Chilling, Thrilling Sounds of the Haunted House*.

We had a conversation in a side corridor and I laid it all out for him. I explained what I had in the works and that Trey would be the ideal person for the lead guitar role. I emphasized the creative contributions Trey could make and the Dead guys' deep regard for him.

I told Coran that I thought this was a legacy moment all around. It would help Phish as well, because if Trey took on the Jerry role, he would put so much thought and passion into it that he would win over skeptical Deadheads who weren't yet sold on Phish.

Coran seemed positive about it (at least based on the nodding of his head) but did not make a commitment. He told me to be patient. Although I am not necessarily a patient person by nature, I have been getting better at it over the years, and I can certainly appreciate how it is often the smart thing to do.

Set and setting are important. It is often about presenting an idea in the right moment. Managers know their clients the best and can be important allies if they believe in what you have to offer. I once approached a manager with a major ask for one of his clients, and he told me it was going to take a little while to receive a response. He added, "If you want a no, I can get you a no right now."

While it seemed like Coran was on board conceptually, nothing was guaranteed. However, Phish tour manager Richard Glasgow, who witnessed our conversation, must have felt that luck was on my side. He grabbed his phone and took a photo capturing the moment just after I said to Coran, "Trey will crush this . . ."

Then I was back into the arena to rock out for the second set and on to the Bowl for the aftershows. Back and forth, it's all one life to me.

That year, we started a tradition that we've repeated each time Phish has played Vegas on Halloween. Working with our team at *Relix*, we have built a number of events around the run. These have included late-night shows, a poster and pin exhibition (in conjunction with PhanArt), a bowling tournament with a charitable beneficiary as well as a special "Lunch You in the Eye" menu, renaming our items with Phish themes, including Halley's Hummus, BLTela, and the Wedge Salad (okay, that last one was a layup).

While our Vegas bookings have included many hip-hop and indie rock acts, I am proud to have created a home for jam/improv music in the center of the Strip. It wasn't easy for the scene to find a place in town because casinos aren't very interested in those audiences who prioritize music over gambling. Building a stage in Vegas was also a powerful way to support all the artists who have been such a major part of our success elsewhere. Plus, I always try to book shows that I want to see.

Another thing about the post-Phish shows at the Bowl in Vegas is there's a vibe that I don't think you would be able to get in a casino. We have this large outdoor area—which is key; most venues don't have that, particularly in Vegas—and it feels a bit like Wook Alley at Bonnaroo. It's like you're in the back of the camping area, where the weird shit is going on . . . except it's on the Strip in Vegas. The Capitol Theatre has an area behind the orchestra that turns into Wook Alley as well. Whether you're in Vegas or Port Chester, Wook Alley feels good.

In 2014, we blew out all our Halloween shows, and the Bowl was hopping throughout the weekend. I imagine that most people believed that the venue was an unqualified financial success.

The reality was slightly different.

Our biggest challenge was that we weren't getting the privates. We faced a struggle because we hadn't established ourselves as a go-to destination for such events, which often pay the bills for a venue like the Bowl. If you are running events for Cisco, Bridgestone, or Twitter and your CEO is flying in, you will want to return to wherever you did it last time, assuming it went well. If you pick a new place and it doesn't work out, someone will ask, "Whose idea was this?"

It's the same reason why film executives book Tom Hanks, Scarlett Johansson, and Dwayne Johnson as often as they do. If you spend $20 million to hire Dwayne Johnson but the movie tanks, you won't get fired. If you hire a new person for $1 million but the movie fails, you're fired.

So people were going back to Bellagio. They were going to Cosmo. No one was taking a chance on the new place.

That increasingly became an issue because our rent was massive. Caesars was recouping the millions of dollars that they had contributed toward our construction. Although they hadn't taken equity, they used a high rent to give them a good return on their investment.

I did receive one important piece of advice from Tariq Shaukat, the chief marketing officer at Caesars. He explained that it was important to win Best Venue in *Las Vegas Weekly*'s Reader's Choice

Awards, because you can leverage that with the people who are booking private events (it helps with agents and managers, too). They want to partner with venues that are well-known and have good reputations.

When Bowl Vegas opened, we didn't have any awards. We also didn't have a robust opt-in email list. Actually, we started at zero. I have come to realize that for a successful midsize live music venue, you need an opt-in email list of about one hundred thousand. We've since exceeded that in Vegas, and we've long had those numbers in Brooklyn and at the Capitol. But it takes years.

The key to launching a new venue is the initial lineup. The lineup is your marketing. It gets people talking and creates awareness within the music community. I even included an artist on our opening lineup ad mat who said that they would play a show but the date remained flexible. Our initial announcement spanned from March to August and included The Roots with Elvis Costello, Chance the Rapper, Jane's Addiction, the 1975, the Avett Brothers, Steve Winwood, Primus, the Tedeschi Trucks Band, the String Cheese Incident, Trombone Shorty, Lettuce, and Phil Lesh & Friends.

We had a great lineup, but it became a struggle to reach potential audience members because we did not have an email list or social followers. In August, we did three nights with the Avett Brothers, who are an arena band in many parts of the country, and we struggled to pull in a thousand paid a night. In that situation, you'd better make sure that the band has a great time because otherwise your venue won't be around long. You need the musicians to report back to HQ (a.k.a. their managers and agents) that your place is awesome.

If we had not initially confirmed so many shows, we would have been dead. With each new show announcement and onsale, we continued to grow our lists. It was a struggle, but we were laboring to launch a big ship.

Unfortunately, as I would discover, this can be particularly challenging if your ship is the *Titanic*. And at eighty thousand square feet, that is basically what we had built.

We were not getting the residencies from the major acts because we could not compete financially with the casinos. They had the ability to top our offers every time, because audience members would not only eat and drink, they'd also go to the tables and give the casinos some more money.

By the time I visited Coran to talk about Trey, Bowl Vegas was hemorrhaging money. So while I was excited about reuniting my favorite band at GD50, I was also feeling the heat. We had no privates and too much overhead.

In the middle of all of this, shortly before we opened, Madison Square Garden hired a new CEO, who had not been part of the original deal. He hadn't approved the funds to develop Bowl Vegas, but the money we were draining was now on his P&L.

So there was a cash call in early 2015 when the new CEO asked, "When do you need more money?"

"Tomorrow," I said.

"We are out," he responded. "You can have the place."

We made a handshake deal that would enable me to give them back a portion of their original investment, and they would give up their ownership, along with their responsibility to cover any future losses.

But nothing was formalized, and before we could come to an agreement, I heard from the senior executive at Apollo, the private equity firm that owned Caesars. Most of their development deals had been with publicly traded companies or entities with fifty to one-hundred-plus retail locations. Since I had been a little guy with one New York venue, I guaranteed the lease in Vegas with the Bowl in New York.

A battle then commenced. We were a couple of weeks past my informal agreement with MSG, and I still hadn't cut them a single check. Meanwhile, Jim Dolan remained pissed about the Sprinkles sign, and his team wanted to wash their hands of the place. So they began pushing for a Chapter 7 bankruptcy, also known as a liquidation bankruptcy. They had no interest in a reorganization, and Jim said to me, "I am sorry, Peter. I helped you, but these are my guys."

At the same time, Apollo told me that since we had not paid the rent, they were going to go to court and take over the Bowl. I had a meeting at Apollo on a Monday, where they explained, "We could take the New York Bowl because you haven't paid rent. But we are not going to do that. We are going to take Vegas, you are going to give us a free license to the name, and you're going to help book it for us."

The Apollo team pointed out, "If you go bankrupt, everyone will know it. It'll be in the newspapers. Your reputation will be muddied. This way, no one will know it didn't really work, and you can still have New York."

I think they genuinely felt like they were doing me a solid.

To my mind, though, they were saying, "You can keep your first child and you can raise your second child, but that one is going to be ours. And that is because we like you."

I'll never forget getting a foot massage at a walk-up nail salon spot on Twentieth Street and Seventh Avenue when an email with the subject line "Sorry Pete" arrived.

This was May 6, 2015. I still have the email.

I think it's worth pausing here to point out that during this time, not only was I still operating in Brooklyn, in London, and the Cap, but I was deep in preparations for Fare Thee Well. On December 11, 2014, when Trey was performing at the Beacon, Richard Glasgow shared some good news. Trey was in.

Fare Thee Well issues were surfacing each day while I was also trying to avoid bankruptcy in Vegas. I find that getting a foot or head massage helps me deal with high stress. It's a good way to face a battle, although my stomach dropped when I read the subject line. I jumped out of the massage chair and headed to the street, where I could pace. Then I called Apollo to beg for time and mercy.

It was all on the edge for a minute, probably a bit over the edge, but I managed to keep it from the abyss. That's the key, really, because once you are back from the abyss and have time for *strategery*, anything can happen.

Strategery is what I call it when I'm methodically considering the steps ahead, thinking and then rethinking how it's all going to work. It's also about getting feedback from your trusted advisers and making extra time to factor that into your decision-making process. Strategery is painstaking, slow going, and essential.

Meanwhile, there was a battle brewing between these billion-aires over the fate of Brooklyn Bowl Las Vegas. Was Caesars going to take over the space, or were we going to go bankrupt first?

What ended up happening was that my investor put me in touch with a bankruptcy adviser. I had the honor of becoming the first client of M3 Partners, which has become one of America's leading bankruptcy advisory firms. They drew up an eighty-page document and made sure I signed it, because everyone was a little worried that I would run away.

Then M3 told me that there was no looking back. I could not take on any future liabilities at Bowl Vegas. I could not call my dad, have him book a birthday party, and give me a deposit. I could not put money down on my credit card like I had done at Wetlands. I could not ask anyone else for money, because the last money in would be the first money out when they sold all the parts of the Bowl. It was over. Or so I was told.

Earlier that same day, I received a call from the general manager of Bowl Vegas, Chris White, who informed me, "We just got a delivery from Caesars. It's a box full of credit card machines. They say *Brooklyn Bowl*, but they are Caesars' machines. Do you know about this?" Meanwhile, the IT guys from Caesars were in the venue checking out the wiring. And we heard that Caesars was preparing a job fair to restaff the venue. The word was out. We were fucked.

I later received another call from Chris with an update regarding a company party we had previously booked. This was going to be our first major party, with a company called NetApp. They had contacted our events team that day because they wanted to ramp it up. It wouldn't be 800 people, it would be 1,800. Rather than just wine and beer, they wanted a top-shelf open bar. They also wanted to add food. All of a sudden, the party budget tripled, and it was the following week.

We had already booked the NetApp private, which meant this wasn't a future liability, and we were allowed to move forward with the event.

I said to Chris, "Tell them they need to send all of the money tomorrow."

He didn't think that he would be able to get 100 percent of it. He thought that 25 percent was a lock and that 50 percent might be feasible, but I pushed him to try for all of it.

As it turned out, he was 100 percent successful.

NetApp sent us all the money the next day, and we used those funds to make payroll. Shortly afterward, I was able to cut new deals with Caesars and Madison Square Garden. We got the rent down. MSG agreed in writing to the terms of our handshake deal where they accepted a portion of the money back. Then I got a little money from my partner Daniel Ziff, and I was able to keep it alive.

We gradually turned the *Titanic*.

In July 2014, we won *Las Vegas Weekly*'s Best of Vegas Award for Best Music Venue. In 2015, we took Best Concert Calendar. In 2016, we won the Reader's Choice Award for Best Music Venue, and we won it again in 2017, 2018, 2019, and 2021. In 2020, when COVID shifted the awards categories, we were named to the All-Time Best of Vegas list (!).

Now we get the privates.

We even turned a small profit in 2018 and improved on that in 2019.

As for 2020, well, at least the first couple of months were strong.

When I see Jim Dolan these days, he'll say, "Yeah, we left you on the island a bit there, but you made it. Good job." I always thank him for believing in us at the beginning.

Jim's instincts were right. There *was* room for a live music venue in the center of the strip to do bands at 2,000 capacity. The Bowl *would* work well for privates. Those predictions were correct; they just took several years to come to pass.

We were a bit thrown off in thinking about Vegas because the launch of the Bowl in New York had been such a phenomenon. It literally made money from day one, and that's not normal. If that hadn't happened, I doubt Vegas would have been funded.

What I can say for sure is that NetApp saved our asses. It made my life a little less stressful at the exact same time that I was headed into the homestretch of Fare Thee Well.

I doubt they are aware of all that, but maybe they are now.

Thank you, NetApp.

I'm not quite sure what it is that you do, but thank you.

37

ATTICS OF MY LIFE

Fare Thee Well: Celebrating 50 Years of the Grateful Dead
Soldier Field, Chicago, Illinois
July 5, 2015

Once again, I got to be a guest at my own party.

Except this time, more than seventy-five thousand people shared a similar feeling, because they were so emotionally vested in it all.

I was standing in the back of the floor at Soldier Field watching the second and final encore on the last night of Fare Thee Well. I had a baseball cap pulled down on my head so I could enjoy these final moments in relative anonymity. People had been fist-bumping me and patting me on the back all weekend. It felt great, I won't lie, particularly given everything that had preceded it. However, I wanted to quietly absorb the conclusion, standing there next to producer Bob Ezrin and my longtime friend Brett Fairbrother as the band launched into "Attics of My Life."

Phil Lesh had selected this song to close Fare Thee Well a number of weeks prior to the event. Unbeknownst to the musicians, we had created a video slideshow that would appear on the giant IMAG screens, tracking the journey of the Grateful Dead from their origins through this final reunion of the Core Four (Bob Weir, Phil Lesh, Mickey Hart, and Bill Kreutzmann), aided and abetted by Trey Anastasio, Bruce Hornsby, and Jeff Chimenti.

We had been a little concerned about whether the video would sync properly with the live performance of "Attics," particularly since the full band had not rehearsed the tune. They had discussed running it at sound checks, but for whatever reason, that never came to pass. This had made Trey Anastasio nervous, since the song featured some complex three-part a cappella harmonies. So he ended up having a chart made from the version on *American Beauty*. Justin took a similar approach, timing his video to the studio recording, which turned out perfectly.

The music and the visuals evoked a swell of emotion from everyone who gathered for this extended family reunion, eliciting spontaneous cheers in a few instances, before the song reached its conclusion.

Then, while the band members bowed and circled for a group hug, I hustled my way from the very back of the venue, through the crowd, to the rear of the stage. I arrived just in time to greet the guys as they stepped off, so I could share my deepest thanks for this incredible run of shows.

The attics of my own life included the life-altering musical experience right here in Chicago back in 1993 that had inspired me to create my student film *And Miles to Go*, which had set me on my path to Soldier Field. Even though I was raised, trained, and educated at Wetlands, I was birthed by the Grateful Dead, which meant they had in effect created the person who would reunite them for their fiftieth anniversary. I still cannot believe that person is me.

Fare Thee Well was more directly preceded by a pitch I had made early in 2005, when I attempted to land a fortieth anniversary Grateful Dead celebration. I sent a letter to Cameron Sears, who managed the band during its final era (and would later become executive director of the group's nonprofit, the Rex Foundation). I wanted to put on a show at Madison Square Garden called One More Saturday Night that would bring everyone together to mark four decades of music. However, no one was in the right frame of mind, and the year passed without any performance to commemorate the milestone.

With the golden anniversary set to arrive in 2015, I began my pursuit during the fall of 2014. Once again, I set my sights on Madison Square Garden, but rather than one show, I was aiming for three. My intent was to put on six in total, with three additional arena dates in San Francisco. The problem was that I couldn't quite thread it with all the sports holds during the late-spring/early-summer period when I hoped to do this. It was long-time Grateful Dead crew member Robbie Taylor, who had gone on to become production manager for Phil Lesh and Furthur, who encouraged me to revise my approach. So I gravitated to the center of the country, and I focused on one weekend rather than two.

I had always enjoyed the epic scale of the Dead summer stadium shows, so I explored Soldier Field in Chicago. Soldier Field also made sense because that is where the final Grateful Dead performances had taken place on July 8 and 9, 1995. However, rather than July 8 or 9, which were a Wednesday and Thursday in 2015, I thought that July 4 would be the right date for the great American band to appear in the heart of America. I figured it would be relatively easy for fans to get there, so my goal became Friday through Sunday, July 3–5, at the last place Jerry played.

Meanwhile, other promoters were floating ideas at the group. One suggestion that gained some initial traction was an event at Golden Gate Park, where the band members would be joined by various guests, with the whole thing filmed for a concert film, akin to *The Last Waltz*. While that approach was ultimately rejected, Phil had never weighed in on the matter, and some folks began to worry whether he would be willing to participate at all. They were finding it difficult to reach him.

I, on the other hand, knew exactly where Phil would be for ten nights in October and November 2014: in my basement.

I had booked Phil & Friends gigs on five consecutive Friday and Saturday nights at the Capitol. So I knew that at some point I would have time with Phil and his wife, Jill, down in catering.

The case I made was that this was the right thing to do for the fans. He hadn't performed a show with Bob, Mickey, and Bill Kreutzmann since a one-off gig in 2009, at Rothbury (the Michigan festival that would evolve into Electric Forest). Plus, ever since Furthur disbanded, he hadn't performed with Bob. It seemed to me that the fiftieth anniversary was the appropriate moment to rectify all of this and celebrate the Grateful Dead's legacy with the group's loyal fans.

But Phil had a different take. He believed that the best way he could serve the greater good was by educating new musicians about the music and the magic of the Grateful Dead. He viewed that as his immediate responsibility, which would have lasting impact on the lives of current fans and future ones.

I did not disagree with him, and yet I still felt this would be the right gift for the people who had supported him over the years. I also suggested that if he wished, he could view it as an opportunity to let everyone know that this would be his final musical statement with Bobby, Mickey, and Billy. I maintained steady, light pressure (a four-dimensional calibration), because I really did believe it was the right thing for everyone. And eventually, I convinced him.

By the end of the year, it was all lined up. Phil, Bobby, Mickey, and Billy were on board. I eventually thanked each of them in person over a meal to discuss general plans for what was to follow.

When Trey signed on, he was eager to begin creative discussions. He wanted as much lead time as possible to prepare so that he could gradually immerse himself in the role.

However, before any of this dialogue took place, we nearly imploded over a matter of miscommunication.

As I saw it (and continue to see it), Phil, Bob, Mickey, and Billy are a band of brothers. However, as someone with two brothers of my own, I'm aware that family squabbles are inevitable from time to time. In this instance, someone outside their circle had started spreading untruths about the contents of Billy's forthcoming memoir. Since the four of them weren't speaking regularly, the issue briefly flared up.

It was a bit surreal observing their email exchanges, yet being helpless to intervene. A promoter's job is to solve problems, yet all I could do was watch. Thankfully, although a bit nerve-racking at first, this ultimately helped to clear the air so that everyone could get down to the matter at hand.

Plus, during this relatively quiet phase before any of the noise that would follow the official announcement, I was heartened by Billy's sentiment on why he wanted to push through and see the event come to pass: "I'm doing it out of love and respect for the Grateful Dead and our fans, the Deadheads, who gave us everything and asked for so little in return."

The other thing that stands out from this stretch is a text from Jill, once we were back on track, featuring a drawing of a Steal Your Face logo with the message "Buckle Up!" I'm tempted to say she didn't know how right she was, but of course she did. I think all of them did. I can't say the same for me.

On January 16, we announced the three nights at Soldier Field. One tricky question was what to call the band. The Grateful Dead name had been retired following Jerry's death in 1995. The incarnations of the group featuring the Core Four that toured afterward were known as the Other Ones and then the Dead. What we would be doing was something altogether different and not necessarily a band proper but rather a multi-night tribute performance. Since my goal is to say what it is—even in this case where we couldn't quite say it—we called the event Fare Thee Well: Celebrating 50 Years of the Grateful Dead. We never identified the seven performers collectively as the Grateful Dead, but we designed the art to feature the words *Grateful Dead* in a way that provided a sense of what was to come.

Another important early decision was maintaining the Grateful Dead tradition of mail-order ticketing. We put their ticket team back to work and reintroduced the personal touch in an era of screens. Deadheads sent their requests to a PO box in Stinson Beach, California, with a money order for the cost of the tickets, a three-by-five-inch index card with the specifics of their show requests, and a SASE. We also encouraged the long-standing practice of Heads decorating their mail-order envelopes by announcing that we would select our three favorites and use these as the commemorative ticket artwork for the shows.

We allocated sixty thousand seats in total for mail order, but we ultimately fielded requests for over five hundred thousand tickets. Our initial plan had been to put additional tickets on sale via Ticketmaster three weeks later, after we had informed everyone whether their mail-order requests would be filled. However, the number of envelopes was so overwhelming that we had to push that deadline by two weeks. We also allocated additional inventory to the mail-order pool by canceling a few online presales we had planned.

The Ticketmaster onsale took place on Saturday, February 28, at 10:00 a.m. I was watching my son, Simon, play soccer when I learned there were over a half million people in queue, more than any other event Ticketmaster had ever sold. The shows went clean within the hour. It felt amazing for a (very) little while, and then the commotion began.

The problem was that tickets immediately were listed on eBay and Craigslist. Seats that had gone on sale for $100–$200 were now being offered for thousands. Some outraged fans thought it was an inside job and blamed us, failing to understand that the whole thing was an arbitrage game. Sellers were offering tickets at inflated prices before they had them, intending to buy tickets from other people to fill those orders, if needed.

We were feeling the heat since a few hundred thousand Deadheads had been shut out. Something had to be done. So even though we had only planned for three Fare Thee Well shows, we began exploring the possibility of adding two dates the prior weekend in the Bay Area. There was no thought to adding shows after Chicago. Those were meant to be the culmination. In the very first article announcing Fare Thee Well, Bob said, "These will be the last shows with the four of us together." We knew we had to honor that appropriately.

We looked into Golden Gate Park, but there was already a Pride event scheduled. So we landed on Levi's Stadium in Santa Clara. This allowed us to get another 150,000 tickets in the marketplace. To thank the band members, we doubled their performance fee even though there would only be two dates, not three. I was able to get the word out by announcing this on *Tales from the Golden Road*, the SiriusXM show hosted by David Gans and Gary Lambert that is a one-of-kind national platform where Deadheads convene every week.

Santa Clara was announced in early April, which meant we didn't have time for another traditional mail order. Instead, thanks to Michael Rapino, the head of Live Nation, which owns Ticketmaster, we were able to have an online lottery. Anyone who wanted tickets had a few days to enter their credit card information, and the winners were selected randomly. It was the first time that all the tickets to a venue of that size were sold by lottery.

I think we received 350,000 entries, which meant that plenty of folks were still shut out.

So since everyone could not get to the shows, we decided to get the shows to everyone. We initially announced a partnership to beam the Chicago performances into movie theaters via satellite. When that didn't entirely satisfy demand—some people didn't have access to a participating theater—we offered pay-per-view options for individuals as well as simulcasts at bars, clubs, and via DirecTV. *Rolling Stone* senior editor David Fricke never made it to Chicago, but he filed two reviews: one from the Capitol Theatre and one from Brooklyn Bowl. All these alternative viewing options eased the pressure for tickets.

Speaking of pressure, I think it's worth noting that during all of this, I was simultaneously knee-deep in turmoil with Brooklyn Bowl Vegas. That's why I never paused to pat myself on the back about Fare Thee Well.

It is a trap to get caught up in the adulation directed your way. It will mess you up. I allowed myself a couple of moments at Dead 50, but if you start to feel that too much, you'll freeze. Things are never as good as you think, because bad things can happen—and they can happen quickly.

Then again, things are never quite as bad as they seem. What's important is that you act and react. When I came close to bankruptcy, I wasn't thinking, *Whoa, I'm going bankrupt!* It was more like, *How do I not go bankrupt?*

Once we locked down Santa Clara, much of the focus turned to Chicago logistics. Here's where my fellow promoters Mike Luba and Don Sullivan of Madison House Presents / AEG stepped up. The two of them had been part of the original Golden Gate Park festival pitch for the Dead 50 event, and after the band put the kibosh on that, they joined forces with me.

Don is a fellow New Yorker who also had attended Northwestern. He settled down in Chicago after graduation to work for Jam Productions and ran the final Dead shows at Soldier Field in '95. I knew Don had a handle on the local politics, which would be essential for the event we were proposing.

As for Luba, we'd been friends ever since the Wetlands days when he managed the String Cheese Incident. We'd gone on to do plenty of things over the years that followed. He's the one I called to connect Pete Seeger with Bruce Springsteen for the Obama inaugural. He later invited me to join him for a memorable train ride with Mumford & Sons that was depicted in the documentary *Big Easy Express*. I appreciate having a friend who calls me and says, "You need to get here now," and holds a spot for me.

Luba's typically spot-on with so many inventive ideas that I feel obligated to take this moment and mention a crappy one. In May 2010, he was working with *Yo Gabba Gabba!* and asked me if I wanted to announce their upcoming tour via an event at the Bowl, which would include a performance and a meet and greet. At the time, they were the biggest thing going, and he thought we could add a little excitement and generate additional press by opening it to everyone on a first-come, first-served basis. This made sense to me for about ten minutes. Think of the firefighter who takes his kids out of school, waits in line all morning, and is the first one shut out. First come, first served at a kids show is never a great idea . . . there will be tears. I also will single out Luba for delivering one of the most memorable lines I have ever heard a band manager say while negotiating a deal: "We need more money and lower ticket prices." (Good luck with that.)

As for Fare Thee Well, by early June, most of the fan frustration had dissipated. The addition of Santa Clara and all the streaming options meant that if you missed out on tickets, you'd still be able to watch the shows (perhaps even with the same crew who would have joined you in Chicago). I understood the nature of the lingering negativity. If you really wanted to be at the shows and you were shut out, you were gonna say, "This thing sucks!" But we were doing the best we could with a finite number of tickets to a limited number of shows.

This is why we made a decision regarding mail order that spiraled out of control rather quickly.

The ticketing office had been inundated with colorful envelopes, and I wanted to do whatever I could to fulfill as many orders as possible. So we eliminated seating on the back half of the floor and made it general admission to increase our capacity. We also sold seats behind the stage for this same reason (on the last night when the musicians took their final bows, they turned and acknowledged these audience members as well, which was a nice touch).

The biggest problem was presented by the folks who had ordered $199.50 reserved floor seats that no longer existed. We didn't want to convert those into GA standing-room tickets, with the assumption that anyone who had ordered a seat wanted a seat (the last Grateful Dead show had been twenty years earlier, and we're all getting creakier). So we reconfigured some of the price points and created additional $199.50 seats throughout the stadium from locations that originally listed for $149.50 or $179.50.

We assumed that most people would rather have a ticket than not have a ticket, and they had already sent in money orders for $199.50. We couldn't change the amount on the money order, and the process of handling all these ticket requests was so time-consuming that we were not able to ask everyone whether they would accept these alternative seats. The short time window also meant that we couldn't request new money orders.

After we sent out the commemorative tickets in early June, a few vocal Heads expressed their displeasure with the situation. We had made the adjustments with the best of intentions. It was not a malicious attempt to pull some sort of bait and switch. Frankly, if it was just about the money, we could have returned unfilled orders and then sold the seats on Ticketmaster at the new price point because the demand certainly was there. I'm also proud of the fact that the GA section closest to the stage was priced at $99.50 and that the most anyone would need to spend for a seat was $199.50.

But as I've discovered over my years as a concert promoter, there are times when no good deed goes unpunished.

The situation in Chicago bothered me because we had attempted to do right by the community. But now we were being criticized by members of the community who were unaware that we were trying to get tickets into as many of their hands as possible.

This in an ongoing issue for me: Do you look at the message boards or not? Is it useful to respond to comments that are untruthful or lack the complete information? In general, my answer is no. This is also why I'm not on social media. It's way too easy to get sucked in and let that become a distraction.

However, I do hear things. In this instance, it was easier than usual because the *Washington Post* ran a story and its principal source was a blog: *The Official Home of Unofficial Grateful Dead and Music News*. So while I usually ignore the chatter, in this case, I became so frustrated that I contacted "Grateful Dean" Sottile, who ran that site. I was exasperated, but I believed that if I could explain to him what had happened, he would understand. Sure enough, he was open-minded and supercool about it, and we remain friends to this day.

When things became really stressful, I would take a long, hot shower and crank up the Grateful Dead. It helped restore my focus, the music really does inspire me. As they say, "If you get confused, listen to the music play."

Ultimately, I went to the band and shared the details, along with the suggestion that we should offer everyone the opportunity for a refund after the shows when things calmed down. They agreed and posted a message that offered an explanation and added, "If you received tickets by mail order and were charged more than the price of such tickets on the seating chart made available at the time [your] orders were mailed and still wish to attend 'Fare Thee Well,' we personally encourage you to attend the shows and sit in the seats you received via mail order. If you're not satisfied that you got your money's worth, we will refund the difference between what you paid and the price of such tickets on the seating chart made available at the time your order was mailed." Ultimately, less than 5 percent of those affected asked for a refund. That number says a lot about Deadheads.

With all of that out of the way(ish) by mid-June, we focused on the concerts themselves. Our main concerns with Santa Clara were gridlock and weather. Levi's Stadium had opened the previous fall, and we were told that traffic occasionally snarled before San Francisco 49ers games. This never became a problem at Fare Thee Well, because people arrived at various times throughout the day, although plenty of them were on hand as soon as the lots opened on Saturday the twenty-seventh and Sunday the twenty-eighth. As for weather, that, too, worked out beautifully, with the rainbow bonus I continue hearing about to this day.

More than anything else, what surprised me about the first weekend at Levi's (beyond the peace sign . . . and the rainbow) was the energy in the stadium. I had anticipated it but hadn't fully appreciated what it would feel like. When you have a 360-degree show and every seat is filled, there's just a different level of energy. Part of the reason I was looking forward to doing these shows was so I could relive that Grateful Dead summer stadium experience where you look out and see all these like-minded people moving along with you. It's very different from an amphitheater show. That initial roar when the band took the stage in Santa Clara remains with me.

I also appreciated the arc of the five set lists over the course of Fare Thee Well. It all began the first night, which offered a nod to the band's origins, since the stadium was fifteen miles from the site of the very first Grateful Dead show (when they were still known as the Warlocks) at Magoo's Pizza Parlor in Menlo Park, California.

I also was able to experience that magical train-leaving-the-station via the travel-themed "Truckin'" opener on night one, which seemed fitting, even if the nature of transport was slightly different.

The second evening closed out in style with my go-to Dead summer favorite, "Sugar Magnolia," followed by "Brokedown Palace," a moving song that always makes me think of Jerry.

While the Santa Clara shows were concerts on an epic scale, Chicago felt like something else. It was a cultural event.

Fare Thee Well wasn't just about the three hours of music each night. It was also the months leading up to shows, thinking about what would go down, and talking it over with friends. Part of the Dead tour experience had been about collaborating with friends planning itineraries and anticipating the adventures that would follow. The same was true of Fare Thee Well, where all that dreaming (and planning) lifted people for a while.

What I continue to hear from folks who attended is "That was one of the best weekends of my life." They generally don't say, "Those were the best concerts of my life," although the music was impressive. It was the entire experience, with reunions upon reunions and cross-generational bonding that made it so memorable.

The city of Chicago leaned into Fare Thee Well. The hotels embraced it. The taxis and ride-sharing companies played Dead music all weekend. The restaurants did the same. Giodano's, the legendary pizzeria, even made custom pizza boxes. There were over fifty aftershows and even some pregames (we made the decision early on to focus exclusively on Soldier Field rather than produce any official late-night events). On Sunday afternoon, I can remember walking from my hotel to a *Relix* party, and everyone I saw on the street was wearing a tie-dye.

Local and even national politicians and administrators were actively involved in preparations for the influx of people.

Speaking of national politicians, longtime city dweller—and then United States president—Barack Obama contributed a welcome greeting in the first of our three free daily programs, writing, "Here's to fifty years of the Grateful Dead, an iconic American band that embodies the creativity, passion and ability to bring people together that makes American music so great. Enjoy this weekend's celebration of your fans and legacy. And as Jerry would say, 'Let there be songs to fill the air.'"

As for the planning of Fare Thee Well, I have a photo of myself in a meeting at Soldier Field. I'm addressing about seventy people—representatives from all the government agencies and entities interested in the event. There were reps from Homeland Security, DEA, state police, city police, the parks department, highway patrol, the fire department, the Mayor's Department of Cultural Affairs and Special Events, and one or two others.

I also spent some time with Mayor Rahm Emanuel. I had reached out to see if we were seeing the world the same way. He was a music fan, and I think he agreed that it made sense for the cops to play zone defense. There was no need to play tight man-to-man.

I didn't witness any of this, but I believe the mayor's office spoke with the agencies represented at Soldier Field. What I can say with confidence is that only three people were charged with marijuana possession during the weekend.

Zone defense had been put into effect.

And zone defense worked.

As for the aspects that we could control, we wanted to make a statement as soon as people entered the stadium. I've found that what seems like small stuff impacts the live music experience in a big way.

This includes how you are treated at the box office, what happens when you enter the venue, your interactions with security, and even your visit to the bathroom. It all matters and plays a role, not just the sound and lights.

So we put the security in tie-dye shirts to change the nature of how they were perceived. This is a prime example of something that I refer to as reverse jujitsu, in which you flip something you think is going to be a negative into a positive. The Wetlands bathrooms were also an example early in my career where we had high-end speakers that piped in the music from the stage, so that rather than missing the show, you were hearing it with clarity while taking a whiz. While the security at a Grateful Dead stadium show had potential for mishap, we transformed it into something that had positive energy.

The vibe outside the stadium was something I hadn't experienced since seeing an actual Grateful Dead show in the '90s. Jeremy Stein from Madison House organized a vendor village during the months leading up to GD50 (while simultaneously producing the Electric Forest festival, which took place a week earlier). The scene then took on its own momentum, with all the Deadheads on the sidewalks and parking lots creating the feeling of an old-school Shakedown Street.

There were also plenty of fingers in the air with folks hoping to land a miracle ticket. One of the things I had enjoyed going all the way back to 1993 summer tour was miracling people in the lots. You can see some of that in *And Miles to Go*. I did it again in Chicago, joined by Bob Weir's wife, Natascha. We'd wander around, fine some deserving Head, and then hand over a ticket. It was a joy to behold.

I had someone else alongside me for a different mission in Chicago. My daughter, Roxy, was nine years old and had one steady refrain throughout the weekend: "Daddy, where's Katy Perry?" We made a few trips through the GA floor to see if we could find her, to no avail.

Katy Perry was one of many musicians who attended Fare Thee Well at Soldier Field. There had been a few in Santa Clara—in fact, when the rainbow appeared, I was standing just behind John Mayer, who was there with Andy Cohen. John was the one who brought Katy to Chicago, where they joined many other fellow artists, including Jenny Lewis, Perry Farrell, Lee Ranaldo, Liz Phair, Renée Fleming, and John Popper.

Phish keyboard player Page McConnell attended all three nights. When I thanked him for being there, he said, "Oh, no, thank *you*." He later mentioned how much he enjoyed watching Trey from the audience, which is something Page can't do in Phish. He also later echoed something I had said to Coran Capshaw while I was pitching him on the idea of Trey's participation: "That opened up a new world to us. I'm seeing a lot of older Deadheads in the audience."

There were many other recognizable faces in Chicago. The person who wins the award for "most resembling an old-school Deadhead who looks just like George R. R. Martin" was, well, George R. R. Martin (I heard the *Game of Thrones* author repeatedly described that way). The world of politics was represented by Al Franken and David Axelrod, while actors included Chloë Sevigny and Bill Murray.

Bill showed up with Jenny Lewis, and he was in his element at Fare Thee Well. He contributed a loose vibe (there's a great picture that Jenny posted to her Instagram of Bill feigning a look of concern while Phil Lesh places a hand on his shoulder), and he even helped sweep up backstage after the final show. I had met Bill two and a half years earlier at the Capitol Theatre when Stevie Van Zandt staged a Rascals reunion. In Chicago, Bill told me he had fond memories of the Rascals gig he had attended (as did I, sitting in the green room backstage with Stevie and Bill, two larger-than-life personalities, who chatted genially while Stevie tended to the tiny dog in a bag on his lap).

Still, the celebrities whose presence at Soldier Field most thrilled me were Mountain Girl and Bill Walton. MG, a.k.a. Carolyn Garcia, was the Merry Prankster married to Jerry for many years and is also the mother of Trixie, Sunshine, and Annabelle. Her energy is strong, and it's easy to understand why Ken Kesey and the Pranksters wanted to hang out with her forty and fifty years ago, just like people want to hang out with her today. She's charismatic, witty, wise, and just plain fun.

As for Bill Walton, I think he's the strongest person I've ever met, both mentally and physically. He's had thirty-six orthopedic surgeries and endured all that pain, yet he evokes such joy. The strength of his heart and his humanity lifts everyone around him. He's someone who shares in the circle of energy. If you give it to him, you'll get it back. I once sent John Mayer a text gushing about Bill's spirit, which led John to respond, "He's a repeater tower!"

Trey is also like that, and I've experienced his generous spirit in multiple ways. His relationship with the audience helps fuel the energy that elevates his music. He gives, they feel it, and they give back. Then *he* feels it, turns it up a notch, and gives it back to them. It's a soaring circle. I've found that's also true on a personal level whether we're at a Rangers game, we're sharing a text thread, or he's about the take the stage at Soldier Field in front of seventy-five thousand people.

There's a photo of Bill Walton backstage at Fare Thee Well having a heartfelt conversation with Trey. I recently learned that Bill was giving Trey a pep talk, telling him, "You've got to *own* these shows!" I believe that Trey took that message to heart.

Here's what David Fricke had to say about opening night in Chicago from his "View from the Balcony" *Rolling Stone* review—the title is a reference to the fact that he watched the show from the front row center balcony at the Cap: "This Dead sounded rehearsed and determined to leave with their legend not just intact, but enhanced. When Anastasio stepped on the gas, harder each time, in his solo choruses during 'Scarlet Begonias,' the rest of the band jumped in rhythmic temper with him. It's a familiar ascension—Anastasio does it all the time with Phish. But punching out of that Capitol PA, spliced on the screen with close-up shots of the eye contact between the guitarist, Lesh and Weir, that kick upstairs looked and felt like new life, a freshly cut road to a reassuring peak."

I'll defer to David on the last night as well, via "The View from the Bowl," his review that captures the experience from Brooklyn Bowl. Here's his take on the concluding "Attics of My Life": "It

was easy to hear, in Weir's plaintive vocal and the supporting harmonies of Lesh, Anastasio and Hornsby, the Dead finally, publicly,
saying a satisfying thank you to Garcia. It was just as easy to imagine Garcia, who wrote the song with Hunter, singing it in 1970
to a greater good: the America that slowly coalesced around the
Dead's music and outlaw idealism, then survived Garcia and his
band. 'When there was no dream of mine,' Weir sang before everyone went home, 'you dreamed of me.' The Grateful Dead ended
their time as a working band on the very date and ground where
their dream came to an unexpected halt, in 1995, with Garcia's
death. But this was not goodbye, just 'See you later—and the next
dreams are yours.'"

My friend Dan Berkowitz said something to me shortly after
Fare Thee Well. Berko, who had handled the VIP packages through
his company CID and also rented space in the *Relix* offices for
many years, declared, "We have peaked! This is it. It will never be
better than this . . . but that's okay."

If that is true, I am fine with it.

But I still want to create new stuff.

38

FORMERLY INTERLOCKEN

LOCKN' Music Festival
Oak Ridge Farm, Arrington, Virginia
September 11, 2015

Something I always keep in mind is that when shit goes wrong, it goes wrong fast.

It is like a lightning bolt, but not a cool Grateful Dead lightning bolt.

I mean this metaphorically, and sometimes I mean this literally as well, because I've had my share of real-life lightning bolts over the years.

Thunderstorms shut down my Earth Day event on the National Mall in 2009.

Snow squalls on the morning of the 2004 Jammys, our first year at the Theater at Madison Square Garden, put an immediate kibosh on all ticket sales, while we still had nearly a thousand to sell.

But my luck broke the right way with Fare Thee Well, starting with the rainbow and continuing through July 4 weekend in Chicago, when the rain held off until Monday.

Maybe it was all my hard work on Earth Day 40, but I finally had nature on my side.

It lasted about two months.

While I had never previously heard the term *microburst*, by Thursday morning, September 10, 2015, I'd heard it dozens of times, typically preceded by an expletive.

For the record, a microburst is a downdraft of air that rushes to the ground from the base of a thunderstorm and then spreads out in all directions. It is the opposite of a tornado.

This is what we experienced on the late afternoon of Wednesday, September 9, just hours before we were going to open the site to ticket holders at the third-annual LOCKN' in the heart of Virginia's Blue Ridge Mountains.

My road to LOCKN' began in 2012 with a call from Dave Frey, who created H.O.R.D.E. with John Popper and served as Blues Traveler's manager back in the day. Dave had worked for both Bill Graham and Ron Delsener earlier in his career, so he has an interesting perspective on the live concert business. Dave managed Blues Traveler through the '90s and would go on to work with other artists like Cheap Trick, the Ramones, Heart, and Brazilian Girls. In 2008, he left New York and relocated to Charlottesville, Virginia.

Dave called me one day to talk about this amazing land that he believed could be an ideal festival site. As it turns out, there have been a couple of times in my career when I've had available financial resources due to investment partnerships. It was during one of these rare flush moments that Dave contacted me.

This was also a period when something had changed in the festival landscape. I was at the first ten Bonnaroos. I attended the first year, had a great time, but said to myself, "Well, I guess I'm not going to get to do the big jamband festival. That's been taken." There was a community of smaller festivals like Gathering of the Vibes, All Good, and High Sierra, but Bonnaroo was operating on a much larger scale, drawing over seventy-five thousand people.

However, by 2012, Bonnaroo had pivoted to the mainstream with Jay-Z, Springsteen, Kanye, Elton John, Eminem, Metallica, and others. The mega jamband festival did not really exist when Dave called me, which is what prompted me to move forward with him to create LOCKN'.

As we developed the festival, one phrase I repeated was "If you don't know Jorma, then you don't know Jack." I wanted to keep us focused on our core base both with the lineup and with the marketing. If you had no clue about the genius of Jorma Kaukonen, then you would have little interest in Jack Casady and their incredible band, Hot Tuna. LOCKN' would have a niche audience of like-minded music lovers, and we shouldn't lose sight of that.

Dave had identified Oak Ridge Farm, a parcel of land in the foothills of the Blue Ridge Mountains. It had its own forest. People could camp beneath the trees rather than on a parking lot or an airport runaway. There was something about the topography that made the clouds distinctive and fluffier. The site had good air.

During our first year, the concert field was located on the site of a horse racing track that had not been used in over a decade. If you look at the original LOCKN' logo, you'll see hints of a track. Our initial idea was to have two stages, with Phish on one end and Bob Weir and Phil Lesh's Furthur band on the other. We received a commitment from Furthur, and although we couldn't lock down a deal with Phish, we decided to move forward with the Dead guys.

I had been to Bonnaroo so many times and I loved it, although some aspects were exhausting. You would be with your friends, and you would all have to decide: Should we see the Flaming Lips here or Beck there or Galactic over there or Wilco way over there? Then the debate began, and the answer sometimes became "Let's just go hang out and drink beer." It was overwhelming. As someone who makes a lot of decisions every day, I wasn't looking to make a bunch more when I was kicking back at a music festival.

At LOCKN', we wanted to avoid that. We would have one band playing at a time. You would be able to see every act without moving.

We would have two stages side by side, and with a nod to the good ol' Grateful Dead, the music would never stop. It would flow seamlessly from one stage to the other and back again. We tried to capture that intent with our original name for the festival: Interlocken.

In early May 2013, we announced that Interlocken would take place on September 5–8. We confirmed three days of Furthur, along with Neil Young and Crazy Horse, the String Cheese Incident, Widespread Panic, Gov't Mule, the Black Crowes, the Tedeschi Trucks Band, Punch Brothers, Col. Bruce Hampton, Keller Williams, Grace Potter, Jorma Kaukonen, and others.

In late August, Neil Young canceled his tour due to Frank "Poncho" Sampedro's hand injury, so we scrambled and then landed the Trey Anastasio Band. Picking up on The Jammys ethos, we announced some collaborative sets such as Widespread Panic with John Fogerty, and the Zac Brown Incident (the String Cheese Incident with Zac Brown). There would be plenty more sit-ins as well, both spontaneous and confirmed in advance.

Beyond Trey's participation, another significant development took place in mid-August. We changed the name of the festival from Interlocken to LOCKN'. Over the prior weeks, we had heard from the lawyers representing the Interlochen Arts Camp, a nonprofit organization in Michigan. They claimed that our name was too similar to theirs, and they deployed a team of lawyers to support that contention. The Interlochen people might be cool, but their attorneys were super hostile. I wondered if the board members were aware of how we were treated. (Then again, maybe they dictated all that aggression; it's easy to hide behind attorneys.)

We were a bit over our skis. That can happen sometimes. Then the question becomes "What do you do next?" We had already announced the festival, and we were just a few weeks out. It's all about the second shot. How are you going to respond when the Interlochen camp threatens to sue a month before your festival?

We ultimately decided to switch from Interlocken to LOCKN', creating a new word in the process. We added a tagline for clarity: "Interlocking Music Festival." While it took a minute and there were some initial speed bumps, LOCKN' has become a small part of the language of live music. It's entered the lexicon.

While the name change was painful, I believe it helped us generate additional press just a few weeks from the festival. In certain respects, we had two bites at the apple. It's like what happened with Social Distortion in May 2018. Their fall tour was about to go on sale when Ticketfly was hacked, which led to a postponement. Then when tickets were made available a week later, they over-indexed, thanks to media coverage of the hack, which had helped build awareness for the shows.

The first year of any event comes with added stress, which in this case was compounded by the name change and our need to find a replacement for Neil Young. Still, going into the inaugural LOCKN', I felt pretty good about our chances.

Ultimately, success would turn on whether we could create some musical magic. Over the course of those four days, it happened again and again. I can point to so many memorable performances from that first year, including the Zac Brown Incident (my wife, Rebecca, was Zac's publicist, which made it all the sweeter), John Fogerty with Panic (which somehow even exceeded our high expectations), Col. Bruce Hampton & Friends (Oteil Burbridge hauled ass following the final show of the Allman Brothers Band tour the previous night and barely made it on time), the Tedeschi Trucks Band and Black Crowes sets (in which everyone sat in with everyone), and Trey's appearance with Furthur (which brought things around to our initial idea for the festival and helped plant the seeds of Fare Thee Well).

In addition to the main concert field, we've always had an additional stage tucked into the woods, which we've used for late nights. That first year, we were still getting our bearings, so what we then called the Triangle Stage was about a mile away from the concert field. On Saturday night at the end of Furthur's set, Phil took off on a golf cart to go sit in with the Terrapin Family Band. (That's why there was no encore, but after "Scarlet" > "Fire" with Trey, what more did you need?) At first, I thought, *Oh shit, people aren't going to make it up there.* And sure enough, there were only a handful of people at the beginning of the set.

But then the Wooks started to emerge. As best I could tell, they were being birthed like gremlins out of the ground. The forest was alive with them. I'd never seen anything like it, and even though it sounds crazy, I know it was real.

The same thing happened one year when I was doing a Phil show at Central Park SummerStage. There is a big rock in the heart of the park near the entrance of the venue, and I was standing next to it before the show, when suddenly, these Wooks began to appear. I had no idea where they were coming from until I finally realized that they were being hatched out of the ground under the rock.

As LOCKN' progressed, it continued to evolve. We purchased the adjoining land and moved the stage to a space much closer to the forest. I mention that we moved the *stage*, singular, because the other thing we did was to eliminate one of them. However, we maintained the "music never stops" principle by using a 360 turntable stage, in which one band rotates off while the next rotates into position. This has been the source of some dynamic musical crossovers, with one band literally segueing into another.

Our lineup maintained a familiarity and consistency. In this respect, the LOCKN' programming philosophy was very different from other festivals. Typically, if an artist is booked at a fest, the performer won't be invited to return for a few years. We took a different approach, turning LOCKN' into a family reunion on both sides of the stage. Along with each of the Grateful Dead guys, we have had annual appearances by Widespread Panic, the String Cheese Incident, the Tedeschi Trucks Band, Umphrey's McGee, Keller Williams, and others, including, of course, Jorma and Jack. On top of that, artists performed multiple days and would often stay with us on-site. This facilitated a general vibe and camaraderie that has resulted in many spontaneous collaborations over the years.

Here is what Matt Busch, Bob Weir's manager, has said about Bobby's approach to LOCKN': "He doesn't even travel to a hotel. He just camps on a bus backstage, and he's there . . . He's probably going to see someone backstage and go, 'I want in,' or someone will see him and go, 'Hey, would you join us?' We make that joke every year: You book him for three, you get four; you book him for four, you get six. That's just how Bob is."

Perhaps the ultimate example of this took place on Thursday night of LOCKN' 2019, when Bobby "sat in" with Joe Russo's Almost Dead . . . on a couch. That year, he rolled in a day early, so shortly after his arrival, during the JRAD set break, Joe and Tommy Hamilton decided to visit him on his bus to see if he'd be interesting in joining them for a portion of their set. They talked with him for a while, but ultimately, he passed because he was settling in.

Meanwhile, Joe had wanted to do something fun with the turntable. At one point, he had suggested, "Just turn us mid-song, and then keep turning us back and forth." However, while Joe and Tom were chatting with Bobby on the bus, I noticed a couch and had another idea.

Just before they started their second set, I told Joe I was going to try to get Bobby to sit on the couch and then rotate him in front of the audience while they were still playing. So while JRAD was performing on one side of the turntable, we set up the other side with the couch, an end table and lamp, some copies of our *LOCKN' Times* daily newspaper, and a book.

Then I shared my idea with Bobby, who is always up for a prank.

He agreed to do it, and I gave Joe a five-minute warning via his drum tech. Bobby made his way onto the couch; we rotated the stage and sent him out there. At first, he was lying on his back, looking at the book, then as he slowly revolved in front of the crowd, he sat up and waved. People went nuts. When he completed the circle, he said to me, "That was interesting. I started doing it before I even knew what I was doing."

I am in touch with that sentiment.

After all the prep work, that is the moment when the train leaves the station.

Unfortunately, in 2015, we had to revise the train schedule.

Shortly after 5:00 p.m. on Wednesday afternoon, Jon Dindas, our production director, noticed some darkening skies and called our meteorologist for a weather update. Dindas was told not to worry because it would only drizzle for a little while. Technically, that was accurate, except the drizzle was followed by torrential rains and wind gusts of sixty-five miles per hour.

The microburst came and went rather quickly. It was localized near the stage, and I missed it because I was up the road running an errand at the Food Lion.

Weather turns quick at LOCKN'. It is amazing land, but like a lot of the world's most beautiful places, it has some atmospheric volatility. This is why our rainbow ratio is rather high—we're the festival league leader. In fact, within twenty minutes of the microburst, a full rainbow appeared, spanning the clear blue sky. This is why many people had no inkling that the brief storm had been so destructive.

However, our site-ops team assessed the situation and identified some damage to the infrastructure. In addition, some of the camping areas were oversaturated with water. They recommended that we postpone the festival by a day.

This was a challenge on multiple levels. We needed to communicate with traveling festivalgoers and coordinate with local officials to identify alternative lodging spots (in some cases, parking lots). We scrambled to reschedule performances, particularly two special sets: Bill Kreutzmann's Billy & the Kids project with guests, and the Doobie Incident, pairing the String Cheese Incident with the Doobie Brothers. And we had to pull this off while ensuring that the site would be habitable for a Thursday opening, with the music to begin on Friday.

Most of what I do on a daily basis is handle problems. Some of the situations are familiar; others are altogether unexpected. The game is to draw on prior experiences while assessing the proper course of action. It helps if you have experienced people on your side who can hold their shit together while things are flying at you.

Had any of us experienced a microburst before?

Negative.

Had any of us even been aware of the term *microburst* before?

No, sir.

The key to getting through a new crisis is not thinking about the crisis that you are in.

Just dig in and do the work. Don't get too high or too low, particularly when it feels like your phone may literally blow up from all the action. Stay in the middle.

We had some weather issues the prior year that helped inform our approach. An intense storm on a Saturday night in 2014 had nearly led to the cancellation of Tom Petty and the Heartbreakers. We had been forced to evacuate the concert field, and when we received the all clear, we needed to figure out how to notify everyone (this was before we had a LOCKN' app).

Eventually, I realized that we had our own low-end civil defense siren in the form of Widespread Panic bassist Dave Schools. I told him to drop some bass bombs to alert everyone out in the hinterlands that we were back in business. The timing worked out perfectly for a full Petty set, which was another early LOCKN' milestone.

My top personal programming priority in 2015 was rescheduling the Doobie Incident. The two bands had been rehearsing in a trailer behind the stage when the microburst hit and, given the localized nature of the storm, hadn't realized its severity. They had been scheduled for Thursday evening and couldn't switch to Friday night because the Doobies needed to be in North Carolina for a gig. However, thanks to a private plane provided by a local fan, rather than close out the music on Thursday, they opened things up on Friday. (Technically, John Popper opened Friday, September 11, with a solemn version of "The Star-Spangled Banner" that he performed alongside first responders.)

LOCKN' proved to be a challenge, particularly on the economic side. There's a saying that if you don't lose money your first year at a music festival, then you aren't doing it right. My experience has been that if you want to do an A-level festival, the deficits can extend into subsequent years as well. A lot of that outlay has been for CapEx (capital expenditures) that we will benefit from in the long run: acquiring land, building roads, bringing in power, and landscaping the forest. This is unavoidable if you're looking to establish a long-term festival legacy.

It's much easier for the big guys to launch new festivals. There's a real benefit to having scale because they can amortize the costs over several events, offices, shows, and tours. This is why you will see the same acts playing multiple festivals owned by the same promoter. LOCKN' is not located in a major population center. It would be economically advantageous to be in Austin (ACL), Chicago (Lollapalooza), Manhattan (Governors Ball), or San Francisco (Outside Lands). Even Bonnaroo is just down the interstate from Nashville. LOCKN' is an hour from Charlottesville (population forty-eight thousand) on a two-lane road and over three hours from DC.

There is certainly some mental strain that comes with maintaining a music festival, but thankfully, there's sweet release as well. I was reminded of this shortly after 1:00 p.m. on Friday, September 11, 2015, when we all started "Rockin' Down the Highway."

As I think back to LOCKN' 2015, it's not the microburst that first comes to mind, it's the Doobie Incident, it's Widespread Panic with Jimmy Cliff, it's Phil Lesh & Friends with Carlos Santana and

Warren Haynes, it's Robert Plant and the Sensational Space Shifters (times two), it's the all-star fifty-year celebration of Jefferson Airplane led by Jorma and Jack, it's the Mad Dogs & Englishmen reunion helmed by the Tedeschi Trucks Band and Leon Russell.

I love LOCKN'.

There is magic in the air.

I just might prefer a little less moisture.

39

JAM THE VOTE

The Preservation Hall Jazz Band & Friends
The Capitol Theatre, Port Chester, New York
November 6, 2016

H aving my own venues allows me to experiment with new ideas.

Things don't always work out the way I initially intended, and they often require more effort than I originally contemplated, but that's the instrument I play. Once other people believe you can deliver, then it opens the door to additional opportunities (a.k.a. other gigs).

I experienced this at Wetlands, which was my first sandbox. I think *sandbox* is an appropriate term, since people thought I was a kid for the first couple of years I owned the place—because I looked like one (see photo section).

As Election Day 2016 approached, I wanted to take all I had learned and try something new to encourage voter turnout. As someone who owns venues, I know the value of advance tickets. You can't count on walk-ups.

The idea that I landed on was something I had never seen before. We would put on an all-star show at the Capitol, two days before the election, and offer a free stream to anyone who logged in and pledged to vote.

Pledge. Stream. Vote.

That was the tagline. And although I would not count it as an altogether successful night, given the election results two days later, it was innovative on the technical side and inspiring on the musical side.

I partnered with HeadCount on Jam The Vote.

I have been a board member ever since the organization launched in 2004 as a 501(c)(3) nonprofit that uses music to promote voter registration and participation. HeadCount was founded by Marc Brownstein, the bass player of the Disco Biscuits, and Andy Bernstein, a journalist and music fan who serves as executive director. Other longtime board members include Bob Weir, promoter Don Strasburg, agent Jonathan Levine, managers Nadia Prescher and Ami Spishock, and tech savant Andy Gadiel. For the past decade, HeadCount has shared the *Relix* office space, and Andy Bernstein is someone I'll often use as a sounding board when I have a new idea.

I have often linked personal special events with HeadCount. On my fortieth birthday in 2012, on the second night of the Cap's reopening week, I pulled together a show that we announced in a rather nondescript manner as Benefit for HeadCount: The Roots and Bob Weir Solo. While we billed it as The Roots and Bobby, this was only partially accurate, as we'd also enlisted some other fine folks to support the cause: Trey Anastasio, Warren Haynes, Grace Potter, and Bobby Keys. The concluding set that night with everyone onstage for "Dancing in the Street," "The Thrill Is Gone," and "Whipping Post" was nothing short of epic, and not only did HeadCount receive proceeds from the door and poster sales, the organization was tagged in the media coverage of the event.

Another cool co-creation has been Participation Row.

As the first LOCKN' approached in 2013, Andy and I discussed what we could do for HeadCount at the festival. I was on both sides of the fence here, which can make a difference in guaranteeing that there's proper touch and follow-through. One of the gratifying aspects about having a venue like the Cap, a festival like LOCKN', or event like Fare Thee Well is that I can use those platforms to assist an organization like HeadCount.

LOCKN' provided an opportunity for blue-sky thinking. Nothing was off the table. We came up with a model where we carved out a section of the festival site for local and national nonprofits to raise dollars and awareness. We called it Participation Row, echoing one of my favorite Dylan songs that the Dead also covered.

The festival drew attention to the nonprofit village through our messaging, and we encouraged fans to engage by offering prizes at each booth. At the end of the weekend, HeadCount hosted a silent auction of signed instruments and memorabilia, then shared the proceeds equally among the organizations.

We also brought Participation Row to Fare Thee Well. That is where my fellow founding HeadCount board member Bob Weir played a guitar autographed by the musicians that later fetched $526,000 in an auction, which represented over $30,000 for each of the seventeen nonprofits.

Jam The Vote seemed like another great opportunity to benefit HeadCount and try to make a positive impact.

The show also offered me a chance to work with Preservation Hall Jazz Band artistic director Ben Jaffe. Ben is a member of the simpatico family. Along with the Jazz Band, he also runs the Hall, and he's one of those people who understands what I go through with the attention to detail and the push for excellence.

There is a certain pressure that comes with running a venue like Preservation Hall, and Ben feels a responsibility to create special moments, just like I do. We have become close friends because we are a similar age, and even though we grew up in different cultures, we see the world the same way. I have a great time hanging out and collaborating with him.

Ben and I assembled a deep lineup that also included the Blind Boys of Alabama, Irma Thomas, Arcade Fire's Win Butler, George Porter Jr., Valerie June, Ivan Neville, Gogol Bordello's Eugene Hutz, Nicole Atkins, and a few of my go-to guys from the Wetlands days: Robert Randolph, Eric Krasno, Joe Russo, and Tom Hamilton.

The music was everything we had hoped it would be (Search "Jam The Vote" on YouTube), and thousands of streamers took the pledge.

The venue itself was not entirely full, though. A headline is that these multi-artist bills do not sell as many tickets as they should. People want to dig in and go deep with their favorites and can be less enthusiastic about a rainbow of musicians. Not me, of course. Rainbows are real, and I'll take them wherever I can.

It was an expensive night, but the good stuff isn't cheap. It's like they say: "You can't do something fast, cheap, and good." It is not possible to achieve all three. You can accomplish two out of three, but that's it. You can do it fast and cheap, but it won't be good. You can do it fast and good, but it won't be cheap.

That's just the way it goes.

But I believed in what we were doing, and I'm still proud of the concept, which no one had tried before.

Plus, it was great working with Ben. Not only is he an exceptionally creative guy, he's the real deal. His parents, Allan and Sandra, founded Pres Hall in 1961, and as he reminded everyone that evening: "The civil rights amendments had not been passed yet, and it was illegal for blacks and whites to socialize, to play music together, to drink together, to do *anything* together. They opened a place called Preservation Hall, and that place was filled with so much love that it became their life's work. It's what I do every day of my life, and it's what these gentlemen up onstage do every day of their life. We can't go back. There's nothing to go back *to*. There's only forward."

When I took the stage, I said, "It's easy to be frustrated. It's easy to not want to be involved. It's easy to want to turn your back. But we can't let that be. We have to stay involved. We have to believe. We have to all participate. We have to all vote."

Then I encouraged everyone in attendance or watching at home to text a friend to tell them about the show and make the pledge to vote. While I was standing there, I texted my high school English teacher Steve Bender, even if I doubt he needed my reminder. He's a music fan, and it's been gratifying to remain in touch with him over the years.

The election results convinced me to up my commitment to HeadCount.

Marc and Andy had been the board chairs from the very beginning. By now, I'd been on multiple boards, including New York Public Radio, the City Parks Foundation, and the Rock & Roll Hall of Fame, so I had some sense about board governance. The two of them had been doing a great job, but you shouldn't have the same chairs in place throughout the life of the organization.

So in June 2019, I became Chairman. We have set it up so that each board chair can only serve for four years, which is important. That way, I can focus my energies, and then someone else can come in and do the same. I'm here to do my part.

While HeadCount still has that Grateful Dead / jamband core, we have also been able to reach many people beyond that constituency. During 2019, HeadCount volunteers were at every Ariana Grande concert and every Billie Eilish show. In fact, Ariana broke the HeadCount record with over thirty-three thousand voters registered on her Sweetener World Tour. In October 2020, Head-Count announced that it had registered over one million voters since its formation in 2004, with nearly half of those during the 2020 election cycle.

When I took over as chair, I said, "When it's done right, the combination of live music and activism, of something that has an element of really meaning something, too, that's powerful."

This is something I learned at Wetlands. These days, it has become more important than ever. And I still believe.

40

BOBBY & PHIL

Bob Weir and Phil Lesh
Radio City Music Hall, New York, New York
March 2, 2018

After GD50, Bob and Phil set off on separate paths. Phil collaborated with a number of younger players and placed a particular focus on working with his son Grahame in the Terrapin Family Band. I continued to do shows with him in my venues and stretched out to other settings as well, like a 2017 Halloween run with the Preservation Hall Jazz Band, Nicki Bluhm, and Robert Randolph that began at the Anthem in Washington, DC, before eventually making its way to the Capitol.

As for Bob, he remained active with Mickey Hart and Bill Kreutzmann, hitting amphitheaters and arenas across the country in Dead & Company, which paired the trio with John Mayer, Oteil Burbridge, and Jeff Chimenti. Dead & Company had been set in motion during the uncertain period leading up to Fare Thee Well, sparked by John asking Bob to join him for a few songs when he guest hosted *The Late Late Show* in February 2015. John was out there on the floor with the rest of us in Santa Clara and Chicago. When Dead & Company launched their initial tour in the fall of 2015, I had an opportunity to be involved, but I was happy to walk away with my memories of Fare Thee Well. Even so, I remained on good terms with everyone, and Dead & Company headlined LOCKN' in 2018. I continue to do things with each of the guys.

It was at LOCKN' in 2017 that a new idea came together. It started when I invited Bobby to join Phil and the Terrapin Family Band for a special set in which they would perform the Grateful Dead's *Terrapin Station* album in its entirety. As part of the deals I made with each of them to appear at the festival, they also agreed to perform a set in the Super VIP tent.

We had one SVIP set per day at LOCKN'. Given the economics of putting on a festival, the ability to sell VIP and Super VIP packages was materially helpful in keeping LOCKN' afloat. The revenue generated from VIP tickets also helped keep the prices lower for GA tickets.

Concert promotion is a tough business—you lose a thousand or win a hundred. Things become a bit easier when you're at super scale, but it's resource intensive, which is why you really only have Live Nation and AEG doing it at that level. They're able to buy up entire tours and cross-collateralize, spreading out expenses, so that the big nights offset the slow ones. They also have more leverage with partners and sponsors. It's hard to close a beer marketing deal for one venue when another company can offer signage in thirty venues. The same holds true for an event like LOCKN'—when AEG and Live Nation each have a bucket of festivals they have available for sponsorships, that's going to be a more compelling meeting for a potential client. It's a tough game.

LOCKN's location in the Blue Ridge Mountains has made for inspiring views and tremendous vibes. There's an actual forest on-site, which is something that can't be said of festivals in New York City, Austin, Chicago, or San Francisco. Then again, those events have millions of people within walking distance, and it is easier for their marketing teams to bring partners out to the event. Over the years, I found if we could bring someone out to LOCKN', they would get it. We quietly nudged our way onto a few top ten festival lists. I would also match the musical moments from LOCKN' against whatever you would find at any other event, whether on our main stage, Garcia's Forest, or the super VIP tent.

My idea for the Saturday SVIP set at LOCKN' 2017 was to pair Bobby and Phil. I am proud of the musical collaborations I have assembled over the years, from Hanson with Bob Weir to Talib Kweli with Phil Lesh (stay tuned). This one seems obvious, but for whatever reason, no one had pushed them to do it before. But when I saw them in the tent at LOCKN', I knew that more people needed to see it again (including me!).

The thing about Bobby and Phil is that they know where they're going and can instinctively weave in and out of each other in a way that's unrivaled. Bobby's playing is idiosyncratic to the extreme, and Phil is right there with him because he is brilliant, talented, and they have known each other for more than fifty years.

Bobby and Phil are a great match in an acoustic setting. During the Furthur years, there was occasional tension because they each had their musical preferences. One of these was stage volume. Phil likes it loud so that he can feel the sound of his bass rig, while Bobby prefers it quieter. Another issue was the pace of the music. Phil prefers the tempo to be faster, while Bobby likes to slow it down. So there was a fair share of push and pull there.

I can remember a discussion at Phil's beach house in Stinson Beach pre–Fare Thee Well. It was part of an ongoing dialogue while preparing for the Dead 50 shows. The conversation turned to the core of the Grateful Dead sound—whether it was more about the music or the songs. Bobby leans toward the songs, while Phil's more music. It had been a little while since they had seen each other, and they were having an impassioned yet brotherly debate on the subject. All of that plays into their preferences about stage volume and tempo. But when the two of them are in an acoustic setting, most of that creative tension dissipates.

For their SVIP set, they started out as a duo, and then a few songs in, they were joined by their old Furthur bandmate Joe Russo on drums. Phil's son Grahame hopped on toward the end, as did Elliott Peck from the Terrapin Family Band (and Midnight North with Grahame). The performance lasted about an hour, and it was incredible. It was everything I had hoped it would be, except it ended too soon. I wanted two sets.

Next up for Bob that evening was a late-night sit-in with Joe Russo's Almost Dead. Before he took the stage, I walked up to Bob, told him how great the set had been, and said we should do it again. He responded, "Yeah, that would be fun. We should do a little run together of classic theaters."

Then Bobby walked up and performed a few songs with JRAD. When he was done, around 2:00 a.m., he made an immediate beeline for me and said, "We should do Radio City, the Chicago Theatre, and that old music hall in Boston."

And that is exactly what we did.

I am amazed by what goes through his head. Apparently, he worked that out between "Black-Throated Wind" and "Jack Straw." Or maybe it came to him in a flash when he was walking over and saw me. I can't be sure.

I was reminded of the first year of LOCKN' when he performed for three nights with Furthur. I was standing there moments after he completed two amazing sets on Friday night, and his first comment to me was "Did you see the University of Georgia flag out there? Nice flag." Then he began talking about the college flag. That's the multidimensionality of Bobby Weir.

Sure enough, in March 2018, six months after Bob named our theoretical tour itinerary, it became our not-so-theoretical tour itinerary. Bobby and Phil played six shows: two apiece at Radio City, the Wang Theatre, and the Chicago Theatre.

Jumping back to LOCKN' 2018, I mentioned that Bobby was there with Dead & Company, and I often think back to an exchange that we had shortly after he closed out the festival with the group. I texted him my thanks about an hour after they wrapped up their final set on Sunday night, and shortly afterward, he answered, "You bet. Good, clean American fun."

That is quintessential Bobby Weir.

It sums up his general approach to live music, and it is aspirational, too. It sets a simple standard that I strive to hit with any of my shows.

The opening night of the tour, March 2, was also the first show I'd ever promoted at Radio City. On one hand, I try to remain in the moment. It's essential to keep my head down and focus on the work. Still, it is worthwhile to have a bucket list if only to remind yourself that there's always another mountain to climb. Just don't forget that while it's sweet to hit the rare air, you should never get distracted by the view. The moment you forget, the wind will knock you over, and there's a long way to fall.

I had been going to Radio City Music Hall my whole life, so I was happy to check off this one. There also was a certain symmetry in putting on that initial show with members of the Grateful Dead. Come to think of it, they've also been a part of similar firsts at the Apollo, BAM (Brooklyn Academy of Music), and Golden Gate Park.

On the first night at Radio City a massive storm walloped us with rain, snow, sleet, and wind. Some folks were worried that we'd lose power or that no one would show up. Everything worked out on both counts, though.

I had a feeling we'd fill the room. All six shows had sold out in a matter of minutes, and when a concert feels like an event, people will get there despite the weather, which then makes it feel like *more* of an event. That happened a second time before opening night in Boston, with six inches of snow in the city and higher totals across the state, but we all pushed through.

That first Radio City show made me appreciate Bobby and Phil, as well as the whole Grateful Dead legacy, in a whole new way. Stripping down the music brought its power out in a new way, which is hard to do with music that's been played for almost sixty years.

The Grateful Dead catalog remains vibrant and vast because it is constantly being reinvented by people who approach it differently. Whether acoustic or electric, duo, trio, or big band, these songs constantly reveal themselves anew when skilled musicians approach them with open minds, hearts, and tempos.

For a minute there, I thought we would do more of these shows. We had talked about West Coast dates, but the scheduling didn't quite work out. I'm not ruling it out down the road, though. It makes so much sense because they play so incredibly well together.

Good, clean American fun.

41

THE APOLLO MISSION

Phil Lesh & Friends with Talib Kweli
Apollo Theater, New York, New York
September 7, 2018

By the fall of 2018, my deal with Phil Lesh had been in effect for five years.

During that time, it felt like I had earned his trust.

There was an article in which he said, "Peter thinks like a musician. He understands the spirit of the music I'm trying to make because he wants to create situations for that music that enhance the experience on many levels."

After putting on ten thousand shows over twenty-five years, I have a sense of what works onstage, not because I'm a musician but because I'm a fan and an intense one, at that. I particularly like improvisational music, which adds a layer to everything. We live in a world where so much is scheduled and planned. But the music that holds the most appeal for me is the music where you don't know what's going to happen. That's where the magic lies.

As part of my fandom, I'm drawn to the unforeseen, which is what has prompted my interest in collaborations, placing musicians in new contexts, which encourages them to respond to each other in the moment.

One of the most satisfying expressions of this approach is introducing my old friends to one another so we can see what develops.

Which is how I brought Talib Kweli and Phil Lesh together at the Apollo Theater.

I've known Talib since the Wetlands days. He was at the club a fair amount during the late '90s. He tells a story about being at a Lyricist Lounge event at Wetlands where Mos Def performed "Children's Story" from their collaborative Black Star album. The song was perceived as a dig at Puff Daddy, who happened to be in the audience, which resulted in "one of the illest conversations I've ever seen."

Talib also recalls his efforts to speak with Common at Wetlands: "I went to the sound check to try and catch him, but he was doing an interview with Joe Clair for *Rap City* at the time, so I didn't get a chance to talk to him. But it's funny, if anyone has footage of that *Rap City*, you see me in the background as Common and Joe Clair are coming out of the tour bus. You see me in front of Wetlands waiting to meet Common."

Here's a fun fact from that Common gig, which took place on July 21, 1999. Common was the late show, but the early show was Mickey Hart and Planet Drum, which captures the diversity of sounds that we had going on at Wetlands, something that I don't think was fully appreciated at the time.

Back to now, I had a feeling that magic would ensue if I could pair Talib with Phil at the Apollo for a special HeadCount benefit we were planning to encourage voter turnout before the 2018 midterm elections. I pitched it to Phil, and even though he was not familiar with Talib, I had earned Phil's trust, so he was down to try it. That is the best part of what I do.

When Phil originally hesitated to do Fare Thee Well, he expressed a preference to work with artists who were not that familiar with his musical approach. So with that spirit in mind, I've done what I can to team him up with the Preservation Hall Jazz Band, Gary Clark Jr., Karl Denson, Luther Dickinson, Anders Osborne, Keller Williams, Stanley Jordan, Josh Kaufman, Eric Johnson, Stuart Bogie, Twiddle, and others..

Back to the idea of old friends, it's been really cool to be able to connect Phil with some of my OG Wetlands crew, including Robert Randolph and Eric Krasno (both of whom played with him at the Apollo). I've seen the impact that playing with Phil has had on these younger guys who have then gone on to explore this music on their own. Robert has worked on a soul-infused Dead project, while Kraz has been a member of Oteil & Friends and has done a couple of JGB things with Lettuce.

I am comfortable making creative suggestions to artists but only if the set and setting is right. I am not going to force something if it isn't going to land well. I would never want to put Phil, or any other musician, in a position that makes them uncomfortable. It's a balance.

I am on the board of New York Public Radio, which oversees a few stations, including one with a classical format, WQXR. I thought it would be interesting to have Phil perform with the Attacca Quartet for a WQXR benefit. For whatever reason, he was reluctant to do this before he finally agreed. What he said to me, though, was, "Okay, if it's important to you, I'll do it." Now, when an artist says something like that, I would not recommend moving forward unless it is *really* important to you. In this instance, there was far less upside than potential downside. So I pulled back and said, "Let's hold off on this for now," because my relationship with Phil was more important to me.

When it came to Talib Kweli, however, Phil didn't hesitate. Some of that I also credit to Grahame, who has been a wonderful facilitator over the past couple of years. He's grown confident so that he can serve as a music director, becoming a voice for his father. Grahame can feel what Phil wants to do, and he can convey that to the guest musicians in a very eloquent way.

Phil & Friends lineups are always at the nexus of dreams and reality. Assembling a roster of musicians can be like playing fantasy baseball. Constructing a Phil lineup is a multidimensional puzzle of who works musically, vibe-wise, has an existing relationship, and who is available when the shows are happening. In addition, as anyone who has ever been in a fantasy league knows, you also need to abide by the salary cap.

Even taking reality into account, it's still about the magic that I hope to experience when I'm out there in the audience, watching it all come together in the moment.

Someone's birthday can be a fun way to support larger goals. This is why I utilized my fortieth birthday in 2012 and this evening in 2018 to raise funds and awareness for HeadCount.

When I'm putting together an event, the fact that it coincides with my birthday can make folks slightly more willing to participate, especially if there is a larger cause. It's tough to know to what extent that was a factor in 2018, because the show was at the historic Apollo Theater (my first as a promoter and Phil's first as a performer in that storied room). It is important to be aware of when the venue is the draw, and in this case, the Apollo was the draw.

We were two months out from the midterm elections, which added meaning to the event as well. We called the evening "Don't Tell Me This Country Ain't Got No Heart: A Benefit for Voter Participation." The proceeds supported HeadCount's stretch run with a number of initiatives, including a program to register voters at high schools, a get-out-the-vote tour of colleges, and direct assistance for local organizations registering voters of all ages. We also facilitated a weekly voter registration drive at the Apollo's famed Amateur Night over the six weeks that followed.

Before the start of the second set, HeadCount's executive director Andy Bernstein addressed the crowd, thanking them for their support. Then Phil came out and encouraged everyone to "get involved, because this is your country, and nothing's going to change until you make up your mind to make it happen. So God bless you all, and dig in, because a change has got to come."

They were joined by my friends in the Terrapin Family Band, Robert, Kraz, and Nicki Bluhm, who came onstage bearing a cupcake, as Phil added, "On a happier note, we have a little ceremony we'd like to perform right now. Well, it's quite simple. Today is Peter Shapiro's birthday, so we're going to sing 'Happy Birthday' to him."

At first, there was some confusion because a few of the musicians were looking at the side of the stage, trying to locate me. Eventually, they realized I was out there in the middle of the audience and gestured for me to come onstage. However, I was quite content where I was, about fifteen rows back, with Rebecca.

I mean, where would *you* be? Backstage, with all the distractions and the muffled sound, or out front, taking it all in and breathing the music?

The second set was about to begin, and not only did we have all those amazing musicians onstage but Talib Kweli and the Harlem Gospel Choir were still on deck.

I gestured my appreciation so they could feel me and then got ready to go to my happy place.

I am still a fan. I love being at the shows. It never fades. Live music just does not get old. At least for me it doesn't.

The process of getting to the shows can be tiresome, but never the shows themselves. That is why I do what I do.

We'd named the night after a line from "Shakedown Street," which was the point during the set when Talib Kweli stepped out and crushed it, during a sequence that also led into his own "Get By." Then it was the choir's turn to elevate the proceedings, which they did during "Knockin' on Heaven's Door," "Turn On Your Love Light," and the "Touch of Grey" encore. If you have any doubts about my assessment, the stream is still up there on YouTube (and after you watch it, why not stop by HeadCount.org to make a donation).

I viewed this night as a continuation of Jam The Vote. While both evenings featured multiple rousing musical performances, this one felt a bit more satisfying on a political level after Election Day 2018, making for a truly successful Apollo mission.

42

THE MAJORITY PARTY

The Majority Party
National Building Museum, Washington, DC
January 3, 2019

After Fare Thee Well, I continued to have a great relationship with Mickey Hart.

A few days before Dead & Company played LOCKN' in 2018, I texted him a five-day weather graphic, sharing the prediction of highs in the eighties, lows in the sixties, with 0 percent chance of rain. He responded, "U can't fool me! Fake news!" I had a few fascinating conversations with him over the weekend to follow, because Mickey always has something going on in the realms of science, technology, and music—typically a combination thereof. After the band closed out their final set on Sunday night, he emailed me a simple, "You did good, kid," which meant a lot.

Then in mid-December, a few weeks following the midterm elections in which the Democrats reclaimed the House of Representatives, I received a voice mail from Mickey: "Is this the greatest promoter in the universe? I thought so. Anybody who can make a rainbow can call Mickey Hart back on his studio phone. So take a deep breath and give me a call if you dare."

With Mickey, I'm always up for the dare.

I returned the call and learned that Mickey wanted me to help throw a party for a friend of his.

That friend was Nancy Pelosi, the date was January 3, and the occasion was her return to power as Speaker of the House, following eight years of Republican rule in the chamber.

I had plans to be with my family in Hawaii at that time, but I couldn't say no. My plan was to fly in from our vacation, spend twelve hours on the ground in DC, and then fly back to Hawaii. That meant about ten hours in the air each way, but it would be well worth it.

I suppose I could have arranged the whole thing from afar, but you can't be there if you're not there.

A few months after I became the HeadCount chair, I made the decision to fly from Chicago to New York on the chance I could have three minutes with Taylor Swift. She was shooting a commercial at the Bowl, and I needed to be back in the Midwest later that same day, but I wanted to try to enlist her for a HeadCount campaign. There's nothing like being in front of the musician, and since she would be at my place, I thought it was worth a shot.

As it turned out, she had an entourage, and I just didn't get the right moment. It is important to have a proper sense of timing and touch; otherwise, things can go backward. I also didn't want to piss off the ad agency and my team in case Taylor complained: "The owner came up to me." That was the risk, and while the reward would have been a HeadCount partnership, I read the room and decided to stand down.

It wasn't the first time I'd flown somewhere to ask a question of an artist. Early in my career, I came to appreciate that sometimes the best way to connect with a touring musician is to get out of town. If you have an idea to pitch, backstage at Madison Square Garden is not the optimal setting. It's filled with distractions, including plenty of other people vying for an artist's attention. So to connect, I recommend a less cluttered environment, away from a major entertainment center. Sometimes you don't need to travel that far. When I wanted to spend some time with the guys in Dead & Company, I went to Hartford, and it was absolutely quiet backstage.

In June 2017, I flew to Louisville, Kentucky, to ask Bono a question. I hadn't given up on the idea of reuniting Led Zeppelin, and I thought we could raise a billion dollars for charity by making tickets available through a lottery, in which people would purchase a chance to win seats. There would be one show, and proceeds would benefit the ONE campaign founded by Bono and Bill Gates to address global hunger.

U2 is the only band I know that schedules a day of preshow meet and greet with their friends, politicians, civic leaders, media members, and celebrities. There is nothing else like that pregame, especially in New York or LA. But they were playing at the college football stadium in Kentucky, where it was only Christy Turlington, Ashley Judd, and me. So I had some time with Bono and talked to him about my idea, which he liked and may yet come to pass.

There was another time when I flew to Lawrence, Kansas, for a conversation with Warren Haynes. I met with him on his tour bus shortly after his band and crew crossed paths with Willie Nelson, who had shared some of his stash.

So I spent some quality time on a very smoky bus. We were reconnecting and shooting the shit for a while, just having fun, when Warren turned to me and asked, "Okay, so what's this meeting about?"

I looked him straight in the eye and realized that I didn't know.

I had made my way to Lawrence, Kansas, to share a business proposal, but I could not remember what it was.

Eventually, some panic reflex kicked in and I realized I was there to chat about his participation on a Jammys tour, which eventually came to pass.

As for Nancy Pelosi, I had initially met her in late October 2018 while visiting a different musical artist in a quiet, smoke-free setting.

We were backstage at the Walter Kerr Theatre, following a Bruce Springsteen concert, and I was deeply impressed with her. She was so intelligent, and her energy level was high.

Bruce was starting to wind down his Broadway residency, and I had asked Jimmy Fallon if he'd seen it. Jimmy hadn't, through no fault of his own, because the dude's busy, so we made plans to go together. I saw the show multiple times over the fifteen-month run, and I still can't believe how Bruce was able to keep it fresh.

What he did was the opposite of what we do in the jam world, where the magic is in the new because you don't know where it's going. Bruce pretty much did the same show, but he performed with such vigor that it felt fresh every time.

Jimmy and I were about the last people to enter. We sat and drank beers in his car outside the theater until everyone had gone in. That's when we were told that we would be invited backstage afterward.

So following Bruce's performance, we went back and spotted the two other people who also had been invited to say hi to Bruce: Nancy Pelosi and her husband, Paul. Nancy was in a good mood, and she explained that she had just seen some numbers leading her to believe that the Democrats would win back the House.

I was looking forward to meeting her again on January 3 to offer my congratulations and remind her of that night.

The idea I shared with Mickey was that we would have a core band and then bring out different guests to take a musical journey through the states and districts that had flipped from red to blue by performing songs from those regions.

We called the event the Majority Party. Along with Mickey we confirmed Idina Menzel, Ivan Neville, George Porter Jr., Sikiru Adepoju, Karl Denson, Eric Krasno, Nikki Glaspie, Giovanni Hidalgo, and Alecia Chakour to join what we'd dubbed the 116th House Band.

We quickly designed some art, featuring the Statue of Liberty, with her lamp replaced by a blue wave to represent the swell of Democratic victories. Whenever possible, I like to create the imaging for a special event in the very early stages of planning. It helps me visualize what we're doing, and it also helps when I'm pitching an artist. If done properly, it can be more effective than words in communicating my intentions.

If a concept is really good, it's worthwhile to spend time creating the perfect name, subtitle, and logo. It lends an additional layer of substance so that it doesn't feel like something you just dashed off.

For the past five years, I've worked with art designer Corinne Guglielmo. Having an A-level designer is one of the most important ingredients to doing what I do the way I hope to do it. Having great early art is like catching the opening kickoff in the end zone and running it back to midfield, so you can start your first drive from there.

With the new Congress only weeks away, Mickey and I continued to refine our plans for the evening. But then on December 22, President Trump shut down the federal government. Many federal offices were forced to close, and employees worked without pay or received furloughs. Given all that was going on, it didn't seem like an appropriate moment to celebrate.

We pulled the plug on December 29. Mickey thanked everyone and said via email, "We will celebrate the new leader of the House at a more appropriate time. Stand by and look for that Bat-Signal."

The Bat-Signal never came.

However, I am prepared to leap into action whenever Mickey calls.

43

EASY RIDER LIVE, BABY!

Easy Rider Live
Radio City Music Hall, New York, New York
September 20, 2019

This one started with a simple forwarded email that arrived out of the blue.

The subject line was "EASY RIDER 50th Anniversary Live Concert."

It came from Nick Lippman, who manages Rob Thomas. I knew him from *All Access*.

Nick posed the simple question: "Any interest for you or your people in getting involved?" This was early December 2018 and *Easy Rider*'s anniversary would take place in 2019.

At first, I almost reflexively answered, "No, I'm too busy."

Things are tossed at me pretty regularly, now more than ever. So I have to figure out which ones makes sense—whether I have the available time and whether it's a situation where I feel I will be able to make some type of significant contribution and have an opportunity for some upside.

As I read deeper into the email, I soon appreciated why I'd want to be involved. Peter Fonda himself, the cultural icon who starred in, cowrote, and produced *Easy Rider* was the creative force behind this project. He was looking to celebrate the classic movie (which is on the AFI's list of 100 Greatest American Films) with a live concert. The email also mentioned that Peter had already started working with T Bone Burnett, who would serve as music director.

They had my attention.

A lot of times, the way I will judge whether I should be involved in an outside project is if it continues to occupy my headspace in the hours after I hear about it. In this instance, I found myself returning to it over the course of the day with any number of thoughts about what we could do and how we could do it.

While I still wasn't sure about the nature of the working relationships and what the expectations would be, I was certainly excited to have a meeting.

So in January, I went out to dinner with Peter, who brought T Bone with him. I went with Jason Miller, an executive at Live Nation New York. Aside from Jason being a friend, this was one of those times when it was smart to partner with someone. I was thinking about having a band play alongside the film at Radio City Music Hall, and I needed additional support. He had a team in place, so we could leverage that infrastructure. Plus, I was pretty sure he could hold Radio City without putting down a deposit, which is a luxury not afforded to an independent promoter like myself.

At the dinner, we talked about life, politics, and the pursuit of magic.

In that setting, you don't start out by discussing the project. You need to get a feel for the people who are going to join you in the trenches. What will it be like to share ideas with them? Will they be open-minded when presented with something new? How will they conduct themselves when shit goes wrong (because shit always goes wrong and you need to be prepared for those known unknowns)?

Peter liked to interweave the conversation about the task at hand with outside topics in order to align the vibe. These were not quite digressions because going off topic helped to create context and build the relationship. It helped to round out the edges, so that if there were unknowns, we'd be on the same page. And all of that would drive the creative.

We did speak about the overall vision, which was to have live music in between the dialogue sequences. The film has clean breaks between dialogue and music, so it was easy for me to imagine, and Peter Fonda got it from the first minute.

As for the name, that came quickly, too.

Easy Rider Live. Say what it is.

I knew it needed to take place at Radio City, which has the largest indoor LED screen in the world. I love large format, and I'd seen it in action from watching all those Christmas shows over the years—it helps to pay attention. So despite all the expenses that came with putting on a show at Radio City, at least we already had a huge screen living there.

Shortly afterward, we got an email from Peter, who thanked us for taking the meeting. Then he shared, "I am very excited about what a great time we're going to have doing this concert. It's been in my heart and head for a few years, now, and I can see it all happening! For the movie, the filmmakers, the musicians, the songwriters, the idea that wouldn't leave my mind or heart until it was put up on the big screen!"

I was still in the process of realizing that vision with Peter when he passed away from lung cancer on August 16. I'd had a great experience hanging with him, and his widow, Parky, told us, "He loved you guys. He loved this project, and he really wanted to see it happen. Let's keep going."

So we continued because it felt like the right thing to do. His final Instagram post from August 1 was an image taken outside Radio City Music Hall with "Easy Rider Live September 20" on the marquee. He added the simple message "Easy Rider Live Baby!!!"

I also very much enjoyed getting to hang with T Bone. At this point, I've been fortunate to work with some incredible musical directors, including T Bone, Steve Jordan, Don Was, and Ben Jaffe. T Bone's approach with the musicians was loose and easygoing. He wouldn't tell anyone to do something in a specific way. Instead, he'd let them take the lead and then gently guide them through energy and vibe. One of the ideas that came out of our very first dinner was to get John Kay (Steppenwolf) and Roger McGuinn (the Byrds). Their voices are deeply entwined with the film, from Steppenwolf's "Born to Be Wild" and "The Pusher" to the Byrds' "Wasn't Born to Follow," Roger's cover of Bob Dylan's "It's Alright Ma (I'm Only Bleeding)," and his own "Ballad of Easy Rider." We later added Peter Stampfel from the Holy Modal Rounders, who performed "If You Want to Be a Bird" in the film. Then I asked Tash Neal and Nicole Atkins to be part of the ensemble, because they're versatile and I knew they'd contribute the proper spirit. Rather than think of this as a one-off, we were hoping that it might be scalable, so we wanted to have a core group who could receive direction from T Bone and then take it on the road.

As September 20 approached, there were still lots of things to work out. Some of these were quite granular, like the question of what we were going to show on the screens when the musicians jammed longer than the original music appears in the film. Should the screen go black? Should there be a live shot of the band? Should we project a still or title card from the film? (We eventually decided to focus on the band.)

While I was working through the logistics and creative thinking for Easy Rider Live, I was doing the same for dozens of other events. The way that this book has been organized into chapters, the shows appear as discrete, independent entities, which is also how they are received by audiences. However, that's not quite how I experience them. I am a juggler. On any given day, not only am I preparing for any number of future projects, I typically have multiple events happening simultaneously. The night of Easy Rider Live, the Black Pumas played at Brooklyn Bowl and Lucinda Williams at the Cap. Across the country in Vegas was an '80s Dance Party featuring DJ CO1. My first Madison Square Garden show was also eight days away.

I keep a file in the notes section of my phone where I list all the major projects I have in the works. This helps me make sure I stay on top of everything and sometimes prompts me to jump into one of them from a clean perspective.

Another challenge with Easy Rider Live was that we could not hold a tech rehearsal inside Radio City a day before the show because the room's too expensive. We were aware of this limitation going in—the cost of paying the in-house crew would have busted our budget. However, we concluded that Radio City was the perfect venue nonetheless. Still, that's why I prefer to do events in my own places whenever possible, because rooms can be expensive if you don't control them (and sometimes even when you do).

This is not to say we didn't rehearse; we just couldn't do it at Radio City. On September 19, we went into SIR, the leading backline rental company that also has studio spaces for this sort of thing—we have used it over the years, going back to The Jammys. But while this helped us work through some of the cues, we still needed to coordinate it all with the big screen at Radio City. So I brought in Dave Gioiella, who I first met at Northwestern and who edited *And Miles to Go* and *American Road*.

Even with Dave on board, the night started with a hiccup. There were a few minutes when we couldn't quite sync up everything. It reminded me of our *Wetlands Preserved* screening at the Ziegfeld. Thankfully, like that evening, it all came together after some brief angst.

All told, it was an incredible night.

The *Hollywood Reporter* will back me up on this one: "It all worked amazingly well, with the film not altered in any way, save for breaks allowing the musicians to perform extended versions of the songs. After the screening ended, the image on the massive screen was that of Fonda, wearing his Captain America jacket with an American flag on the back, taken from the original cover of the soundtrack LP."

Before Peter passed away, we had plans to present Easy Rider Live in Vegas on July 4. But that became too difficult to pull off even before coronavirus.

I still believe in the fundamental concept.

There is good soil there; I just need to cultivate it.

The pandemic slowed us down (although it did get me thinking about drive-in theaters).

While I hope to bring it back one day, if I never do it again, it was an honor to have dinner with Peter Fonda and work with him on this.

His dream was to see it at Radio City, and although he wasn't there in person, we pulled it off together.

Easy Rider Live Baby!!!

44

THERE'S A REWARD

There's a Reward: A Celebration of the Life
and Music of Neal Casal
The Capitol Theatre, Port Chester, New York
September 25, 2019

I'd often go to Becca's family's cabin on Lake Michigan right after LOCKN'. Sometimes I liked to drive, but in 2019, I flew.

I'd been there for less than a day when I received a call on Tuesday morning with the news that Neal Casal had taken his own life.

It was shocking news, as I had just spent a few days with him at LOCKN', where I had seen him smiling throughout the weekend. He had been part of two amazing performances at the festival, which I look back on with warmth.

On Thursday, his band Circles Around the Sun performed late night in Garcia's Forest. I remember hopping in a golf cart with Joe Russo and Tommy Hamilton to see the set. Neal saw us watching and invited Joe to sit in, which was a cool moment.

Neal also was part of the Oteil & Friends set. It was Oteil Burbridge's fifty-fifth birthday, so we had put together a special lineup that included Neal, Melvin Seals, Eric Krasno, Jay Lane, Jen Hartswick, Natalie Cressman, Duane Betts, and Jason Crosby (and a cake as well). It was a lot of fun, and Bob Weir even sat in for a few songs, which was a big deal for everyone involved.

Neal was a sweet soul. We'd become friendly over the previous five years, and he even had called me a few times asking for advice on this and that.

We had connected through Justin Kreutzmann. In early 2015, I was trying to figure out what to do during set break at Fare Thee Well. What do you play between two sets of the fiftieth anniversary of the Grateful Dead? How do you hold people when they're sitting there beneath the fluorescent lights, freaking out? We began with the idea of creating unique film presentations for each of the five shows. Then the question arose about what to do for a musical score. Justin's idea was to call his friend Neal, who called *his* friends Adam MacDougall, Dan Horne, and Mark Levy to form what became known as Circles Around the Sun.

I got to known Neal through his gigs with the Chris Robinson Brotherhood and Phil Lesh & Friends. I had also seen him in Ryan Adams's band back in the day, including a memorable version of "Wharf Rat" at The Jammys in 2005. Still, I was unprepared for the richness and depth of what he'd create for the set breaks at GD50.

We'd given him a nearly impossible task because we wanted set break music worthy of the occasion that wouldn't distract from the main event. Here's what Neal said in *Relix*: "This was all of us going deeply into our Grateful Dead influence and bringing it forth, and trying to walk that fine line between being reverent and staying within the sounds and staying within that color palette. There is a palette of Grateful Dead musical colors that is there to work with, and if you go too far outside of it, then it doesn't feel familiar. It doesn't feel right, but if you just mimic or if you just kind of paint by numbers, then it's too close to the source and somehow it undermines the mission. So there's this really fine line that we tried to walk and a small window to try to fit ourselves through. The sensitivity of these musicians is what made it successful. We did it all in two days. We did it all live. There are no overdubs. We just caught lightning in a bottle."

That he did.

One of my many pleasant surprises at Fare Thee Well was looking into the crowd at halftime and watching a sea of moving colors because people were getting down to the music.

During those set breaks, dozens of people asked me, "Who *is* this?"

Neal and his friends had initially created these sounds solely for the purpose of accompanying Justin's videos, but the music quickly took on its own momentum. So Rhino Records released *Interludes for the Dead*, a 2-CD soundtrack that immediately produced a fan base for CATS beyond the people who had made it to Fare Thee Well.

I kept telling Neal, "You guys really need to play a show." I'm proud to say it finally happened at LOCKN' 2016 in the woods. From there, they would go on to record two additional studio records, which expanded the nature of their sound, and we did a lot of shows together. Their final gig with Neal was in the forest three years later.

As soon as I learned of Neal's passing, I called his manager, Gary Waldman. I've known Gary since the Wetlands days, when he was Robert Randolph's original manager.

Gary was heartbroken in that moment but said, "I'm going to do the best fucking tribute of all time to my friend." They were close friends who had known each other since Neal was a New Jersey high school student.

I immediately volunteered the Capitol. That is the benefit of having a stage of your own. You have the ability to make commitments on the spot, whether they are somber occasions such as this one or more joyful instances like one I pursued early on with Stevie Van Zandt.

Stevie was looking to put together a multimedia concert event, in which he would reunite the original members of the Rascals for the first time in forty years. He wanted to bring it to Broadway, but that was expensive, and he needed proof of concept. I met him while we were still in construction, through Marc Brickman, who helped design our lighting. Marc worked with Pink Floyd and later on two Olympics as well as *All Access*. He suggested that I speak with Stevie, and we eventually premiered *Once Upon a Dream* over six nights at the Cap in December 2012 with Marc supplying the visuals.

When I first sat down with Stevie, his enthusiasm was contagious. I didn't know all that much about the Rascals, but he enlightened me. Sometimes when you get to the creative side with an artist, it's hard to say no because they're so into it. Stevie was *really* into it.

He had an elaborate vision for *Once Upon a Dream*, and the project drew on my strengths. There are three elements to developing something like this. First, you have to create it. Then you need to execute on the creation. Finally, you need the proper platform for the execution.

Some of my favorite moments on the project were sharing meals and ideas with him (they still are). I remember a lunch at the Breslin, which was my lunch spot in the city (my dinner spot is Carbone—I guess I also build relationships with restaurants). We had a bottle of wine, which I don't normally do at that time of day. But when he asked, "Should we have a second bottle?" of course the answer was yes.

After opening at the Cap, Stevie eventually did take *Once Upon a Dream* to Broadway. I could have been involved, but the budget was too high for me. After a brief run, it toured as a road show. Ultimately, *Once Upon a Dream* was the product of Stevie Van Zandt's artistry and ambition that was achieved through my platform.

After Neal Casal passed, I was able to offer that platform to Gary Waldman. I was also able to tell him, "Whatever it costs, I will cover it." There were a fair amount of expenses involved with bringing in all the artists, but that was our contribution.

We also streamed the show, so it reached a couple of thousand people at the Cap along with tens of thousands at home. It also served as a benefit for MusiCares, and we raised over $25,000. We also made a $10,000 seed donation to Backline, the nonprofit organization that now "connects music industry professionals and their families with mental health and wellness resources."

At one point during the night, I announced that we would be renaming the stage at Garcia's Forest in Neal's honor, to celebrate his circle around the sun with us at LOCKN'.

So many people participated out of friendship and respect for Neal, including his bandmates in the Chris Robinson Brotherhood, Beachwood Sparks, and Circles, as well as Steve Earle, Dave Schools, Scott Metzger, Eric Krasno, Citizen Cope, Leslie Mendelson, Todd Sheaffer, and many others.

Neal was a gifted photographer as well. Before the music started, we shared a slideshow of his work, which included intimate portraits of musicians like Phil Lesh, Jackson Browne, Billy

Gibbons, and Dave Navarro, as well as images that captured the flow of everyday life. He had a great eye.

Neal left behind a detailed note that included a section about what he hoped his friends would do in his immediate absence. We posted it on the screen before the show, and we made a point to follow through on it: "Have an epic party for me and play my favorite records, and remember all of the good times we had, the music, images, and waves we caught. That's all. Play *Exile on Main Street* from beginning to end, and especially, play 'Moonlight Mile.' It's my song, always has been, it's me. I used to lay with my headphones on and listen to that song over and over again and it would make me cry and inspire me to live and create. It's beautiful and elegant and tough and sad and hopeful all at once. Everything I ever wanted to be."

We called the night There's a Reward, after the final song on Neal's 2005 solo album, *Return in Kind*. It is a cover of Jamaican reggae artist Joe Higgs, but Neal made it his own with a solo acoustic performance of this deep ballad, which encourages the listener to keep the faith despite the sorrows that may haunt us from time to time.

I also viewed the title from a personal perspective. There's a reward for putting in all the sound and lights so we could offer the Capitol as a turnkey venue on short notice for an event that needed it. There's a reward for installing all the cameras and streaming technology that allowed us to share this night with the world. And, of course, there's a reward in just hosting the Neal Casal memorial.

It was an important show. Not a happy show but an important show. I feel both honored and obligated to do those.

Over at the Bowl, we've had weddings, birthdays, funerals, bar mitzvahs, memorials—all types of events that capture the range of emotions in the human experience. Sometimes a music venue provides a more important function than offering a stage for a performing artist—it becomes a holy place.

45

MADISON SQUARE FUNK

Vulfpeck
Madison Square Garden, New York, New York
September 28, 2019

The live music world is going to be different in five to ten years. A lot of the rock acts who have been playing arenas for decades, who helped to define what it means to play arenas, won't be touring anymore. The Stones, Roger Waters, the Eagles, Aerosmith, McCartney, Billy Joel, Elton John, and Springsteen will likely hang it up. Petty and Prince are already gone.

This will create an opportunity for new acts to find their way into the big rooms.

In the fall of 2019, we demonstrated how that can happen through a show that inspired a *Billboard* article titled, "How Funk Band Vulfpeck Sold Out Madison Square Garden Without a Manager or Big Label."

Vulfpeck at the Garden. That sounds particularly satisfying because we were able to bring a Wetlands / Brooklyn Bowl–style full-on funk throwdown to MSG. We presented a night of instrumental-heavy grooves in the world's most famous arena, and the room was full.

Vulfpeck's Garden party was not inevitable given the group's prior plays in the market. After debuting at Rockwood Music Hall's Stage 1 in 2013, a 70-capacity room, the group advanced to Rockwood's Stage 2 (200 capacity) later that same year. Vulfpeck then became a regular at the Bowl in 2015 and 2016. The band moved on to the 1,800-capacity Brooklyn Steel for three nights in 2017, followed by two gigs at Brooklyn's 3,000-capacity Kings Theatre in 2018. Then, rather than taking the natural next step, which was Terminal 5, a 3,000-capacity room in Manhattan, Vulfpeck set their sights on MSG.

Ultimately, their ambitions were realized, in partnership with my company, Dayglo and Bowery Presents. We spent minimal money on advertising, and we still sold fourteen thousand tickets. I had a good feeling about this one from the start because I was familiar with Vulfpeck, and I also knew how many Vulfpeck fans we could reach through email lists and socials.

When we put tickets on sale, our Dayglo social platforms and email lists cumed at a million each. While I don't have a personal Facebook or Instagram account, I do appreciate the value of our socials, and I've encouraged their growth. And from experience, I know the email list is even more important. The number of our followers is on par with any other venue out there, including arenas, so I suppose you could say that even though I am not on, I am on in a big way.

While I don't have my own socials, if there's ever something I want to share, I always can reach out to the person who runs point on a particular channel or platform. I don't do this often, but it's always an option.

For an artist, it makes perfect sense to do a co-pro with Dayglo and Bowery. The deal points are the same as if there were only one promoter. However, you get double the promotional support with the platforms of both companies without having to pay for it, and that hopefully helps you sell more tickets.

Vulfpeck has succeeded through their boisterous funk, affirmative vibes, and spot-on social media instincts. They posted an album of silent tracks to Spotify in 2014, and so many of their fans "listened" to *Sleepify* on repeat that Vulfpeck earned $20,000 in royalties, which they used to support a tour where they played for free.

I was quite aware of their dynamic live show because we had done a few dates with them, including multiples at LOCKN'. They're gifted musicians, and the individual band members seem to release a new record every month or two. It's a challenging environment out there, but Vulfpeck seemed to have found the perfect lane.

There are multiple paths to success, and they are often quite distinctive. Hootie & the Blowfish is a great example. They're a great bar band, maybe one of the best ever. I don't say that lightly, and I mean it as a compliment. But part of the reason they achieved success is because they were really good dudes. Early in their career, they would take their van from market to market and go out at night with the college reps and radio promo people. This wasn't phony or contrived, and based on a hang we had at Wetlands, I can confirm that they'd be the last men standing. So when their album *Cracked Rear View* was released, they had a huge network of supportive people who'd been out with them until 3:00 a.m. in Sioux City or Boise or Gainesville. I think that had meaningful impact.

Vulfpeck has a special connection with their fans that they've nurtured through their email list and socials. When we added ours to the mix, we were able to reach a massive audience in a direct, cost-effective manner.

The Dayglo email lists are strong because we have built them over twenty-five years. We have clean lists because they weren't generated by random contest entries where the recipients can't quite figure out how they signed up. So not only are our raw numbers high, but so are the open rates of our emails, because people are interested in what we have to say. So everybody wants the email, and anybody who doesn't probably unsubscribed years ago.

The Brooklyn Bowl list began as the Wetlands list in 1998, and then we ramped it up starting in 2009. We had had someone walk the streets of Williamsburg before we opened, collecting emails (when you're collecting emails, you don't need to ask for a name—the email address and ideally a zip code will suffice—requiring a name can be off-putting). The Cap list started in 2012, *Relix*'s list is twenty-five years old, and all of that really cumes up. We're also in the process of building a new national list through Rock and Roll Playhouse, which is in over forty cities.

Vulfpeck was able to utilize all of that, in addition to the Bowery Presents' sizable online presence.

The band was also smart about the ticket price. The ticket price is set in direct relation to the money guarantee we are paying the artist. Vulfpeck was smart about keeping their financial demands low so that we could do the same, with tickets in the $45–$60 range.

The band made it even easier by treating us like true partners. Rather than demanding an advance, which is standard operating procedure, they said, "You don't have to pay us until you break even." For this show, we'd hit that mark at about ten thousand tickets sold, and Vulfpeck had faith that we would reach that figure.

The night turned out to be a win for everyone.

I don't want to overlook the fact that this was my first show in the big room at Madison Square Garden. Four years earlier, I'd done five sold-out stadium gigs, but MSG is my hometown arena. It's where I saw Madonna in 1985. I love going to other cities and seeing arena gigs, but I've never felt the energy anywhere else like I've experienced at Madison Square Garden.

The Vulfpeck show provided a perfect opportunity to work with the Bowery Presents guys. Even though we compete, we are very good friends. It's super fun when we're on the same side, which happens occasionally but not too often.

As I previously mentioned, I've known John Moore ever since he was at Mammoth Records in the mid-'90s, and I'm always up for a Jomo hang. When I am in my living room and look up, I actually see Bowery cofounder Jim Glancy across the way (I can say no more; I'll explain in the next book).

Working with Bowery also means working with Johnny Beach, who was my intern back in the Wetlands days. He has gone on to book the Mercury Lounge, the Bowery Ballroom, Terminal 5, and many other rooms. People tend to float in and out of this business, so you never know if or when you'll see someone again. Johnny was still a teenager when he was my intern, and he probably weighed ninety-seven pounds at that time, although he's grown . . . as have all of us (d'oh!). Having said that, competition with friends is still tough. I've experienced it with Bowery going all the way back to Wetlands, so the times we can work together are sweet.

Looking back on Vulfpeck's success at the Garden, it now seems inevitable, but there was still risk involved. While I had a good feeling about what we were doing, there were plenty of naysayers out there who thought it was an overreach. So it felt particularly good to move ten thousand tickets on the onsale.

While Vulfpeck was still largely unknown to the general public, we had the ability to ensure that everybody who knew about Vulfpeck knew about the show.

And that is really all you need.

46

JIMMY FALLON'S ALMOST DEAD

Joe Russo's Almost Dead
The Capitol Theatre, Port Chester, New York
February 23, 2020

Fare Thee Well was intended to be an ending, but it became a new beginning.

The event led to a heightened enthusiasm for the music of the Grateful Dead.

It's not just that Bobby, Mickey, and Billy rolled their collective energy into their next project, launching Dead & Company with John Mayer, Oteil Burbridge, and Jeff Chimenti less than four months later.

Phil Lesh had been delivering master classes for years with his various lineups of Friends and now an increasing number of artists, many of whom weren't old enough to have seen Jerry Garcia, were taking the music in new directions.

It's exciting to me that so many younger musicians continue to be inspired by the Grateful Dead, and they apply that enthusiasm to reimagining the Dead's incredible songbook. They all do it a little differently, adding their own nuances to songs that have become standards.

It never fades.

When I travel to another city where I'm not putting on a show, I typically go out to see music. That often means I will check out a cover band, and my preference leans toward Grateful Dead cover bands.

I love cover bands.

I understand that not everyone shares this sentiment—at Wetlands, whenever Chris Zahn booked the Dave Matthews Tribute Band, he referred to it as a "rent party" (yes, that was their actual name—it was a clever marketing ploy that helped with SEO on Ticketmaster).

Sometimes you have to help cover bands by rounding out the edges. A '70s tribute band called Cougar Magnet did really well at Garcia's, but before they could move into the big room, I told them that they would need to change their name. I suggested 8 Track, and that became their name. 8 Track can play the Capitol, Cougar Magnet can't.

A number of arena rock artists will be retiring in the near future, and people still want to hear their music performed live. I know that *I* do.

One of my favorite cover bands features some friends that I've known since the Wetlands days. The members of Joe Russo's Almost Dead were a steady presence at the club during my era, although the groups they played in at the time didn't draw on the Dead catalog. Still, Joe Russo (Fat Mama, Benevento/Russo Duo), Scott Metzger (RANA), Tom Hamilton (Brothers Past), and Marco Benevento (Benevento/Russo Duo) all contributed an energy that kept the club vibrant even during its final days (the group's final member, Dave Dreiwitz, was touring with Ween during this time). Joe and I have become so close that I asked him to share a few remarks when I was honored at the 2016 BRIC Celebrate Brooklyn Festival Opening Night Gala (I also asked Eric Krasno, someone else who has been with me on the journey ever since Wetlands).

The formation of JRAD was a happy accident (or perhaps it was more of that Grateful Dead serendipity). It took place in January 2013 when a last-minute cancellation at the Freaks Ball XIII, an event put on by the long-standing NYC Freaks list, led Joe to pull together four of his buddies, most of whom were unfamiliar with the Dead catalog. Joe had envisioned this as a one-off gig, but the response to that performance at Brooklyn Bowl was overwhelming, so we did a second show eleven months later at the Cap. Once again, the audience was blown away by JRAD's approach, which brought a speed and intensity to the songs, at times embarking on musical journeys that stretched the material to the brink.

The demand for more JRAD performances was immediate. The band members eventually agreed to carve out time for the project to the point where they're now a full-time band. Their success has been a blessing not only for the elevated music they've been able to offer but also because the band members' participation in the group has opened the doors for them to explore some of their passion projects (which has brought even more elevated music into the world).

On February 23, 2020, when JRAD closed out their three-night run at the Cap, I watched the show up in my box with someone else I had first met at Wetlands: Jimmy Fallon. I was standing outside the entrance one night in early 2001 when Jimmy walked up. At that point, he was a couple of years into his run at *Saturday Night Live* and had just started hosting Weekend Update with Tina Fey.

That evening at Wetlands made a particular impression on future JRAD guitarist Tom Hamilton, who was performing with Brothers Past. Tommy explains, "When I got offstage, a buddy told me Fallon was there watching us and that he was now at the bar in the lounge. I went over and found him and said, 'Hey, man, not tryin' to be *that guy*, but I really love what you're doing on Update.' He was supercool and appreciative: 'Oh, dude, thanks! Wanna beer?' Then he ordered PBRs for the two of us. We shot the shit for a bit as I fanboy'd out about a De Niro walk-on, then I left him alone. He could not have been any more nice, earnest, or genuine-feeling, and that made a severe impression on me and how I treat folks."

Tom's point about the way Jimmy treats people is something that I've learned from him as well. He's the best I've ever seen at making others feel good, always looking everyone in the eye when talking to them. He also remembers a lot about other people, which always impresses me.

Jimmy and I spoke for a little while at Wetlands, and then over the years, we kept running into each other. We have a similar vibe to the way we roll. There's not a "job him" and a "personal him," there's just him. That's how I walk through life as well.

Another thing the two of us have in common is we're always game for an adventure. That might mean hopping on a plane to go to Wimbledon, and then to see Neil Young and Bob Dylan in London's Hyde Park. Or flying to Tennessee on a Thursday night to see a Dead cover band at Bowl Nashville before returning home the next morning. Or it could be a spontaneous hang at the *Relix* office, where Jimmy walked past a live performance by Dispatch's Chadwick Stokes while heading to the bathroom, and the next thing I know, he's sitting in on a Dylan cover ("It Ain't Me Babe").

An additional benefit of becoming the *Relix* publisher in 2009 has been the in-office performances. For a while, they took place in my office, which meant that I literally had the best seat in the house for music from Bob Weir, Grace Potter, Dawes, Chris Thile, Blues Traveler, and hundreds of others, including Rusted Root, who came in at my request early on, letting me relive my fandom at Northwestern. Beyond my office, we've also had performances on the roof, the boiler room, the basement, and the dedicated recording space (another former office), where Jimmy sat in.

We rented an entire floor in our building, and the *Relix* space has also felt like an incubator as we've subleased to other music-related entities, including CID and HeadCount. It's been a journey, and I'm appreciative to Rachel Baron, Josh Baron, Mike Greenhaus, and my coauthor Dean Budnick for encouraging me to get involved in 2009. I should also thank Brad Tucker, who first joined me as my assistant shortly after I started the gig and has come into his own as a project manager, connecting with many of the younger artists who entered the fold during his tenure.

Back to the Cap on February 23, 2020, Jimmy was really enjoying the show and at set break we began discussing the possibility of him sitting in during the encore, talking about potential Dead tunes or songs by The Band. What eventually happened, though, was when we came down to the stage after the second set, Chris Harford, who is a friend and mentor to the JRAD guys, pushed for Neil Young's "Fuckin' Up." Jimmy didn't know the lyrics, but he's a gamer, so they worked it out for a few minutes while I went back up to watch.

The promoter's job is to deliver the assist.

It's the artist who scores, but I'm here to put them in position to do so.

For instance, at LOCKN' 2018 before Sheryl Crow performed, I gave her a quick sense of the vibe around the festival because these things matter to her. I described Garcia's Forest, and two songs into her set during the introduction to "Everyday Is a Winding Road," she called out, "This is awesome! I want to be in the forest tonight, listening to some Jerrrrry!" The crowd went nuts.

Sheryl always plays varsity ball, but a timely assist can help.

I can be particularly hard on myself when I miss something. So when Jimmy walked out with JRAD holding a beer, I was disappointed that I hadn't thought to take it away from him. He nearly tripped over a mic wire because he had the cup in his hand. Not only that, but when Jimmy commits, he *commits*. So when he dove to the floor, I didn't want people to think he was drunk, which he wasn't. He was just going all in, which is what he does.

I've had plenty of well-known people come to my shows, and they'll often show up with a PR rep or some kind of minder to ensure that they don't do anything to "hurt the brand." Jimmy isn't like that. He's there to embrace the moment, and I think people sense that about him. He also happens to be the most talented extemporaneous performer I've ever seen. (I was reminded of this in February 2022 after breakfast at Tootsies in Nashville when he spontaneously joined two separate bands at the honky-tonk for classic rock covers, then continued up Broadway for more of the same.)

Chris Harford sang lead on "Fuckin' Up" as the JRAD encore started, with Jimmy chiming in on the chorus. After a couple of verses, during which Jimmy finally handed his cup to a crew member, he removed the mic from its stand and stepped to the front of the stage for some call-and-response with the audience (like my favorite artists, he instinctively connects—he's a call-and-response kind of guy). Then he let things fly, leading the band into portions of "Born to Run," "You Can Call Me Al" and "Hey Jude" before bringing it back around to "Fuckin' Up." During the Springsteen portion, he even pulled Dino Perrucci, our house photographer, out of the pit for a spontaneous Courteney Cox "Dancing in the Dark" moment.

Despite my brief initial nerves, it was an amazing encore.

I love a great encore.

There are some tricks to the encore trade, like making sure we don't play house music and keeping the stage lighting on while the audience remains dark. That helps nudge things along because while the fans are cheering, even if the artists are back in the green room, they can hear it.

Sometimes I will be more direct. In August 2015, Duran Duran finished the first of two nights at the Cap and then went upstairs. The crowd was applauding wildly, but the band didn't come back. So I stepped onto the stage and raised my hand, gesturing to keep the audience going, then went up to see the musicians. They were starting to get undressed because they felt like they'd given it their all. However, I believed they had a bit more in the tank, so I pointed out the crowd reaction. Then I went back down and resumed coaxing the audience. Finally, almost ten minutes after Duran Duran left the stage, they returned for their encore.

You can find the video on YouTube where Simon Le Bon acknowledges, "You guys made me put on a pair of sweaty pants and a T-shirt that is going to be sweaty to go home in. But that's okay, because we are Duran Duran, and if you cheer loud for us, we'll always come back." Which they did the next night as well, without my prompting.

Sometimes a band will play their encore and I will still want more. In certain instances, particularly with musicians I know really well, I have dropped some cash to make it happen. I definitely did that once with Umphrey's McGee, promising them $500 so they'd keep playing.

That way, we all get to enjoy some more music.

Plus, double encores are good for the bar, so it almost pays for itself (ha!).

On March 7, 2020, I took these things even further by paying for an additional set. Melvin Seals & JGB were appearing at the Cap, and I really wanted to be there.

Melvin played organ in the Jerry Garcia Band from 1980 until Jerry passed in 1995. I spent time in San Francisco one summer during college, and a highlight was seeing Jerry's band with Melvin at the Warfield. A decade after Jerry's death, Melvin and JGB released an album titled *Keepers of the Flame*, a description that still rings true.

These days, Melvin's performances touch on the Grateful Dead as well as the Jerry Garcia Band (and so much more). Returning to my earlier point about the variety of Dead cover bands, whenever I hear Melvin play a Dead or a Jerry song, it's different from the way that JRAD plays it or Dark Star Orchestra or Oteil & Friends or Grateful Shred. They all approach it differently, so for audiences, there's always something new to observe and absorb.

When I realized I had family commitments that night, I wondered whether I would be able to make it in time to see Melvin. Since he had an opening act, he was going to play one long set.

Larry Bloch was a big believer in two-set shows, which he required of all his weekend headliners. I've never gone quite so far as to mandate it, but I'm definitely a strong advocate. I believe that bands should play longer, and I'll occasionally make that suggestion. If we have all gathered together from different corners, then why play a short show? When an artist puts it all out there, those are the shows that people remember.

Even dividing one long set into two usually results in more music given the way set lists are built. Plus, with two opening songs and two closers, the opportunity increases for hitting those higher highs.

So we bumped up our offer to Melvin, which meant that he would take a break and collect some extra money (which again would be partially offset by the bar). It also meant that the night would extend at least forty minutes longer, giving me a much better chance to see him, which is exactly what happened. I left the city around 10:15, but I made it in time for Melvin's entire second set.

When I walked in the door that night and looked out into the audience, it was obvious that something was happening. We had sold close to five hundred tickets within the final twenty-four hours, including hundreds of walk-ups, which is beyond the statistical range of normal.

It seemed that people were viewing this as a last hurrah.

COVID-19 cases were fast on the rise, and we were starting to hear about local governments trying to mitigate the spread by shutting down restaurants and music venues.

Sure enough, that evening would be our final performance with an in-person audience for quite some time.

I feel like we entered the COVID era in style because Melvin and the band picked up on the crowd's energy and sent it back with passion and fire. I had a great hang with Melvin after the show, and he told me he thought they had taken the music to another level that night.

I am glad we all were able to experience that show, because our opportunities for collective musical inspiration were about to end.

Initially, we postponed Phil Lesh's eightieth birthday run, which had been set to begin on March 13. The remainder of our upcoming schedule soon followed.

We eventually placed a sign on the marquee that read, "This is only a set break. The bands will be back soon."

And so they were.

A year and a half later.

47

BE IN THE STREAM

Jason Isbell and Amanda Shires
Brooklyn Bowl, Nashville, Tennessee
May 15, 2020

"**S**ometimes the leftovers aren't better," Jason Isbell announced from the stage of Brooklyn Bowl Nashville where he stood alongside his wife / musical collaborator, Amanda Shires. "This is not a pot of chili. This is not your grandmama's lasagna. The leftovers aren't better. We need it fresh, and we need it now."

Jason was embracing the moment, celebrating the release of his new album, *Reunions*, with a special free livestream on my new streaming platform FANS.live. It was also our first show at Brooklyn Bowl Nashville.

He was playing to hundreds of thousands who had tuned in, some of whom were waving and holding up signs from the ends of the bowling lanes. These people were not there in person; they had been projected onto the wall behind the lanes, sending greetings from across the globe, with the youngest member of the audience only a few days old.

The show would be named to the *New York Times* list of 10 Best Quarantine Concerts Online, and a *Rolling Stone* review noted, "For a world of music fans stuck at home, worried about the dangers that lurk just outside our front doors, this was the kind of reunion we needed."

It was also a reunion that almost didn't take place.

Ten days prior to our opening party on March 13, a tornado tore through the Germantown section of Nashville where we are located and damaged a building across the street from us.

Then COVID hit, and by mid-May 2020, it was clear that the pandemic would be devastating to the live music industry. Our livestream was not even possible until Nashville mayor John Cooper ended the city's "Safer-at-Home" order on May 11 (after fifty-seven days), allowing for phase one of a limited reopening.

Oh, and just moments before the livestream was set to begin, our site crashed due to overwhelming traffic.

All in the name of PTSD, I suppose.

Of course, it all worked out just fine, other than perhaps a lingering twitch (and not the good kind of Twitch).

Jason Isbell at Nashville Bowl on May 15, 2020, also represented the first performance I had attended in over two months. This brought an end to the longest period I had gone without seeing live music since I was eighteen years old.

After Melvin Seals at the Capitol, I attended two more shows before COVID shut it all down.

On March 10, I was at the Garden for a concert celebrating fifty years of the Allman Brothers Band, a variation of the event that Butch Trucks had pitched me back in 2017. Although Butch and Gregg Allman had since passed away, it was great to see Jaimoe, Warren, Derek, Oteil, and Marc back together.

While I was at the show, a number of people asked me what was going to happen with LOCKN'. Earlier that day, Goldenvoice, the promoter of Coachella and Stagecoach, announced that those festivals would be postponed from the spring until the fall (they would later move to spring 2021 and eventually spring 2022).

I had no answer as yet. Coachella and Stagecoach were slated for April and early May. LOCKN' wasn't scheduled until June 19–21.

In previous years, I would not have needed to worry about this for a few months, because LOCKN' had taken place in late August or early September. However for 2020, I had decided to move it to June because I no longer wanted to be among the last festivals of the year. Since I owned the land and operated the event independently, I could make that call (unlike Live Nation or AEG, where dramatically adjusting the date of a single festival would have major repercussions for their entire slate, requiring a lot of internal politicking).

LOCKN' had originally launched on the weekend after Labor Day because that's when Furthur was available. We moved it a couple of weeks earlier in 2016 to accommodate Phish's tour schedule. In 2020, we responded to the late-summer festival fatigue (and wallet fatigue) that some music fans experience.

In January, we made our announcement and had our biggest onsale of any LOCKN' to date. That was an entrepreneurial lesson eight years in the making, but at least we were iterative and open-minded.

Our LOCKN' roster was built around Phil Lesh's eightieth birthday. He would appear with a new lineup each day, starting with his classic Quintet (Warren Haynes, Jimmy Herring, Rob Barraco, and John Molo), then it would be the Q with special guest David Crosby, and finally, JRAD with Phil and John Mayer.

On March 10, I wasn't ready to postpone LOCKN', although the next day, I made the call on Phil's eightieth birthday run at the Cap, a postponement that ultimately extended from March 2020 until October 2021.

However, as news outlets continued to report on COVID, I felt increasingly uncomfortable about the road ahead. Beyond the human tragedy, when it came to business operations, I could see the moving targets. Timelines would be dependent on health variables, along with the shifting responses of national, state, county, and city officials. So I needed to be cognizant of what was happening in DC but also in New York City, Port Chester, Nashville, Las Vegas, Arrington, and Philadelphia (where we were moving toward construction of the next Brooklyn Bowl).

Despite all of this swirling inside my head, I was able to focus on another charitable venture. Love Rocks is an annual fundraiser that takes place at New York's Beacon Theatre to support God's Love We Deliver, a nonprofit organization that began during the AIDS crisis and delivers over two million meals per year to those who are suffering from severe illness. The 2020 participants included David Letterman, Dave Matthews, Jackson Browne, Chris and

Rich Robinson, Derek Trucks and Susan Tedeschi, and Warren, along with a house band led by Will Lee, which included Larry Campbell and Eric Krasno.

On March 12, the day of the benefit, organizers announced they would restrict attendance due to COVID concerns. The live audience would be limited to working personnel along with a few friends and family members. The financial implications looked dire, in part because they needed to reimburse ticket holders. I'd previously spoken with Love Rocks executive producer Greg Williamson (who founded the show with John Varvatos) about a potential stream that had not materialized, but now I was able to step in and offer a solution.

Love Rocks reached a substantially wider audience than it otherwise would have, thanks to a quick pivot: a free livestream on the Relix Channel (and we did it all again in 2021).

This would be the final show I attended for two months. At one point, I stood between musician Ivan Neville and New York Knicks TV producer/director Howie Singer, both of whom contracted serious cases of COVID, landing each of them in the hospital. Although somehow I avoided it, this still demonstrated how dangerous and crazy everything could be.

The online platform we used to share Love Rocks represented something I had been working toward for years. It would prove beneficial to bands and nonprofits along with my staff, as we were able to make payroll on multiple occasions solely through streaming revenues.

During our construction at the Capitol Theatre, we installed cameras that would allow us to record every show (we eventually did the same at the Bowls). Initially, we only broadcast the feeds live inside the building (at the bars, green rooms, and catering). However, we also archived the performances, which became cheaper over the years as the costs of terabyte storage came down.

I'm pretty sure there are no other venues out there with comparable archives, particularly given our high-end sound and visuals. That's one limitation of venues with corporate ownership. Irving Plaza is not going to store its shows, because the person in charge won't be there in five years and doesn't want the expense to appear on their P&L.

Still, we needed a platform to share all these amazing performances, past, present, and future. Thankfully, we had already set that in motion.

There had been a few attempts that preceded us. In 1996, Michael Dorf and Andrew Rasiej founded the Digital Club Network to present music from multiple venue partners—a fine idea about twenty years too early. Butch Trucks created Moogis ten years after that, but the bandwidth still wasn't available to most people. Brad Serling's Nugs.tv eventually moved into this space, and for a few years, they hosted our livestreams (back when we all called them *webcasts*), starting with LOCKN' 2013.

Eventually, we wanted our own platform for the shows that originated at our venues. We moved our free livestreams off Nugs and onto YouTube starting with a Drive-By Truckers show at Brooklyn Bowl in October 2017. We became a premium YouTube content partner, building a subscriber base and awareness.

Then, starting with As the Crow Flies at the Capitol in April 2018, we started offering pay-per-view livestreams at Relix.com /live (TourGigs initially provided white label service for us on the back end). In November 2018, we also moved our free streams to Relix, which helped build our email list. We remained active on YouTube, though, posting highlights of the shows.

Up until this point, we had branded everything as the Relix Channel. However, some of the performers had no direct connection to Relix, and we wanted to expand our focus. So it made sense to create an independent platform to host the streams. This was when I realized I already had a site with the perfect name: FANS.com.

I had been inspired to create FANS the morning after Robert Plant played Brooklyn Bowl in 2014. I woke up at 6:00 a.m. and grabbed my phone to search for photos and reviews, but I could not find anything. The existing social media platforms did not make it easy for people to chat about live music. As I began to think about it, I realized that while a site like Facebook can connect family and friends, you might not want to share your account of the earth-shattering Mastodon show that kept you raging until 5:00 a.m. while you basked in its aftermath if your boss or grandma might be reading the post.

While community is a vital part of the live music experience, it had not fully translated to the online world. Artist news, event databases, touring information, and music streaming all existed in separate silos, with no single place for fans to congregate. So I decided to create one.

I saw the value from multiple perspectives. As a music fan, I wanted to be able to check in easily on what my favorite bands did the previous night. As a venue owner, it would be helpful to reach those fans. Of course, this also would benefit the bands. It seemed like a great opportunity to lift all boats.

I raised money from people who shared my view and developed a social networking site for music fans.

In August 2016, I wrote a letter that explained: "FANS is an online community for you to embrace your passion for live music, celebrate your personal concert history, discover new experiences and connect with like-minded fans. Whether you're a seasoned concertgoer or a casual listener, music provides a powerful path to happiness, community and memory. FANS is an open forum for self-expression and new discoveries for music-lovers of all stripes. FANS is the place I would have liked to have been able to go after seeing Dylan and the Grateful Dead perform all those years ago."

That's all still true. However, by March 2020, while our total registered users exceeded one hundred thousand—the leading interests ranged from the Grateful Dead to the Tedeschi Trucks Band to LCD Soundsystem to Backstreet Boys(!)—I had to accept that we couldn't generate enough traction for FANS to remain an active enterprise, given the expense of hosting and staffing. It was tougher than I had thought to break through the hegemony of the existing social media platforms. So we informed our users that something new was cooking and provided the means to download their existing concert histories.

When our new version of FANS launched in April 2020, I wanted to do more than present music. My goal was to add the experiential to the virtual. At the core of this was our Be in the Stream concept, enabling people to interact with the music and each other in a way that elevated the experience.

Be in the Stream provided an option to do more than just watch the show. Fans could enter a Zoom room from which we selected them to appear alongside and sometimes within the performance feed.

Plenty of people decked out their living rooms, tossed on their show clothes, and opted to "Dance like everybody is watching" (our initial tagline for Andy Frasco's I Wanna Dance with Somebody livestream party). It gave all of us in quarantine a sense of community and connection.

In thinking about COVID and how to respond to it, I visualized the whole situation as a bouncing ball that steadily moved up and down until it hit a rock and abruptly ricocheted. This forced us to chase after it and reposition ourselves. The relaunch of FANS was one of those occasions when I anticipated the errant bounce and remained in perfect sync.

Be in the Stream debuted during FANS' debut event: a moe. marathon. By this point, we moved our back end off TourGigs because we had finally built our own. We streamed five archival sets, with intervening live Q and As drawing on audience questions selected by Dean. The evening concluded with moe.'s performance from the Cap on February 2, 2018, with a full-on Be in the Stream immersion.

Six weeks later, we hit new heights with FANS' first livestream: Jason Isbell and Amanda Shires at Brooklyn Bowl Nashville. We had always planned to have Jason play the Bowl around his record release, but we had anticipated this would have been our fortieth or fiftieth show. Instead, it would not only be a debut for FANS but for the venue itself.

Details for the stream remained fluid as I sat behind the wheel for the one-thousand-mile trek to Nashville with Jonathan Healey riding shotgun and doing prep work for the stream he would direct.

I love long drives. I find that road trips help clear the head and can be useful when brainstorming. As I have said, I do a lot of my thinking in bed staring at the ceiling—that is my version of watching Netflix.

Healey and I left NYC on the morning of the fourteenth, with plans to break up the trip by staying at LOCKN' on the nights before and after the Isbell show. He needed to oversee our streams on those other evenings, including three on the sixteenth (Sheryl Crow's 2018 LOCKN' set followed by Tom Petty at LOCKN' in 2014, then the Frasco dance party).

As I drove, my mind ran through potential interactive opportunities during the Isbell performance. While our Be in the Stream functionality placed audience members in front of their peers, I wanted Jason and Amanda to connect directly as well. My initial idea was to host a contest in which people could draw their own versions of the *Reunions* album cover, and then Jason and Amanda would select their favorites. Everyone signed off on that, but I wasn't sure it went far enough.

Meanwhile, I was also wondering what we should do after Jason and Amanda finished a song. Silence would be awkward, and a smattering of applause from the people in the venue would not help. Then it came to me: We'd put the Be in the Stream participants onto the screens at the end of the bowling lanes. They'd be muted during the music, but we'd unmute them at the end of each song so that they could cheer. This would enable Jason and Amanda to see some of their audience, hear the responses, and maybe offer some banter. We would also share Jason and Amanda's visual perspective of those screens.

I worked that out during the car ride, but Healey wasn't sure if the cameras we had installed at the Bowl were properly positioned to capture the screens at the end of the lanes. Thankfully, he had the ability on his laptop to remote into the system and view the camera angles. As it turned out, we couldn't get the shot. So after Traci Thomas, Jason's manager, signed off on the plan, Healey ordered another camera for the next day (and I put the album art idea into my back pocket for another day). All of this happened while I was behind the wheel.

The first leg of our road trip brought us to LOCKN' Farm in the late afternoon. There are year-round accommodations, so we would be able to get a night of sleep and do some work before our six-hundred-mile push into Nashville the next day.

Our arrival on the farm coincided with some rain showers. We had not anticipated a storm, but the weather turns fast in the area. Having spent enough time on-site, I also had a sense of what might follow. The sun came out within the hour, and knowing what to expect, I oriented myself in the proper direction and, sure enough, caught a rainbow.

I was snapping photos and texting them to friends, feeling pretty good about our general prospects until the moment arrived for the Jazz Foundation of America benefit stream. We were hosting a fundraiser to support the JFA's COVID-19 Musicians' Emergency Fund, which had been created to supply basic living expenses to musicians and their families. I had offered up our platforms because we had so many more subscribers than they did.

The event came to me from former Jammys line producer / hero Dan Parise (who would pass away five months later) and JFA artistic director / drummer extraordinaire Steve Jordan.

I was thrilled to provide assistance but less than thrilled when I heard Healey say, "We've got a problem." It turned out that one of our streams didn't fire right away. Healey was unable to launch it, and after the big push we had made to build awareness for the fundraiser, I was starting to feel uncomfortable. Before I became too agitated, though, Healey had it up and running. The night was a success, generating over $100,000 for the emergency fund.

On the way home from the Bowl on Saturday, we had another issue, this time with the Frasco stream. The I Wanna Dance with Somebody Dance Party had been one of my earliest ideas after we came up with Be in the Stream. It was a perfect fit for Andy's energy and vibe. Plus, Healey and his team regularly outdid themselves in locating ridiculous videos that they would cut to throughout the two hours. Perhaps not this night, though, because Healey informed me that the computer at the Capitol Theatre had crashed. Something had happened with the software, and the show file disappeared. He did not think he would have time to rebuild the graphics he had created over the preceding week. Eventually, through a reboot reminiscent of what we had done at the Ziegfeld Wetlands premiere, he was able to salvage the situation and launch the stream.

While both of these incidents induced stress, the collective discomfort was still a fraction of what I experienced in Nashville on May 15.

I had a lot on the line that day. It was the first live show we would be streaming from FANS, the first time people could see my venue, and we were showcasing our new interactive element. I had been told that a number of Warner Records employees were encouraged to tune in for a sense of what it would be like for an artist to stream in a venue without a crowd but with full-on production.

I have said that I try not to get too high or low, but this is one of those instances where I was kind of pumped. Not only was it a big night for us, I would be seeing my first show in two months.

Just before it started, I told a few people, "Okay, we did the tornado, we did the pandemic. We should be good now."

I felt like I was flying.

Then, moments after Jason and Amanda walked onstage, I crashed back to earth.

There were about two dozen people in the venue—members of our staff along with Jason's crew and management. As 8:00 p.m. arrived, one of the younger people working for Traci Thomas came over to me holding his phone. He couldn't connect to the stream. I told him that it was probably our in-house internet, but after someone else approached me with the same issue, I noticed that my own phone was blowing up with texts from people sharing this problem.

It turned out our site had remained stable right up until show-time. Anyone who logged on early made it in just fine, but due to the influx of traffic, anyone who tried afterward was unable to connect.

We had notified our hosting company that this might be an issue, but the number of would-be streamers far exceeded our projections. While this seemed like an easy problem to solve, when we called the company to upgrade our disk space, we were told that we needed to provide a PIN. The problem was that none of us knew the PIN, and none of us could figure out who had the PIN. Meanwhile, additional people approached me holding phones with spinning icons.

I had a pit in my stomach, kind of like the one I had when I was screaming into my pillow after I lost my chance to work on the John Kerry inaugural concert. The situation also reminded me of opening night at Brooklyn Bowl Vegas when I was feeling so good until I was told, "No, you're fucked." Or when lightning arrived at LOCKN' and we had to evacuate the show field. Things turn fast.

I stepped into the bathroom, where it was quiet, so I could focus.

We were probably ten minutes into all of this, and my head had already gone to "Well, at least we'll have it online tomorrow."

Still, that was a far cry from what I had hoped this night would be.

Just as I started thinking about the statement we would release, I began getting texts from friends who had finally made it in.

It turned out that one of the developers who had helped build the Relix back end and still did some maintenance on the site was our official contact with the hosting company. He was hanging out with his family when we finally figured it out, and he provided the PIN.

It was a victory, but it was very close to a complete disaster. By this point, I was physically and emotionally spent. Thankfully, from there, just about everything came off as we had hoped.

The one exception was the applause. We couldn't put that audio in because of a delay produced by our routing of the Zoom feed. Still, our Be in the Stream participants held up signs with messages for Jason and Amanda, who responded in between songs, cuing the audience members to do more of the same.

The two of them were on their game throughout the night, truly being present.

At one point, Jason looked around the room and deadpanned, "This is a lot like all the CD release shows we did before *Southeastern* came out."

When asked about it later, he joked, "I've played to empty venues before, so it wasn't a new experience for me."

I love being at my shows, but I also love the feeling when they are done. I love getting the first review. It is less about what the review says than the feeling that whatever happened cannot be changed. I remember flying home from Fare Thee Well, thinking, *No matter what, the event is done. Now it is a memory. It is baked in.*

At the end of the night, Jason addressed the crowd and said, "I hope you guys have a great weekend. It's gonna be a weird weekend, but that's okay."

It had been a weird week. A weird month. A weird year.

There was plenty more to come.

48

RESCUE SQUAD

Trey Anastasio Band
Beacon Theatre, New York, New York
October 9, 2020

As the summer of 2020 arrived, it became clear that musicians and their fans would not be returning to traditional live music settings anytime soon.

Nearly twenty-five years earlier, I had started my career at Wetlands, where I did a show every single night of the week (and two on Sundays). By the time the pandemic shut down our venues, I was juggling multiples between New York and Vegas (with Nashville about to come on line). So it was a major adjustment for me as I altered the rhythms of my life.

Even when I am not at my shows, they still require some energy. As long as I have something going on, I need to be available. So if I am with my family and the phone rings, I need to look at it. No one contacts me when everything is fine. They only call when things go sideways.

COVID provided a break from those calls.

It also allowed for additional family moments. My building has a roof deck, so I had the chance to play street hockey with my son, Simon, and teach him how to Rollerblade. I drove out to Westchester with Roxy for tennis, which was also a great way to change the scenery. Becca and I shared date nights at restaurants outside under a heat lamp.

I was still feeling internal pressure to keep my businesses afloat. I had already been through a near bankruptcy in Vegas, and I remembered how that had felt. One upside of coming through that experience, though, is I have been able to focus on long-term decision-making since there have been limited opportunities for me to take out profits in the short term.

I worried about my musician friends and those who worked in the concert industry. However, I aimed to remain positive and let everyone know that we would come out okay on the other side.

Throughout all of this, Trey Anastasio regularly reminded *me* that we would come out okay on the other side.

He would send kind words my way, pointing out what we had done together in the past and emphasizing what we would do together in the future. Then he would thank me for facilitating "all that joy."

Mickey Hart lifted my spirits in his own way. He sent me a text referencing the Fare Thee Well rainbow and promising me that if I would use my "magical powers" to stop the coronavirus, he would "play your bowling alley every day for the rest of time." Then he sent me an update, reporting that Jerry was on board as well: "He really likes you Peter BUT you need to deliver on this."

My friendship with Steve Jordan also grew during COVID. We first worked together in February 2020, when he served as musical director of a B. B. King tribute show we hosted at the Cap.

I knew the people at Blackbird Presents, who packaged the event. It looked like Keith Richards and Ronnie Wood would participate, which grabbed my attention, as well as the opportunity to work with Steve.

Blackbird was targeting one night in LA, but I countered with two nights at the Capitol, offering more money. Plus, they wouldn't need to pay any costly origination fee to record or stream the show, which is something I can add to any deal.

It was a little tricky because the Seva Foundation was holding one of those dates for a benefit, with Derek Trucks and Susan Tedeschi already on board. However, this felt like kismet because Seva cofounder Wavy Gravy (a.k.a. Hugh Romney) had been given his nickname by B. B. King. Also, Derek and Susan maintained long-standing relationships with B. B. right up until his death in 2015.

So I found out how much Seva was looking to raise and personally guaranteed that sum, adding the organization to the event as a beneficiary.

Originally, The Thrill Is Gone: A Tribute to B. B. King was going to take place on Sunday, February 16, and Monday, February 17. We announced a series of musicians who would participate, but Blackbird didn't want to specify which night anyone would appear. It turned out that the Monday lineup wasn't quite coming together, and ticket sales were a little light, so at a certain point, I decided to make it all one evening.

This meant that the finances were upside down, but it was still the right thing to do, because there's finances and then there's energy in the room. You can't have a half-full B. B. King tribute. If you are hosting an event, it means you are responsible for what happens, even if you are not fully in control of what happens. The right way is the hard way.

While it was a financial hit for me, Seva did just fine. I was holding out hope for Keith and Ronnie until the very end, but the show was full of highlights, thanks to Buddy Guy, Jimmie Vaughan, Ann Wilson, Stevie Van Zandt, Robert Cray, Robert Randolph, and many others.

Plus, it established my relationship with Steve Jordan. As a drummer, he approached his role as musical director differently from some of the others I have worked with. He focused on being in the pocket, so he would be a little more specific when he spoke with everyone, but then he let them go.

As a result of my connection with Steve, I hosted the JFA stream in May. Then a month later, we began a more active collaboration. I immediately discovered that he enjoys the creative back-and-forth, just like I do. We enthusiastically swapped clips via text and email while assembling videos for Red White Black & Blues, a "16-hour journey through Black American live music" (it ended up being closer to seventeen because we could not stop ourselves from making additions until the last possible moment).

Dr. Dean Budnick and Kirk Peterson (who helps book my venues) were in on the action as well. I had met Kirk at Northwestern where he had impressed me with his musical knowledge. In 2001, Cheryl Liguori, the CEO of the Boulder Theater (who had been one of Larry Bloch's initial employees at Wetlands), called me out of the blue to ask if I had any recommendations for a talent buyer. Kirk was in the area doing something else, but I put her in touch with him. He worked there until 2013, when he joined me.

Our editor on *Red White Black & Blues* was Sam Blakesberg. He crushed it, which pleased me and also his dad, photographer Jay Blakesberg. Jay has documented much of my journey and created coffee table books for Fare Thee Well, LOCKN', and the Capitol Theatre. During COVID, he started hosting a *Photos with Stories* stream for the Relix Channel where he interviewed his peers.

Red White Black & Blues originally was going to be a one-day, twelve-hour event slated for July 4. Then we revised this to five nights of programming in shorter installments. Eventually, we returned to the idea of a single extended stream (that stretched to nearly seventeen hours) for maximum impact. We also pushed it from July 4 to July 25 so that we would have the time to do right by the subject matter. Again, iteration is essential.

Since I served as both creator and platform, I had freedom of control during an era when so much else was out of my hands.

My career has included a fair number of opportunities that failed to materialize. People who talk about all the things I have done are often unaware of near misses (and not-so-near misses).

For instance, I have come close on a couple of other Brooklyn Bowls. We had a building in Chicago's West Loop we were going to convert. However, as costs rose to $20 million for what would have been two floors and forty-eight thousand square feet, I had second thoughts. On the nights when we'd book a big artist, we would do just fine. But you have to think about whether you can make it work on a Tuesday in February. I ultimately passed on the space, which was taken over by Punch Bowl Social.

I had plans for a Bowl in Boston. It was going to be in the Hub on Causeway complex, right next to the TD Garden arena. We diagrammed it out, but when we paused to sort out the financing, someone else grabbed the space.

I almost took over Dangerfield's, the New York comedy club, which opened back in 1969. It all began one afternoon when I dropped Roxy off at UES for a birthday party, then went for a walk. I found myself at Rodney's old place and decided to take a look. I thought the room had a cool vibe and called in Jimmy Fallon for counsel. He went in there one Sunday night, where he ended up doing a brief set for five people in the club. I took this as a positive sign (that Jimmy approved, not the five patrons) and entered into negotiations. At one point during the fall of 2019, I thought I would be taking over in the spring. But everything changed with COVID, and I came to the realization that comedy is not my world and I needed to remain focused on music.

COVID also altered my plans for an epic Earth Day 50 on the National Mall. Ten years after the Climate Rally, I was going to serve as executive producer of an event that would span the globe, with additional participation from performers, activists, and citizens.

In January 2017, I had returned to the Mall, running point on streaming for the Women's March (which was an honor but became a near disaster at times, like the moment we realized that the person in charge of closed-captioning forgot to bring the proper cable and we had to manufacture one on the spot). Three months later, I was executive producer of the March for Science, which offered a chance to support an important cause alongside another extraordinary musical director: Jon Batiste.

Following those experiences, I had big plans for Earth Day 2020 on the National Mall, which I pivoted into Earth Day 2021 on the National Mall . . . until that was canceled as well.

There have also been any number of festival ideas that, unlike Earth Day 50, never made it to the announcement phase. For instance, before we created LOCKN', we made a pitch to Led Zeppelin for an event on the same site that we would call Arrington, after the town where the farm is located (the name had a certain ring to it). I later tried to orchestrate an R.E.M. reunion at the University of Georgia football stadium. I came close to launching a Wetlands festival on Governors Island, which seemed fitting since there is an actual wetlands there. After Woodstock 50 was canceled, I scrambled to pull together a weekend event with some of the artists in Flushing Meadows Corona Park, the home of the 1964 World's Fair (amazing site, awkward name).

On the subject of festivals, I once made a serious attempt to re-create the Grateful Dead's legendary Wall of Sound at LOCKN'.

We would maintain the same size and scope on the exterior, but Meyer Sound would supply contemporary technology on the inside. I still love the idea, even if retrofitting six hundred speakers turned out to be impractical. But who knows, these things come around. In the interim, we hosted Anthony Coscia's Le Petite Mur De Son ("mini wall of sound"), a one-quarter-scale model, at Garcia's before Phil Lesh's October 2021 rescheduled birthday run.

I even had dreams of developing a multimedia showcase for Wayne Newton. I spent some time with Mr. Las Vegas, and the stories just spilled out. I wanted to take that old-school vibe and place it in a new context—a New York theater—rather than a lounge in Vegas. I believed then, as I believe now, that this would be equally appealing to older people who had grown up seeing him and younger people who might only be familiar with his name. We met a few times to discuss it, but he was not interested in traveling east for an extended period of time.

When it comes to artists, as I've said, nos often lead to yeses. So when a musician passes or drops off a show, I am always of the opinion that they will come back around. Neil Young stepped away from the inaugural LOCKN' due to Frank "Poncho" Sampedro's hand injury but eventually played two dates for me in 2018 at the Capitol (and one day, I will get him to perform *Harvest Moon* under the harvest moon, if I haven't just jinxed it). Bob Dylan, who passed on our first New Year's at the Cap before pitching us on opening the venue, later returned for a three-night run after I made him an offer for ten shows. So there's a lesson: sometimes you ask for ten to get three. A 30 percent yes is a pretty good no.

In 2019, we announced a Cap date for another icon, Larry King, which unfortunately will never come to pass. His appearance was originally slated for May 2019 and, at his request, would have included a portion of the evening where I interviewed him. We were forced to postpone because of his scheduling conflicts and then due to COVID. Sadly, he later contracted the virus, which hospitalized him in December 2020, before he died three weeks later of sepsis.

I first met Larry over breakfast at the Nosh in Beverly Hills. I had won the opportunity to join him and his regulars through a 2016 auction at the Grand St. Settlement Centennial Gala.

I waited nearly two years for our calendars to align, and it was everything I had hoped it would be. Sitting with Larry and his guys was another one of those moments when it felt like I was in a movie. When he introduced me to his crew, it sounded like I was a guest on his show (which I suppose I was—ha!). We mostly spoke about current events, and it went so well that Larry invited me back. It still fires me up to think that I had earned my seat at the table.

My initial breakfast with Larry in July 2018 represented another milestone because I had him sign the term sheet as the witness for my joint venture deal with Live Nation. This agreement would help me build additional Brooklyn Bowls. New York was still mine, but we would share resources on future Bowls.

I am not afraid to partner with the big companies. I have done that off and on over the years, threading the needle as an independent. As I have said, "Sometimes you want to go down the slide alone, and sometimes you want to go down the slide with the big kids."

Partnering with Live Nation means that I can enter a market like Nashville or Philadelphia without worrying that I don't have a local email list or socials. I can't launch a venue from zero again. I tried that in Vegas, and we almost didn't make it.

I could go into Nashville and open a cool 180-person cabaret club on my own. However, I would not be able to build a 1,200-cap room in a city where I have never done business and compete with the most powerful institution in live music.

So I feel like I am leveraging them. A benefit of scale is it lifts the team. Smaller business is often about the founder. As things gets bigger, I find it becomes a bit less about me. Sometimes, I kind of want it to become bigger so I have less to do (ha!).

From Live Nation's perspective, they recognize that we live in an increasingly experiential world, which is the appeal of a place like Brooklyn Bowl.

I can understand why some people view Live Nation as a big faceless corporation. It *is* a publicly traded company, which means that it faces certain pressures to turn a profit. However, it is also comprised of individuals, and the people I've dealt with, like Jordan Zachary, have done right by me and the Bowls.

One small downside of the joint venture was that the Bowls couldn't qualify for PPP loans during COVID. I *was* able to get PPP for LOCKN', the Cap, and *Relix*.

Even so, I still needed to pursue additional revenue streams for all the businesses. We were able to step up our merch game (thanks to my creative wingman, Chris Kovach), with posters, pins, and T-shirts that synergized with a revamped Relix Marketplace ("Goods for Heads").

We also explored other ideas, such as selling engraved entryway tiles at the Cap. We allowed people to select a name, a favorite show, and the date it took place (I picked opening night, Bob Dylan, on September 4, 2012). We spread the word through our socials and sold a couple per day until a New York TV station ran a news report, and that number increased exponentially. It is not always easy to predict what will set self-propulsion in motion. The same is true for shows, although I have found that the best marketing is the person who buys a ticket and tells a friend.

The tile sales reflect another important lesson that I was reminded of throughout COVID: It matters if you treat people right. The news producer was someone who enjoyed what we do and was eager to help out by spreading the word. It's good to have friendlies. We are everywhere.

It can be frustrating to watch certain people turn quick profits by screwing over others without a second thought. However, I continue to believe there is another way that will still get you where you want to go, even if it may take longer to arrive. While the journey may be more stressful, it is also communal and far more gratifying.

So when a friend sends you an unprompted text that says, "The troops are ready to help repay the debt we all owe u," it makes you feel great. When that friend is Trey Anastasio, it also gives you confidence that it will happen.

Which brings us to the Beacon Jams.

As I began contemplating additional revenue opportunities, streaming was always at the top of my list. I not only had my archives, I also had my venues, fully equipped for live broadcasts. I began speaking with potential partners, including Twitch, which was looking to move into live music.

I was in the middle of drafting our Twitch programming grids when a friend texted and asked if I had heard about the Trey run at the Beacon. Although it had yet to be announced, Trey was going to perform a weekly residency at the theater, which eventually would take place from October 6 through November 27. Someone we know had been contacted about it because Trey wanted to stream these shows for free, and to maintain high production standards, his team needed a sponsor.

I thought I could help.

At the time, Trey was thinking about streaming on Facebook or perhaps YouTube, but I called Patrick Jordan, his comanager, and suggested Twitch.

What I said to Twitch was "If you want to get into live music, there is no better way than streaming Trey once a week for two months at the Beacon."

I was in a unique position to facilitate this because I had relationships with Twitch, with Trey's team, and with MSG, which owns the Beacon.

The Relix Channel on Twitch was set to launch in October, and at first, it looked like we might even have the Beacon Jams as part of our programming. However, Trey eventually decided that he wanted to create his own channel. In cases like this, the artist always leads (and if it ever comes down to it, the artist wins ties as well). So the Beacon Jams wound up on the Trey Anastasio Channel.

The residency was a tremendous success because Trey was overflowing with pent-up energy and creativity. Beyond the music, he raised over $1 million to build a drug treatment center in Vermont.

Trey was kind enough to mention me a couple of times during the run, and *Relix* also received some nice plugs. They even gave me a sales commission, which I had not anticipated and says something about the integrity of everyone involved.

The eight livestreams drew over 1.8 million viewers who watched nearly 50 million minutes of music. In addition to the core members of the Trey Anastasio Band, Trey welcomed a number of guests, including four musicians that he introduced as the Rescue Squad Strings. The name referenced Phish's New Year's Eve show at Madison Square, when Trey found himself stranded above the stage on a platform that failed to descend during a production sequence, necessitating help from crew members whom Trey dubbed the Rescue Squad.

The Beacon Jams offered hope to many of us. Trey was inspiring and forthright. As he said in between songs on the third night of the run: "When life gives you pandemic, make pandemic-ade."

For two months during quarantine, we gathered together each week and collectively embraced the moment.

That special Trey Anastasio feedback loop was in full effect for our mutually supportive Rescue Squad.

49

GRATEFUL MAHALO

Billy & the Kids with Billy Strings and Carlos Santana
Banana Beach House, Kauai, Hawaii
May 4, 2021

I was lying on a massage table at Chris Blackwell's GoldenEye resort in Jamaica when I received some advice.

"You need to open your heart," said Lyndale, the resort's "intuitive therapist," as he worked to release my stress through a deep muscle technique.

I had thought I was in a good place spiritually, so I wasn't sure what to make of Lyndale's remarks. Chris's girlfriend, Marika, had recommended him, and the experience had been everything she said it would be, other than this comment.

It was February 2021, and I had made my way to GoldenEye for five days to recharge and receive Chris's counsel. He carries himself like no one else I know; he's refined and classy yet still rock and roll. He is also a hip and thoughtful progressive, so it is a pleasure to sit with him and talk about any of my ventures, any of his ventures, or none of that at all.

I had anticipated that this would be an intense and demanding year, so my time at GoldenEye provided some welcome peace of mind.

Which it did . . . until it didn't.

Due to COVID protocols, when I returned to the United States, I needed to be tested. The most convenient location was at a cardiologist's office. Since I was there (and perhaps because of

Lyndale's remarks), I mentioned that I had recently experienced a tightness in my chest some mornings. I scheduled an appointment, which led to a follow-up and finally a CT scan.

As it turned out, Lyndale's diagnosis was correct, except he wasn't speaking metaphorically. I *did* need to open my heart because one of my coronary arteries was 90 percent blocked. The doctor informed me that the occlusion was in my left anterior descending (LAD) artery, which is also known as the widow-maker, because when the blockage leads to a heart attack, the results are typically swift and fatal.

I had plans to join my family in Colorado for a skiing vacation, but the doctor told me to cancel. He said that I would be endangering my life, given the altitude.

The situation was so serious that he instructed me to visit an emergency room immediately if I experienced any discomfort. He also indicated I should refrain from exercise. I mean, how often does a doctor say no exercise?

A few days later, I had an angioplasty to insert a stent into my artery and open the pathway.

Before the procedure, I took some comfort in learning that my doctor had seen Galactic at the Bowl, while one of my nurses had been there for Pigeons Playing Ping Pong.

From my session with Lyndale on through my angioplasty at Mount Sinai, I felt like I was in good hands all around.

Within a day or two of leaving the hospital, I learned that Ben Taylor, the general manager of Front Gate Tickets, had died of a sudden heart attack at age thirty-eight.

So I would encourage anyone who experiences a tightness in their chest or who feels even a little out of sorts to schedule a doctor's appointment. You may need to open your heart as well.

Prior to my stent surgery, the cardiologist told me that I would feel much better afterward. I couldn't imagine there would be much of a change, but sure enough, I *did* feel much better.

My heart issue may have been partially a product of my family history, but my lifestyle certainly contributed. In this regard, I respect what Bob Weir has been able to do for himself. He will bring his exercise gear on the road and schedule gym time in his daily itinerary. He also takes a holistic approach and regularly practices meditation. I was making the rounds early one day at LOCKN', and there he was sitting outside on the grass without a shirt, legs crossed, eyes closed, and motionless in the early morning sun.

I have modified my eating habits, easing up on steak and swapping in more fish.

I have also tried to moderate my alcohol consumption, as this is an occupational hazard. One of my favorite ways to offer a quick thank-you to my staff or salute a band is through a round of tequila shots. It is a quick, fun way to bond, and I still love to do it with the team . . . with bands . . . with fans . . . and with my friends. I have also upped my physical activity to some degree. Apparently, seeing three shows a night at three separate venues doesn't count (ha!).

Even during COVID, though, I played sports. Along with street hockey and tennis, I would hop into my car for a round of socially distanced golf with Jimmy Fallon or Ron Delsener (unfortunately, never Jimmy Fallon *and* Ron Delsener, but I will dare to dream).

While I am not a frequent golfer, I enjoy the hang. I should give my parents credit here. When I was twelve years old, they shipped me off to Stanford University golf camp for a week—the complete antithesis of the Skinner Brothers wilderness experience. I had no interest in golf, and I probably did not play for ten or fifteen years afterward. However, I can hit a ball because I learned it when I was young. It's like skiing: if you do it when you're a kid, even for a week, you will remember it twenty or thirty years later.

I have always been someone who doesn't like to remain sedentary, even if that means walking around with a phone pressed to my face. Maybe that is why on the day after my angioplasty, I checked out of Mount Sinai and went directly to the Capitol Theatre. There I masked up and joined Senator Chuck Schumer for a fist bump as he announced that "help is on the way" for independent venues via the American Rescue Plan Act. Congress had also passed the Save Our Stages Act four months earlier, although it came too late for over seventy-five venues that were forced to shut down permanently, as per a tally in *Billboard*.

I would have felt the heat more acutely but for our streaming efforts. This is where the jam scene finally caught a break. Many jambands had trouble selling their recorded music back in the heyday of the CD, but they supported themselves through their live shows. So the recording industry's transition from physical to digital didn't disrupt them. Prior to the pandemic, many of these groups had even successfully streamed their live shows, since no two sets are identical, which keeps their supporters coming back for more.

In February 2021, we streamed six nights of Billy Strings at the Capitol. The Déjà Vu Experiment riffed on the Grateful Dead's six-date run at the venue in 1971. Each night, Billy encouraged fans to project a specified image to a "receiver" during set break, paralleling the dream telepathy experiment conducted by Stanley Krippner at the Dead's '71 shows.

Four of the streams were pay-per-views, and we sold over twenty thousand tickets to watch on FANS.live (we had been renting the FANS.com domain, and this new URL, which we owned, more closely aligned with our current approach). We offered both the opening night and the finale for free on the Relix Twitch channel, drawing in another two hundred thousand viewers.

Our other platforms supported these efforts, since we typically offered the first fifteen minutes for free via the Relix Facebook page (and any suitable venue pages).

It was due to our successes with Bob Weir & Wolf Bros, the Hold Steady, Dark Star Orchestra, St. Paul & the Broken Bones, and Margo Price that I decided to try something different . . . the destination stream.

To celebrate Bill Kreutzmann's seventy-fifth birthday, we presented three shows with his group Billy & the Kids (Tom Hamilton, Aron Magner, and Reed Mathis) in a natural setting that overlooked the Hawaiian coast.

We recorded the performances a couple of days in advance because I wanted them to end at sunset, when it would be too late in the east. I was also nervous about potential internet issues on the island of Kauai.

I credit Benjy Eisen, who manages Billy & the Kids (and coauthored Bill's memoir) for planting the seed a year earlier. He had envisioned the whole thing, including the announcement video (which involves a smokable message in a bottle—you can find it on YouTube). Benjy even had a name, Grateful Aloha, although I changed it to Grateful Mahalo, which sounded better to me (*mahalo* is a word for "thanks").

The show expenses ran into six figures once we factored in everyone's travel (flights, food, and accommodations) as well as our production needs and backline gear. So it wasn't until we had established our platforms with their own emails lists and socials that I felt comfortable moving forward. We rented Sylvester Stallone's former home on the island to record Grateful Mahalo, which also helped with sleeping arrangements.

We announced in advance that Billy Strings would appear with the group. (In the video, he was on the receiving end of the joint in a bottle, prompting him to declare, "Oh my god, I know what this is. It's a distress signal from Billy Kreutzmann! He needs to play a gig right now!") We also revealed Carlos Santana's participation a day before the first stream.

We had confirmed Carlos and Billy by putting ourselves in a position to get lucky. We approached each of them after we had already committed to Grateful Mahalo. So rather than saying, "We're going to do this *if* you do it, too," our pitch was "We're *already* doing this. Do you want to join?" It is a much lower-key ask, which places less pressure on the artist.

James Casey later joined on sax after we learned that he was quarantining in Hawaii.

So less than five weeks after I had been advised not to go to Aspen, I flew to Kauai. Plane travel is pretty easy for me; all I need is a window seat and Wi-Fi (Economy Plus helps too). Since my phone is my main computer, I can get a lot accomplished. Back in the days before Wi-Fi was available in the air, I'd stress over the emails and texts that would be awaiting me when I landed. These days, I love knocking them out while I am flying—sometimes I visualize it like I'm playing an arcade game.

It is helpful to pick an airline. In 2019, I flew more than one hundred thousand miles (in 2020, considerably less), and I'm a Premier 1K member on United. This means if a flight is canceled or postponed, I can call an 800 number while everyone else is running to the gate or the customer service desk.

Whenever I fly, another helpful skill is that I am able to sleep on demand. I have built up so much tiredness that I can turn on a dime and fall asleep, anytime and anywhere.

Jonathan Healey joined us in Kauai to direct the stream. This is something that he is doing more frequently now that we own portable gear—traveling to Red Rocks, for instance. On the flip side, thanks to the technology at our venues, he can also direct a Nashville stream from his home in Connecticut (although we are training more of our own people so that we can share the load).

The Hawaii shows came off without a hitch, other than the heat being so overbearing that we needed to take a couple of breaks. When Carlos joined us on the final day, he served as DJ during these intermissions, pulling out his phone and sharing some heavy jazz.

As Healey remembers it, during one of these jazz baths, he heard a voice next to him say, "How cool is this?" When he turned his head and realized that the person addressing him was Bill Kreutzmann, Healey's thought was *How cool is* that?

All in all, Grateful Mahalo offered a few days of mutual appreciation and admiration for where we were and what we were doing.

Considering where I had been and what I had been doing just five weeks earlier, I was particularly grateful to be there.

Mahalo, Lyndale.

50

WEEKENDS DON'T HAPPEN EVERY DAY

Dawes at LOCKN' Farm > WE ♥ NYC >
  Goose at LOCKN' Farm
Arrington, Virginia > New York, New York > Arrington, Virginia
August 20–22, 2021

"I think we are going to do a lot of shows. And then we are going to do a lot more shows." Those were my words on New York's channel 5 in July 2021.

At that point, we had more shows on the books at the Cap for the six-month period that would begin in September with our official reopening than for any other six months in the venue's history.

Nine of those shows would be with Phil Lesh. It felt great to have him finally returning to the room.

In the interim, he performed three well-received July dates in Nashville with my friends in Dawes. I love expanding that world, and I had every faith that the Goldsmith brothers could pull it off.

Griffin texted me his thanks for the experience midway through the run, and Taylor shared a memorable conversation he had with Phil. When Taylor asked who should take a solo on a particular song, Phil responded, "Everyone. And no one."

That pretty much says it all about the mystery and majesty of Phil and the Grateful Dead. Phil wants to be in the moment, and he is not interested in working out too many details in advance.

By the time we opened Nashville Bowl following a fifteen-month delay, I was thrilled to move past the planning stages as well. Our original opening night on March 11, 2020, would have been Soulive and George Porter. On June 25, 2021, Old Crow Medicine Show finally did the honors.

Our two first weekends were representative of what was to come. Old Crow blended country and jam with my own predilection for special guests (including Jerry Douglas, Molly Tuttle, and Joshua Hedley). Then we had "NOLA in Nash" (as Stef May described it), featuring the Rebirth Brass Band with Ben Jaffe, who drove up from New Orleans and appeared throughout their set. (As Ben later explained, that is the custom where he comes from.) The next weekend, we had the Travelin' McCourys, joined by Del McCoury, Billy Strings, and Sierra Hull. I couldn't be there, but Del sent me a video message telling me how much he liked the place ("This is uptown. Even though it's downtown, it's uptown here"). We juxtaposed that show with Sparkle City Disco's ninth anniversary party. Same church, different days.

On opening night, as our new staff members welcomed concertgoers, I noticed that the lines were growing too long for comfort. So I walked over and offered a small piece of advice: Whenever possible, the person checking IDs should be different from the person giving out wristbands. It is a simple way to keep things flowing that I have picked up over time.

While I prepared to bring my existing venues back online, I continued working on new projects. In February 2021, we debuted our new Relix Studio with a free stream from Garcia Peoples. After years of hosting sessions at the office, we moved our gear into the former home of the Jazz Standard, which had been unable to reopen after the pandemic.

Around this time, I walked past the Good Stuff Diner on Fourteenth Street between Sixth and Seventh, which had closed a few months earlier. As I paused and peered in the window, I had a vision for what I would call the Jazz Diner. We would serve Miles Davis's chili recipe and have an amazing sound system, perhaps with high-end speakers at each table, where people could control their musical menus.

I contacted Steve Jordan, thinking that we could work on it together with some of the proceeds directed to the Jazz Federation of America. The idea went through a few iterations until I recognized a major problem with the diner's location: the street was closed to auto traffic from 6:00 a.m. to 10:00 p.m.

However, and this can be filed in the "obvious is obvious until you miss it" category, I looked at the ground floor of our new Relix Studio that had previously housed Danny Meyer's Blue Smoke and realized this could be an ideal future home for what I would call Jazzlands.

Meanwhile, I continued planning any number of new projects while maintaining the day-to-day on my current ones. At a given moment, you might find me working on a Garcia's jazz club in Chicago or a tribute band–themed concept or Brooklyn Bowl Philadelphia (where we eventually opened on November 4 with Soulive and George Porter, just as we had hoped to do in Nashville, along with a special Bowl Train performance by Philly native Questlove).

Streaming remained part of the plan as well. FANS continued to grow, which produced more growth. Sometimes you will hit critical mass and not even realize it. Whenever you start something, all the calls are outgoing. But if you build it right, you get the incoming.

While a number of venues contacted us, I also did my own outreach with the new Westville Music Bowl in New Haven, Connecticut. I could see the potential for competition with the Capitol during the summer months, but rather than be adversarial, I opted for the reverse jujitsu move to become part of what they were doing. So we streamed their shows, which further built our profile while Relix had great presence on-site.

I attended a number of gigs at Westville, but one of my most memorable moments involved a battery run. Billy Strings was playing two dates, but he had been limited to a single set on the first night because people were late to enter the venue. So his manager purchased a megaphone on Amazon that would enable Billy to cruise around the lot in a golf cart and encourage people to go in early. However, when the package arrived, they realized they were short two D batteries. With time running out, I drove to a nearby convenience store, where the clerk sold me two unwrapped Ds that he pulled out of a plastic bag. I was back in time for Billy to make his tour of the lot (wearing a Capitol Theatre bathrobe), and he played two sets that night.

I've known Bill Orner, Billy's manager, for a while, so this was all part of blending friendship and business. Later that evening, I soft floated the idea of Billy returning to the Cap for another Déjà Vu Experiment. A few days later, we began working out the details for what would become Déjà Tu. That says something for showing up and pitching in, because I do believe that batteries matter.

As for our streaming efforts, although the numbers came down once the quarantines lifted, they were still higher than pre-pandemic. I am not convinced that it is a self-sustaining business, but it makes sense as a complementary piece of something larger. The deals are revenue shares where the musicians typically receive between 70 and 90 percent, so the margins are small. However, it is another point of contact to build relationships.

Since I enjoy interacting with artists, a few people approached me during COVID about becoming a manager. I appreciate the ask, but I don't want to be in a position where I turn someone down and then they won't play my venues. (I'd miss out on those celebratory fist bumps—I am proud to have been an active fist bumper pre-COVID). I have put in my one hundred thousand hours working on live shows, and that is what I do best.

When I'm at shows (both mine and others), I take a lot of pictures on my phone. I will capture a moment and send it to an artist, an agent, a manager, or a family member. It is a fun way to connect. I typically tweak the images by turning up the contrast, black point, brightness, saturation, noise reduction, pretty much all of it. When in doubt, turn it up.

If I am watching a stream, I'll take screen grabs and send those around. Matisyahu played a Chanukah show at the Capitol in 2020, and while he was singing, there was a cool overlay effect with a dreidel. I texted that to him, and he ended up posting it to his Instagram. As I continue to add venues, connecting by screen-shot has become another part of what I do (and I also use streams to provide notes on the lighting in the venue and at times on the stream itself).

Of course, my favorite way to connect with an artist is direct and in person. Since 2013, I have had plenty of those opportunities at LOCKN', where artists often appear for multiple days, so they have time to slow down and enjoy the family gathering. There is also magic in the air, which is why despite my struggles to turn a profit, I could not give up on it.

In early April, we rescheduled to the last possible weekend the weather would permit: October 1–4, 2020.

LOCKN' 2019 had been a memorable one, anchored by Derek Trucks and Susan Tedeschi with the Trey Anastasio Band, then Trey with the Tedeschi Trucks Band. It seemed like a perfect musical match as well as interpersonal one, since they're all givers. The idea was to make it feel fresh but also familiar. I'm drawn to that approach, particularly at an event like LOCKN', where Derek, Susan, and Trey had appeared multiple times going back to the very first year.

The weekend culminated with Trey and TTB, joined by Doyle Bramhall II for an epic performance of Derek & the Dominos' double album, *Layla and Other Assorted Love Songs*. I knew something big was planned, but they never told me directly what it was. At one point, Patrick Jordan texted me to ask about the curfew. I told him, "It's a late curfew. Planning to go to 12:30. There is some room." He responded, "Planning greatest set ever." I answered, "Then there is no curfew." (Ha!) As I've said, the goal is to put yourself in position for something incredible to happen, and in this case, I believe the two nights made a difference.

I had some big ideas for Phil in his eightieth birthday year, so I was hoping to salvage LOCKN'. I came to realize that the key would be rapid testing for COVID. Here is where I thought we finally had an advantage over those festivals based in the big cities. Since people were traveling specifically to LOCKN', I believed we could have a reduced-capacity event limited to people who camped on-site following a negative COVID test.

After we announced this plan, I was contacted by the office of Trump testing czar Admiral Brett Giroir. He was eager to use us as an example of the administration's success. The problem was that we were unable to find a cost-effective, reliable way to process that many tests on a reasonable timeline. Not only that, but after putting the idea out there and taking the temperature of the room, I realized that people were not prepared to attend a music festival until vaccines became readily available. So I announced we would postpone LOCKN' for a year, until October 1–3, 2021.

Except that did not happen either. As the spring arrived, I began to worry that it might be unrealistic to host a full-capacity event in October. Once I began thinking about decreasing the scale of the festival, I wondered if we should modify our overall approach. LOCKN' had been through many iterations since we initially envisioned it as the Interlocken Music Festival with Phish and Furthur swapping sets from opposite sides of a racetrack.

Once again, the idea was to keep it fresh but familiar. This led to three mini-fests held over successive weekends built around individual artists: Joe Russo's Almost Dead (August 13–15), Goose (August 20–22), and the Tedeschi Trucks Band (August 27–29). I had wanted to call the middle weekend Camp Goose, but they preferred Fred: The Festival, so I yielded (artists always lead, and talent wins ties). The name runs contrary to my "say what it is" philosophy, but the band did permit a slight tweak so that we could bill it as Goose Presents: Fred the Festival.

In early June, a few days after we announced this, I learned that Clive Davis was planning a concert to celebrate the reopening of New York. My friend Jason Miller was producing it on the Live Nation side. I soon began working with Clive's son Doug and Jason on the name and logo. The initial working title, the Official NYC Homecoming Concert in Central Park, was a bit unwieldy; plus, the event was only a homecoming if you had gone away.

I began searching for a more concise name that carried an emotional resonance, and I ultimately landed on WE ♥ NYC. I developed the logo with my in-house designer Corinne Guglielmo, and in the spirit of collaboration akin to adding *Goose Presents*, the official title was We Love New York: The Homecoming Concert.

Corinne also did a fine job with our new LOCKN' Farm imagery. While the mini-fests wouldn't be LOCKN', they certainly had the LOCKN' lineage, so we emphasized that the festival site was called LOCKN' Farm. We had taken an event and converted it into a place.

I think this will continue to evolve. A few soggy days in August led me to realize that we need the flexibility to move indoors. Who knows? Maybe in the spirit of the LOCKN' turntable stage, we will create something that can rotate into a covered space when the weather goes awry. Plus, some festivalgoers might enjoy returning from a day of music to small cabins we could build on the land (I trust in Dayglo's Chris Moody to sort it out).

I began contemplating all this in earnest following the opening JRAD weekend. I keep multiple weather apps on the home screen of my phone throughout the summer months, so while I was not able to make it there until Sunday, I held my breath from afar watching the satellite imagery. It can be a tough feeling when I am not at a show, but I can see what's coming, especially after the microburst. We ended up losing our Friday and Saturday evenings, which led to ten hours of daytime music on Saturday and Sunday. In response, we allowed anyone at the event to use their ticket for free entry at either of the next two weekends.

The weather turns fast at LOCKN'. But there is opportunity in danger. Both magic and beauty appear with that threat.

The next weekend during Goose, there was a moment when it felt like we were in Kansas, although the storm blew by without touching us (taking the heat and humidity with it, which was much appreciated). Seven days later, one of our nights with the Tedeschi Trucks Band was cut short due to lightning in the area.

On Saturday, August 21, I could see lightning from my vantage point on Central Park's Great Lawn. The air was thick and humid due to fast-approaching Hurricane Henri, and my weather app told me the chance of rain was 100 percent.

The WE ♥ NYC concert then stopped abruptly with Barry Manilow still in the middle of "I Can't Smile Without You." He later performed an encore over the phone for CNN's Anderson Cooper. By all accounts, that postshow performance was just as compelling as the concert itself, and talks began almost immediately about a second go-round to finish the event.

The longer I am in this business, the more it seems that weather is becoming a factor, in part due to climate change. If I have a show or even if I'm at a show, I find myself checking my weather app in an addictive way.

Still, I am appreciative that the one time I absolutely needed the weather to cooperate, everything worked out fine. We were five for five at Fare Thee Well, and I attribute a portion of our success to the mild days and clear skies (augmented by a rainbow on one occasion). We will see what happens over July 4 weekend in 2025 (spoiler alert!), because I have Soldier Field on hold for GD60 (!!).

As I look to the horizon, while I know that our venues will still face a fair share of challenges in a world that's been altered by COVID, I believe that our fundamentals are strong. I am also of the opinion that as long as you do right by everyone, venues do not fade over time, they institutionalize. Unlike restaurants or night-clubs, they strengthen as people return to their favorite venues to see their favorite bands and find new favorites as well.

I do know that when we finally began opening our doors, I received more hugs than ever before.

I was on a bike ride with my son, Simon, recently, and in a true Yogi Berra moment, he dropped some wisdom on me.

It was one of those perfect late-summer afternoons that are meant to be enjoyed with loved ones. COVID had changed our perspective on daily life for so long, making it feel flat and repetitive. But as Simon and I savored our time in the sun, he reflected on the moment and informed me why it was so special: "Weekends don't happen every day."

Later that night, I was back at my inspiring grind. Here's the thing: Even after putting on ten thousand shows, I still love the shows. It is still hard, and I still get that pit in my stomach when I walk up to a venue. There are so many intangibles, and none of this is a science. You need to put in the work because the details always matter. But you also need to remember that it is not a widget and it will never be a widget. Once you treat it that way, you will screw it up.

I am one hundred thousand hours in, and I continue to have the passion for it. I am still stressing the details, I still need to sell tickets, and I am also still searching for magic.

That is why after I saw Dawes on the opening night of Fred: The Festival, where they performed a set of Black Sabbath covers, I woke up early the next day and, anticipating flight cancellations due to Hurricane Henri, I drove home so that I could be there in time for the WE ♥ NYC concert.

Then the day after that, with New York airports closed due to Henri, I drove to Philadelphia, flew to Charlottesville, and took an Uber to LOCKN'.

After all, you can't see it if you're not there.

Since weekends don't happen every day.

And the music never stops . . .

ACKNOWLEDGMENTS

Thank you to everyone who crushed it behind the scenes, sharing guidance and insight during the creation of this book. In particular:

The intrepid Paul Lucas, Eloy Bleifuss, and Luke Janklow at Janklow & Nesbit.

The steadfast and patient Ben Schafer, Carrie Napolitano, Fred Francis, and Jen Patten-Sanchez at Hachette.

The kind-hearted Budnick and Barrett families.

As well as everyone who created the music, provided the inspiration, worked the shows, and shared the magic over the years . . .

PHOTO CREDITS

Dave Bartlett: 10 top

Andrew Scott Blackstein: 8 bottom, 14 top

Jay Blakesberg: 5 top, 5 bottom right, 8 middle, 9 middle, 15 middle

Phil Bruell: 1 middle

Danny Clinch: 1 bottom

Scott Harris: 6 top left, 11 top left

Erik Kabik: 16 bottom

Neal Meltzer: 6 middle

Marc Millman: 9 bottom, 11 bottom left

Dino Perrucci: 11 top right, 14 bottom

Peter Shapiro: 1 top, 2 top, 2 left, 2 right, 3 top, 4 middle right, 4 bottom, 5 bottom left, 6 top right, 6 bottom, 7 top, 7 middle, 7 bottom, 8 top, 9 top, 10 middle, 12 top, 12 middle, 12 bottom, 13 top, 13 bottom, 14 middle right, 14 middle left, 15 top, 15 bottom, 16 top left, 16 top right

Rob Stricker: 13 middle

C. Taylor Crothers: 2 bottom, 3 bottom, 4 middle left

Geoffrey Tischman: 10 bottom

Dave Vann: 11 bottom right

Tim Warner: 4 top